Praise for *Change the Culture, Cha[nge the Game]*

"This is the most important book on leadership that I have read in over twenty years. Connors and Smith's brilliant and simple step-by-step approach will help any leader effectively engage the entire organization in changing its culture and ensure the delivery of results."
—ROMAN J. BOWSER, executive vice president, American Heart Association

"*Change the Culture, Change the Game* provides the methodology and approach every leader must master in order to achieve a culture based on accountability and focused on achieving key results. A must-read for every team interested in ensuring that they deliver and perform at the top of their game."
—PAUL J. BYRNE, president, Precor Incorporated

"I've lived through dramatic performance improvements enabled by the approach of Connors and Smith—it's nothing short of a miracle! *Change the Culture, Change the Game* provides a certain path to creating accountability for achieving goals and objectives normally beyond our grasp, using a proven, commonsense approach that energizes people at every level of the organization."
—DAVE SCHLOTTERBECK, chairman and CEO, CareFusion Corporation

"This book presents Partners In Leadership's approach to achieving results through cultural transformation and is the *absolute best leadership process* I have ever seen! We have employed it in organizations large and small, both inside and outside the United States. If you know the results that you and your team want, this process is the way to get them."
—FRED MCCOY, vice chairman, Synecor, LLC

"Using the Results Pyramid model to accelerate culture change, Connors and Smith don't just state what we all know to be important—they take it a step further and detail *how* it can be done. *Change the Culture, Change the Game* gives leaders a methodology that works for building and sustaining a high-performance organizational culture."
—CLINTON A. LEWIS, JR., president, U.S. Operations, Pfizer Animal Health, Pfizer, Inc.

"As the recognized experts on workplace accountability, Connors and Smith ratchet it up another notch in *Change the Culture, Change the Game*! Building on the success of their previous books, *The Oz Principle* and *How Did That Happen?*, they now detail how to accelerate culture change with a process that delivers lasting results."
—AMBASSADOR GREGORY J. NEWELL, former U.S. Assistant Secretary of State

"*Change the Culture, Change the Game* outlines practical and powerful tools that our management team embraced early in our company's formation. I am confident that applying these concepts and creating a Culture of Accountability will propel us to success in the difficult world of start-ups and prove vital in realizing our vision to transform an entire industry."
—TODD M. POPE, president and chief executive officer, TransEnterix, Inc.

"Culture change is never easy, but with the tools and insights we take from *Change the Culture, Change the Game*, we are seeing rapid progress."

—WYMAN ROBERTS, president, Chili's Grill & Bar

"Bottom line: If you keep doing what you've been doing, you'll keep getting what you've been getting; but if you want to change the game . . . you need to read this book. *Change the Culture, Change the Game* lays out an actionable approach that every leader should master. So, if you're tired of trying leadership techniques that are not effective and new programs that don't work, then stop and read this book."

—GINGER L. GRAHAM, former CEO, Amylin Pharmaceuticals

"With the process described in *Change the Culture, Change the Game*, in less than two years we tripled revenue and substantially increased our profit by 75 percent. We became a 'believing' organization. We believed we could succeed, we believed we could win in the market, we believed we could deliver products on time, we believed we could exceed customer expectations—and we did. This book presents a high-impact plan that every leader can follow to transform their culture and create accountability for results at every level of the organization."

—HAROLD A. BLOMQUIST, president and CEO, Simtek Corp.

"Connors and Smith's latest book lays out the plan for achieving results-driven accountability in a quick and readable format. Their specific examples of how leaders can cut through their natural filters to focus with precision on underlying issues will hit home for senior leaders interested in accelerating culture change and driving business results."

—JIM MAZZO, president, Abbott Medical Optics

"The go-to guide on culture change with proven, practical ideas for leaders looking to accelerate change, strengthen their teams, and achieve success."

—LAURIE ANN GOLDMAN, CEO, Spanx

"A great read with practical pointers and relevant industry examples of application and impact. Notable takeaway: all behavior is rewarded."

—DAVID P. HOLVECK, president and CEO, Endo Pharmaceuticals

"*Change the Culture, Change the Game* is the definitive guide on culture change and offers a powerful yet practical approach to changing your organization's culture and achieving your results."

—TIMOTHY VIG, president, USKH, Inc.

"Every book in the Oz series just keeps getting better. *Change the Culture, Change the Game* provides pertinent real-life examples about how companies have implemented the culture change necessary to achieving their desired results. The book is filled with case studies that illustrate how to do it, providing a clear road map for implementation. A great read that will convince the naysayers who exist in every company that culture change is not an option, it is a necessity; and mastering that process of change will bring competitive advantage."

—WILLIAM A. BRIZEE, president and CEO, Architects Hawaii

"*Change the Culture, Change the Game* provides leaders with a clear and intuitive step-by-step guide to understanding and shaping your corporate culture, the critical component of every organization's formula for success."
—LOUIS J. WOOLF, president, Hebrew Senior Life

"Connors and Smith have once again shown us a proven and effective way to align around and achieve key corporate results! A great read for every executive interested in building a strong culture that maximizes results."
—JOE H. HOHNER, senior vice president, chief of staff, and chief information officer,
Blue Cross Blue Shield of Michigan

"*Change the Culture, Change the Game* is a priceless must-read for any experienced or aspiring leader. There is no better guide on how to leverage your organizational culture and make a giant leap in performance. This is a pragmatic and practical approach that will make a real and lasting difference in any organization."
—KELLI VALADE, chief operating officer, Chili's Grill & Bar

"*Change the Culture, Change the Game* gets right to the heart of what it takes for organizations to succeed and provides an invaluable guide to safely navigating the economic turbulence of our time. Building on the foundational concepts of their earlier works, Roger Connors and Tom Smith provide a pragmatic and reassuring framework to assist leaders in developing a culture that is both results-producing and sustainable."
—MARTIN C. LOWERY, chief learning officer, Apollo Group, Inc.

"You've cut the costs, optimized the process, and taken other steps toward improvement, yet the desired results remain elusive or hard to sustain. Connors and Smith make a compelling case that the reason is staring leaders right in the face: it's the culture. This well-structured book focuses on hard realities and practical applications. It isn't a soft, 'let's all play nice in the sandbox' look at organizational behavior. Rather, it provides culture management tools you can put to positive work in your company today."
—CHRISTOPHER FAWCETT, vice president, general manager, Sony Electronics Inc.

"Every experienced leader knows that having the right organizational culture is crucial to his or her success. That fact makes this book required reading for anyone in leadership and everyone who is aspiring to become a leader. *Change the Culture, Change the Game* provides the best approach that I have seen on how to engage people to get sustained behavior change and results."
—MELISSA STRAIT, senior vice president, HR, Training and Development,
Arby's Restaurant Group

"This book provides an amazingly simple yet powerful methodology for building a motivated organization that is focused on getting results—an essential priority for every organization in today's tough competitive environment. Convincingly, the authors back up their assertions with compelling examples that support their claim: change the culture and you change the game!"
—STUART MAGLOFF, vice president, Planning and Supply Chain Systems Strategy,
MD&D Supply Chain, Ortho Clinical Diagnostics, Inc.

"After working with the concepts in *Change the Culture, Change the Game*, I believe that no other approach to culture change is as powerful in its simplicity and effective in its application. Every leader who is serious about culture change should read this book."

—JEFFREY GERSTEL, senior vice president, Dress Barn

"Everyone knows that you have to plan in order to succeed. Unfortunately, many leaders do not adequately plan on managing their culture—perhaps the single most consistent factor of success for most organizations. *Change the Culture, Change the Game* provides the most complete and practical blueprint any leader can use to ensure that their organizational culture is working for them and is producing the results they need."

—LYNN TAKAKI, vice president, Human Resources, Precor Incorporated

"At the end of the day, being successful in business is about getting results, and managing the organization's culture is key to getting this done. *Change the Culture, Change the Game* provides leaders with the key ingredients and the practical tools necessary for creating a Culture of Accountability, where people are engaged, in a very personal way, in ensuring that the organization succeeds and desired results are delivered."

—BERRY CARPENTER, director, Talent and Leadership Development, PETCO Animal Supplies, Inc.

"A vital addition to every library on leadership and organizational performance with powerful tips on every page to transform your organization into one that consistently achieves its key results. It's rare to find a book that contains a step-by-step approach to ensuring personal and organizational success; this is that book!"

—WAYNE A. SHARRAH, managing director, Esurance

"There are myriad methodologies in the literature on change, but Connors and Smith provide what I believe to be the best framework ever presented in a leadership book on how to accelerate culture change. They reveal the 'missing' pieces that are the essential differentiators between success and failure of any change effort. *Change the Culture, Change the Game* is the most practical approach to leadership I have ever read."

—SALLY TURNER, director, Patient Centered Care, Aurora Health Care

"*Change the Culture, Change the Game* provides practical guidelines and techniques, which serve as an actual organizational road map to greater accountability. The premise of the book is unarguable: follow the accountability path and results are guaranteed!"

—SUSAN LEVINE, executive director, Hospice of the Valley

CHANGE THE culture

The Breakthrough Strategy for
Energizing Your Organization and
Creating Accountability for Results

CHANGE THE game

Roger Connors and Tom Smith

PORTFOLIO / PENGUIN

PORTFOLIO / PENGUIN
Published by the Penguin Group
Penguin Group (USA) Inc., 375 Hudson Street,
New York, New York 10014, U.S.A.
Penguin Group (Canada), 90 Eglinton Avenue East, Suite 700,
Toronto, Ontario, Canada M4P 2Y3
(a division of Pearson Penguin Canada Inc.)
Penguin Books Ltd, 80 Strand, London WC2R 0RL, England
Penguin Ireland, 25 St. Stephen's Green, Dublin 2, Ireland
(a division of Penguin Books Ltd)
Penguin Books Australia Ltd, 250 Camberwell Road, Camberwell,
Victoria 3124, Australia
(a division of Pearson Australia Group Pty Ltd)
Penguin Books India Pvt Ltd, 11 Community Centre, Panchsheel Park,
New Delhi – 110 017, India
Penguin Group (NZ), 67 Apollo Drive, Rosedale, Auckland 0632,
New Zealand (a division of Pearson New Zealand Ltd)
Penguin Books (South Africa) (Pty) Ltd, 24 Sturdee Avenue,
Rosebank, Johannesburg 2196, South Africa

Penguin Books Ltd, Registered Offices:
80 Strand, London WC2R 0RL, England

First published in the United States of America by Portfolio /
Penguin, a member of Penguin Group (USA) Inc. 2011
This paperback edition published 2012

13 15 17 19 20 18 16 14

THE LIBRARY OF CONGRESS HAS CATALOGED THE HARDCOVER EDITION AS FOLLOWS:
Connors, Roger.
Change the culture, change the game : the breakthrough strategy for energizing your organization and
creating accountability for results / Roger Connors and Tom Smith.
p. cm.
Includes index.
ISBN 978-1-59184-361-0 (hc.)
ISBN 978-1-59184-539-3 (pbk.)
1. Organizational behavior.   2. Corporate culture.   3. Responsibility.   4. Management.
I. Smith, Tom (Thomas A.)   II. Title.
HD58.7.C6276 2011
658.4'063—dc22
2010032892

Printed in the United States of America
Set in Janson Text

To our children.

May this book provide a lasting reminder that you
can make a difference in the world:
Allyse, Bryanna, Katie, Josalyn, Michael, Brent,
Seth, Stephen, Kimberly, Mary, Audrey,
Jerry, and Starla

Acknowledgments

THERE ARE MANY TO acknowledge who were associated with this project. First, Adrian Zackheim, along with the team at Portfolio, including Brooke Carey, Emily Angell, and Will Weisser, who provided tremendous support and enthusiasm for this book. We appreciate most the fact that the Portfolio team gets it: accountability produces results.

To Michael Snell, we express our heartfelt thanks and friendship. His flexible and ever supportive collaboration has been helpful indeed. We appreciate the true partnership he brings to the game.

To our colleagues on the Partners In Leadership team: John Jacobsen, Tony Bridwell, Tanner Corbridge, Craig Hickman, Maury Hiers, Jared Jones, Kirk Matson, Marcus Nicolls, Tracy Skousen, Brad Starr, Don Tanner, Jennifer Zarback, Michelle Murray, Pete Theodore (a vendor, but a key member of the team), Robert Haws, and Denise Smith, we express our appreciation for their contributions and support. Without them, this project could not have been completed. The writing of this book, like each of our other books, has always been a team effort. Thank you, team!

We continue to value the amazingly loyal support of our clients. We particularly appreciate those with whom we have partnered since the beginning and who have so successfully applied the principles in *Change the Culture, Change the Game*.

Finally, we must acknowledge the support, enthusiasm, and encouragement of our wives, Gwen and Becky, and our children and grandchildren. They make it all worthwhile!

Contents

Acknowledgments ix

Introduction 1

PART ONE

Implement the Results Pyramid to Change the Culture

CHAPTER 1 7
Creating a Culture of Accountability

CHAPTER 2 29
Defining the Results That Guide the Change

CHAPTER 3 49
Taking Action That Produces Results

CHAPTER 4 67
Identifying the Beliefs That Generate the Right Actions

CHAPTER 5 89
Providing Experiences That Instill the Right Beliefs

PART TWO
Integrate the C² Best Practices to Accelerate the Culture Change

CHAPTER 6 113
Aligning a Culture for Rapid Progress

CHAPTER 7 133
Applying the Three Culture Management Tools

CHAPTER 8 153
Mastering the Three Culture Change Leadership Skills

CHAPTER 9 173
Integrating the Culture Change

CHAPTER 10 193
Enrolling the Entire Organization in the Change

Index 217

CHANGE THE culture

CHANGE THE game

Introduction

THOSE OF YOU WHO are familiar with our previous books and know our work on accountability already appreciate the fact that we, along with our ever-growing list of clients, are die-hard believers in the impact that greater individual and organizational accountability has on both business results and company morale. Accountability produces amazing results, and our books, based on over twenty years of our own experience consulting for and training leaders in the top companies in the world, document the fact that greater accountability can and does lead to game-changing results.

Unfortunately, in many organizations, accountability has become something that happens to you when things go wrong. That kind of accountability never works. However, real accountability, achieved through a proven step-by-step process, makes things go right. It will assist you in your quest to achieve organizational results. Far from being a punishment for missteps and failures, it is a powerful, positive, and enabling principle that forms the very foundation on which you can build both individual and organizational success. It is not an option; it is not a fad; it is a basic requirement in today's complex and fast-changing business environment. The way we hold one another accountable defines the very nature of our working relationships: how we interact, what we expect of one another, how we "do things around here."

Creating an organizational culture where people embrace their accountability toward one another and toward the organization should occupy center stage in any effort to create successful organizational change. Without accountability, the change process breaks down quickly. When it does, people externalize the need to change, resist initiatives designed to move them forward, and even sabotage efforts to transform the organization. With accountability, people at every level of the organization embrace their role in facilitating the change and demonstrate the ownership needed for making true progress, both for themselves and their organization.

Our experience proves that accountability, done the right way, produces greater transparency and openness, enhanced teamwork and trust, effective communication and dialogue, thorough execution and follow-through, sharper clarity, and a tighter focus on results. Accountability should be the strongest thread that runs through the complex fabric of any organization. It is the single biggest issue confronting organizations today, particularly those engaged in enterprise-wide change efforts. At the end of the day, greater accountability produces greater results. And when you build a Culture of Accountability, you create an organization filled with people who can and will get game-changing results.

You may have read our previous bestselling book on accountability and culture change, *Journey to the Emerald City: Achieve a Competitive Edge by Creating a Culture of Accountability*. In that book, we addressed the subject of using greater accountability to accelerate culture change in support of desired organizational results. Since the publication of that book and after many years of intensive work with clients, we have learned a great deal more about how to use accountability to speed up culture change. Our clients' ownership of the Culture of Accountability Process has been beyond compare. Many of them have taken the process to the next level as they have applied our methods, innovated, and passionately pursued changing the culture in their own organizations.

We have felt compelled to share this learning and promote the best practices associated with creating a Culture of Accountability. To accomplish that, we have not merely revised *Journey to the Emerald City*, but have thoroughly rewritten and updated the book. While we still use many of the models that first appeared in *Journey to the Emerald City*, we have added to them and have surrounded them with fresh insights, deeper understandings, and brand-new client stories. Consequently, we think you will see even more clearly how the accountability best practices can produce game-changing results for you and your organization. Perhaps even more important, we hope this new book helps you sharpen your expertise, leadership capability, and proficiency to *accelerate* organizational culture change.

As in our other books, we have filled *Change the Culture, Change the Game* with real client examples that bring all the principles to life. Whenever we can, we refer to the company by name. However, some clients understandably prefer to remain anonymous. Because we highly value our relationship with those clients, we honor their wishes by presenting a few anonymous cases in which we have disguised the client's identity with a fictitious name set off in quotation marks, like "CorpAnon." Rest assured, however, that in those instances, you are still reading a true story with only the names changed to ensure confidentiality.

Throughout the book, we will show you the best practices associated with creating the C^2 culture, including B^2 beliefs, R^2 results, and a whole array of culture-management models, tools, and skills. When it comes to culture change, as with most things in life, experience truly is the best teacher, and our hard-won experience over the past twenty years has taught us a lot about what works and what does not work. The diagram on page 4 brings together all of the pieces presented in *Change the Culture, Change the Game*. The C^2 Best Practices Map offers an overview and summary of the best practices you will need to accelerate the culture change and sustain it over time.

Our many years of experience with numerous clients, many of whom we have highlighted in this book, have convinced us that these C^2 best practices do work when correctly implemented and integrated into the organization. Culture has an impact on results, and the right approach to culture change accelerates that impact in a way that brings *game-changing* results.

Change the Culture, Change the Game describes the Culture Track component of our comprehensive Three-Track approach to creating

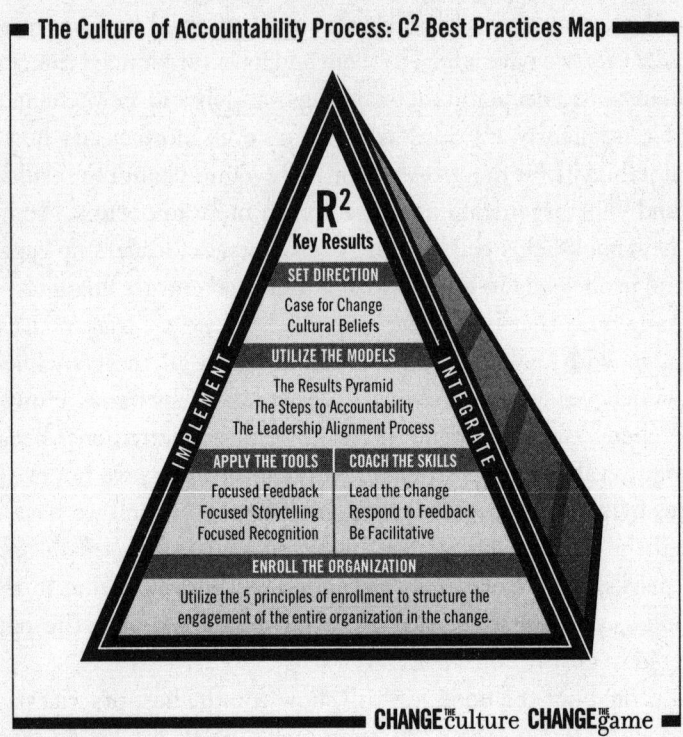

■ The Culture of Accountability Process: C² Best Practices Map ■

R^2
Key Results

SET DIRECTION
Case for Change
Cultural Beliefs

UTILIZE THE MODELS
The Results Pyramid
The Steps to Accountability
The Leadership Alignment Process

APPLY THE TOOLS
Focused Feedback
Focused Storytelling
Focused Recognition

COACH THE SKILLS
Lead the Change
Respond to Feedback
Be Facilitative

ENROLL THE ORGANIZATION
Utilize the 5 principles of enrollment to structure the
engagement of the entire organization in the change.

IMPLEMENT

INTEGRATE

■ CHANGETHE**culture CHANGE**THE**game ■**

greater accountability for results. When you base culture change on accountability and adopt a process designed to produce your desired results, you not only create a competitive advantage, you gain the tools you need to sustain that advantage far into the future. The pages ahead will show you exactly how to do it.

Let the journey begin!

Implement the Results Pyramid to Change the Culture

Part One of *Change the Culture, Change the Game* shows you how to use the Results Pyramid to accelerate the change in culture you need to achieve your key organizational results. We will show you how to implement both the top and bottom of the Results Pyramid to create a Culture of Accountability. In the pages ahead, you will also read numerous client stories and examples of successful best practices around each level of the Pyramid: Results, Actions, Beliefs, and Experiences. We feel confident that you will soon agree with our basic premise that a Culture of Accountability produces game-changing results.

CHAPTER 1

Creating a Culture of Accountability

WE BEGIN BY INTRODUCING our core belief: Either you will manage your culture, or it will manage you. What do we mean by *culture*? Simply stated, organizational culture is the way people think and act. Every organization has a culture, which either works for you or against you—and it can make the difference between success and failure. Managing the organizational culture so that leaders, managers, team members, and employees think and act in the manner necessary to achieve desired results has never mattered more. Doing it well is not an option; it's a necessity. Optimizing the culture should command your attention every bit as much as your effort to achieve performance improvements in manufacturing, R&D, sales, and every other organizational discipline.

Experienced leaders know that changing the culture can mean changing the game by growing faster than your rivals, beating a bad economy, revolutionizing the value proposition of your organization, or a host of other competition-beating achievements. Managing the culture so that it produces the results you are looking for has become an essential role of leadership and a core management competency. Neglect it at your peril.

The story of Alaris Medical Systems illustrates our point. You may not have heard of them, but you have probably used one of their products if you have spent any time at all in a doctor's office or hospital. Alaris, one of the top medical device companies in the world, produces and sells some of the most widely recognized brand names in their categories.

The Alaris story is about a company that transformed an organizational culture and, as a result, literally changed the game in a way that significantly influenced an entire industry. Ultimately, it generated an increase in share price from 31¢ per share to $22.35 per share in just three years, growing revenue as much as 15 percent a year in a market where competitors were achieving a mere 3 percent. Purchased by Cardinal Health, a Fortune 20 company, Alaris eventually became the nucleus of a company called CareFusion, a spin-off from Cardinal and one of the largest medical device suppliers in the world. The Alaris story is also about CEO Dave Schlotterbeck, who valued the transforming impact of culture on what he characterized at one point as the "most difficult job" he held during his distinguished forty-year career.

When we first met Dave Schlotterbeck, he was presiding over a merger between IVAC and IMED, the most highly leveraged medical device company in the world, with $350 million in revenue and $525 million in debt. Prior to Alaris, Dave had spent two decades effecting successful company turnarounds in the world of manufacturing. Previous experience had shown that he was good at what he did, developing what he considered a repeatable "recipe" for optimizing performance in manufacturing organizations. He had become adept at clearly seeing a company's problems after simply spending time with a set of financials. He learned to spot "sloppy systems" and to identify when people were failing to pay enough attention to the details.

Early on, Dave learned a fundamental lesson: To generate cash for a struggling company, you must optimize manufacturing. He knew that in companies failing to deliver results, manufacturing was often a big part of the problem. This conclusion was proving true at Alaris as well. Relying on his hard-won experience, Dave began his efforts to improve performance by doing those things he knew would generate the cash needed to deal with Alaris's enormous debt. However, those early efforts to generate the needed cash produced shocking results. As Dave put it, "It turned into a scenario that I'd never seen before: The company actually took what I directed them to do and ended up consuming cash!"

It was beginning to look as if Alaris deserved the reputation it had earned on Wall Street: a company with good ideas but unable to execute. Dave began to spend an inordinate amount of time on the details as he worked to improve execution, leaving him precious little time to run the business. Despite his initial efforts to turn things around, the company continued to head toward bankruptcy. As 20 percent losses piled up month after month, Dave began to despair. Why was everything still heading in the wrong direction? He felt trapped in an irreversible downward cycle that was becoming graver by the minute and appeared almost impossible to reverse.

One day, while walking back from a lunch picnic at the park next door to the corporate offices, he fell into a conversation about the company's predicament with a manager in Marketing. As they walked, the conversation turned to the people who were making things happen, in spite of the performance of the company. Yes, a lot of go-to people still worked for them. At that very moment, Dave had an epiphany: Imagine how catastrophic things would be if Alaris lacked such talent, and how successful they could be if everyone in the company were a go-to person. He began to consider whether they might even reverse the dangerous downward spiral in which they seemed trapped. Mulling over the conversation with the marketing manager, he reached an inescapable conclusion: To improve performance, Alaris needed a new culture, one that consistently produced go-to people.

He had known all along that the organizational culture was an issue, but only now was he beginning to appreciate the impact of current behaviors and attitudes on Alaris's results. Now he more fully recognized the price the company was paying when people avoided taking risks and altogether shrank from any high-visibility opportunity for fear of being sacrificed when things went wrong—which everyone knew they almost assuredly would! What was the cost to the organization of heavily punishing failure and prohibiting people from having fun while they worked? What was the senior management team missing when the most eager staff members avoided opportunities to be exposed to upper management, because such exposure was always a negative experience? The situation had grown dire, a fact Dave recognized now more than ever.

The Alaris culture had fostered a mentality of survival; people worried more about protecting themselves than getting the results the company needed. When Dave decided he needed help with the problem, he began to read as many books as he could find on the subject of culture change. Every weekend his wife would find him walking about the house with his nose buried in a book on culture. Shaking her head incredulously, she would ask, "What are you doing, Dave?" Not lifting his eyes from the latest tome, he'd mutter, "Reading another culture book." Dave later observed, "The way these culture books were written was always, 'Here is the way it was and here is the way it is now, and look at what a big change in performance occurred.' But they never explained how to do it." When he began reading *Journey to the Emerald City*, the predecessor to *Change the Culture, Change the Game*, he finally found what he was looking for: "This culture book was different than all the others, because it showed me what to do." After Dave finished reading the book, he invited us onto the scene to help him implement our culture change methodologies to transform the Alaris culture so that it produced go-to people and teams that could execute the strategy and change the performance of the organization.

At that point, Dave made a conscious decision to stop focusing on financial performance. The company had racked up thirty consecutive months of losses, and he knew that similar financial results would no doubt continue for the foreseeable future. For the last eighteen months, he had been focusing on changing the financial performance of the company, a process he knew like the back of his hand, but it hadn't made any difference. "In fact," he said, "it was getting worse, and I was getting frustrated. I thought, why frustrate myself?" Instead of getting frustrated, Dave chose to concentrate his efforts on changing the culture, something that was new to him as a manager and leader, something that was clearly missing from the Alaris management team's focus.

THE RESULTS PYRAMID

Dave and his team successfully implemented the culture change process detailed in the pages ahead. Central to their effort was a simple model we call the Results Pyramid. In the business of culture change, simple is good. In fact, we like to remind our clients that simplicity is on the other side of complexity! Just because something is simple does not necessarily make it less potent, versatile, or effectual. Quite the opposite. In the very simplicity of the model, you find its power and sophistication to enact real change in an organization. The Results Pyramid will help you better understand, change, and then manage your organizational culture so that you achieve the bottom-line results you are accountable to deliver.

The Results Pyramid presents how the three essential components of organizational culture—experiences, beliefs, and actions—work in harmony with each other to achieve results. Experiences foster beliefs, beliefs influence actions, and actions produce results. The experiences, beliefs, and actions of the people in your organization constitute your culture, and as the Results Pyramid demonstrates, your culture produces your results. This bears repeating. Your organizational culture produces the results you are getting. If, like Dave Schlotterbeck, you need to change your organization's results, we recommend you consider applying the culture change process we present in the pages ahead that helped Dave and the Alaris organization energize their people and create accountability for results, which they delivered in a most convincing and unprecedented manner.

In *Change the Culture, Change the Game*, we will examine scores of situations and examples to illustrate how you can use this model to accelerate a change in culture. In Part One, we will show you how to implement the culture change by tackling one piece of the pyramid at a time and employing the best practices to implement each level of the model effectively. In Part Two, we will introduce specific Culture Management Tools needed to accelerate the change in culture, and we'll show you how to integrate these tools into the daily business activity and ongoing management process of your organization.

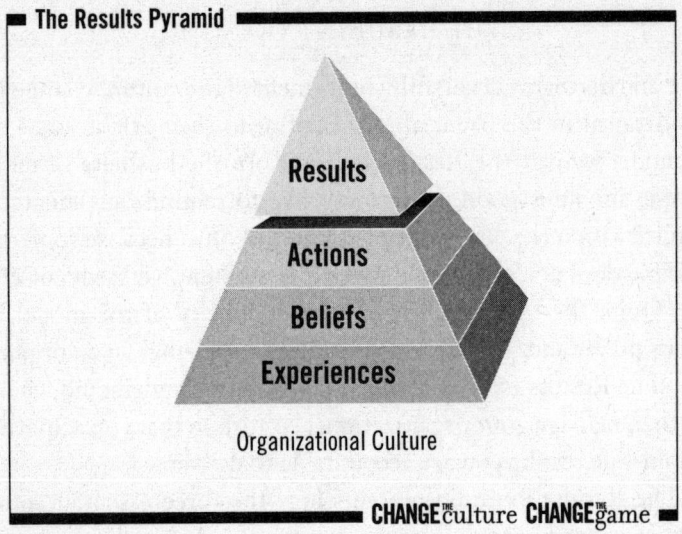

The Results Pyramid

Results

Actions

Beliefs

Experiences

Organizational Culture

CHANGE THE culture CHANGE THE game

Whether managers realize it or not, they are creating experiences every day that help shape their organizational culture. From promoting someone or implementing new policies to interacting in meetings or reacting to feedback, these experiences foster beliefs about "how we do things around here," and those beliefs, in turn, drive the actions people take. Collectively, their actions, with few exceptions, produce their results. It's really that simple, and it happens every minute of every day. Whether your organization is a robust and healthy one or one that needs to change, learning how to make sure the culture is working for you will result in creating greater competitive advantage. Always!

That's exactly what happened at Alaris. About three months into the change effort, Dave began to see signs of progress that would quickly evolve into a major turning point. While he could not measure them as precisely as the usual financial indicators, he began to see more of the go-to attitude he and the marketing manager had visualized spreading throughout the company. People were starting to "get things done." While it was not as apparent to others in the company, Dave recognized real change was beginning to occur. But would it stave off disaster?

Possibly not. The banks had finally run out of patience and wanted to put the company into bankruptcy. Alaris had broken its debt covenants on eight different occasions, resulting in punishing 16 percent interest rates and large fees. As far as the banks were concerned, it just looked like "business as usual" at Alaris. Hoping to change that impression, Dave boarded a flight to New York to meet with the bankers and plead for more time. In a scene right out of a high-stakes thriller, he sat at the end of a long conference table surrounded by thirty-five bankers who wanted to know what was happening with their money. Armed with only one data point, his sense of the change that was beginning to take hold at his company, Dave announced, "The turnaround has started." He could see the quizzical frowns of the bankers around the table. Someone exclaimed, "Are you out of your mind? You still owe a ton of money, and you have broken your covenants. We think the company should go into bankruptcy." Amazingly, but with only that one unsubstantiated data point in hand, Dave managed to buy a little more time.

Meanwhile, Dave and his team, using the Results Pyramid as a guide, enrolled every Alaris manager in the process of creating the right experiences to foster the desired beliefs, produce the most effective actions, and bring about the intended results. As the culture change effort went into full swing, management quickly enrolled everyone at every level of the company. Within six short months, the financial indicators turned positive as Alaris began posting monthly profits. These results were, in and of themselves, an important experience that reinforced the belief among the company's people that they really could execute and turn their performance around. People felt energized, optimistic, and eager to do whatever they could to get results. Dave felt just as enthusiastic. He could see clearly that only when they started working on the culture did the financial picture begin to change. Changing the culture was literally changing the game for Alaris.

Alaris's game plan included an innovative concept and product for enhancing patient safety and preventing medication mistakes by health care providers. When the marketplace eagerly adopted the concept, large institutions began to place big orders. Essentially, the same people at Alaris who had formerly stumbled in their attempts to implement such strategies were now executing them flawlessly. For Dave, it was a breathtaking change. With the game at Alaris changing so significantly, he was finally able to pull away from the details and focus on the bigger picture, the business itself.

In time, customers preferred purchasing from Alaris because it had established its brand as the gold standard in patient safety. One afternoon, a manager from the Alaris Safety Center marched into Dave's office and announced, "The customer wants to see you." Dave thought, *Uh oh, this can't be good. Customers don't generally summon the CEO unless they're angry about something.* When Dave entered the boardroom, he found a contingent of clinicians and their chief nursing officer waiting for him. The CNO started, "I only have one question." Dave thought, *Oh, here it comes.* She continued, "What have you done with your organization? We are so impressed that we want to do the same thing with our organization. We have never seen anything like it before." At this point, Dave knew Alaris had so fully internalized the change that their customers could see it just as clearly as he did. From that day forward, that admiring group became the company's biggest and best customer.

Dave had never really talked to the bankers and financial analysts about the culture change because he thought that the number crunchers would disdain such a soft topic. True or not, whenever the analysts visited the reinvigorated company, they would always ask, "What's going on here?" Everyone who came into contact with Alaris saw the change. The company was hitting and exceeding its financial numbers, it had become the employer of choice in San Diego, and it attracted visiting executives who wanted to see first-hand a manufacturing operation where industry best practices and high morale ruled the day.

Dave had also avoided sharing the culture change project with the board of directors, because, in the beginning at least, he didn't think he could sell them on investing in a soft strategy in such hard times. Of course, he didn't need to do much selling two years later when Alaris's stock price had shot from 31¢ per share to $14 per share. They were now the heroes. Nothing could have delighted the board more than that bottom-line result.

It got even better when Cardinal Health, one of the largest medical device companies in the world, paid $2 billion for a company with a market cap of $15 million. That represented a whopping 7,000 percent return on equity investment from the day Dave and his team started working on the Alaris culture to the day they sold the company to Cardinal Health. Today, the company's technology and products protect over 1.5 million patients each year! How did it happen? Dave Schlotterbeck and his Alaris team created a culture that allowed them to flawlessly execute a game-changing strategy.

They got the desired result. They changed the game by creating a culture filled with go-to people and teams that can execute the company's strategy and enhance its performance. The outcome for Alaris: unmatched performance in the industry. The outcome for our company, Partners In Leadership: another very happy client and a superb case study to report. *Change the Culture, Change the Game* introduces a proven strategy for energizing the workforce to create a Culture of Accountability for results by describing what happens to people like Dave Schlotterbeck and companies like Alaris when they manage their culture with knowledge, determination, and a methodology that accelerates change and produces results.

We have helped hundreds of organizations like Alaris Medical Systems implement organizational change efforts that brought about similar game-changing results. Our experiences with companies in every major industry category, including some of the top-performing organizations in the world, have proven our assertion: If you change the culture, you *will* change the game. In the pages ahead, you will meet many people, like Dave Schlotterbeck, who have done just that.

THE CENTRAL IDEAS

As we help organizations, large and small, change their culture, we commonly hear two questions:

1. How do you change culture in a way that will get organizational results?

2. How do you do it quickly enough to enhance the bottom line?

The answers lie in the application of the Results Pyramid and its associated methodologies and tools, which enable organizations of any size and any type to implement and integrate the culture change needed to create competitive advantage. Before we proceed, however, we'd like to emphasize a few central ideas:

- Leaders must create the needed culture.

- The culture produces the results.

- The most effective culture is a Culture of Accountability.

- The Results Pyramid will accelerate the transition to a Culture of Accountability and create competitive advantage.

We have not encountered a single situation in which these basic ideas do not hold true. That's why we work to drive them home early. We firmly believe that leaders and managers who understand and accept them will much more easily and quickly develop the leadership competency of managing culture. Leaders must manage culture. Culture does produce results. A Culture of Accountability is the most effective culture. And companies that create such a culture get the results they want and need to have.

LEADERS MUST CREATE THE NEEDED CULTURE

Either you manage your culture, or it will manage you. In our work, we continually meet people, at every level of an organization, who get batted around by their company's culture. Their culture undermines their attempts to get the results they want. They long for stronger customer focus, but they can't get it. They desire diversity, but they can't create it. They appreciate the need for regulatory compliance, but they can't attain it. They plan for growth, quality, productivity, and profitability, only to end up disappointed by a lack of performance. When the culture is not working, it poses a formidable obstacle to achieving results.

Every company has a culture. That culture either came about as the result of a methodical effort to build it, or it has developed willy-nilly, for better or worse. Whether it arose from a deliberate process or not, you must ask yourself one all-important question: If everyone in the organization continues to think and act in the same manner as they do today, can you expect to achieve the results you need to achieve? Overwhelmingly, organizational leaders answer this question with a resounding, "No! We must shift the way we think and act!"

Will your culture produce the results you've promised? Will it deliver the results you need in the future? If you don't think it will, then changing the culture is not an option, it is an imperative; and you need to begin doing it now. As an organizational leader, you must take the initiative. You might be tempted to appoint a "chief culture officer," but that would just rob the leadership team of one of its most vital responsibilities. Culture does not change in a "one and done" event, nor is it something you can relegate to your Human Resources department. From long years of experience, we know that the leadership team must shoulder the responsibility of shifting culture. Developing the leadership competency to accelerate the change effectively and then sustain the culture over time is the never-ending role of leadership. You can exclude no one. Culture building will and must involve every single leader in your organization.

Not infrequently, leaders who fail to manage culture find that when the game changes, as it always does, sooner or later, they are forced to play catch-up, which is almost always a costly and risky endeavor. Just look at the American automobile industry. In the case of General Motors, the game changed so drastically over the past few decades that the once dominant manufacturer found its market share slashed from 50 percent to 20 percent. Ed Whitacre Jr., appointed chairman of General Motors by the White House on June 1, 2009 (the same day GM filed for Chapter 11 bankruptcy), took on the unenviable task of changing the stagnant GM culture so that the company could once again compete and win. In his first round of communications with GM employees, the former AT&T boss told GM people that he expected to see visible, positive changes in the company within twelve weeks. Managers, he insisted, would be held accountable for making real progress toward immediately fixing GM's deficiencies and inadequacies. That was a tall order for a company wallowing in a stagnant culture characterized by bureaucratic decision making, management by committee, a lack of individual accountability, and a fear of taking risks. Whitacre felt certain that without a major shift in GM's culture, the company would never reverse the $80 billion dollar losses that had accumulated in the years preceding the bankruptcy and put GM into this bleak situation.

An Associated Press article reported Whitacre's message to GM workers: "Make decisions. Take risks. Move fast. Be accountable." Like Dave Schlotterbeck, Whitacre appreciated the need for sure and swift culture change. He, too, needed an organization filled with go-to people. The GM board liked what he was doing enough to ask him to take the helm as CEO. Will he succeed at the daunting task of teaching this old elephant new tricks? For GM, it's a game of catch-up, but one that Whitacre stands to win if he is able to master the competencies of culture change. Learning how to manage culture is, for the best of business reasons, an essential management skill that brings us to our next principle.

THE CULTURE PRODUCES THE RESULTS

Your organization's culture determines your results, and the results you want should largely determine the kind of culture you need. Culture depends on results; results depend on culture. Leaders can build a company culture around any set of desired results: market dominance, sales growth, technological excellence, ease of customer interaction, best-in-class quality, or stable earnings, just to name a few. Once you clearly define the targets, then you must move quickly to build a culture that produces the right experiences, beliefs, and actions to achieve those results.

The leaders of a well-known retail brand, which we'll call "Lauren-Smith" or L-S for short (to provide the requested anonymity), consistently delivered on their performance metrics. The owners of the firm had made it abundantly clear to their senior managers that they were accountable to solve problems and get results and that if they did not solve problems, they were "not doing their jobs."

To produce and place reports of excellence on the owners' desks, a practice evolved in the culture that amounted to "Potemkin visits," a term that conjures up the image of lovely but sham villages supposedly erected by General Potemkin's troops and repeatedly moved from place to place along a road in eighteenth-century Russia to fool Catherine the Great into thinking that the newly conquered Crimea was prosperous when, in fact, it was nearly desolate.

In the case of L-S, when the time came for executive inspections to ensure that L-S products were advantageously displayed in stores, the managers selected stores grouped near one another in a straight line to the airport, minimizing any obstacles to the quick and hopefully uneventful trip. Any variance from the preplanned route could cost the sales associates their jobs. With advance warning prior to each planned store visit, the area's sales associates would scurry around erecting knock-their-socks-off merchandise displays to give the appearance that the brand was being promoted in the intended way, only to see these displays dismantled within hours of the store visit. On top of that, associates were told never to raise any thorny issues or problems during the visit, for management was not coming to solve problems but to see that everything was going as planned. In one especially egregious case, L-S associates ran the scam at every store within fifty miles of the North American Sales Meeting. People flew in from all over the country to make it happen. It all went smoothly enough, but it cost the company some $400,000 in free merchandise! The result: only perfect scores on the store visit report to top management. From the top, it appeared that problems were being solved and the brand presence in the stores was proceeding as planned.

Out of curiosity, we recently asked a sales associate who had worked at L-S for thirty-five years if he still set up Potemkin visits.

The veteran laughed. "Sure! I just spent the last two weeks getting ready for one we ran just yesterday." How, you might ask, could this go on year after year? Wouldn't someone at the top wonder why all twenty stores in an area always received perfect scores during an audit? Apparently not. The Potemkin visits had become a part of the culture. Imagine the results the culture could have been producing if the company had eradicated such inefficiencies? Optimizing the organization's culture in order to operate at the highest level of performance will always yield a competitive advantage, validating our central idea: The most effective culture is a Culture of Accountability.

THE MOST EFFECTIVE CULTURE IS A CULTURE OF ACCOUNTABILITY

Our first book, *The Oz Principle: Getting Results Through Individual and Organizational Accountability*, became the classic book on workplace accountability because people do recognize that greater accountability, done the right way, can make all the difference in terms of bottom-line results. *The Oz Principle* presents a hands-on guide to creating that kind of accountability for yourself, your team, and your organization.

Central to the message of *The Oz Principle* are the Steps to Accountability. A clear line separates accountable and nonaccountable behavior and thinking. Above the line are the Steps to Accountability, to See It, Own It, Solve It, and Do It. Below that line is the all-too-familiar blame game or victim cycle. The Steps to Accountability lead to what we call Above the Line actions and thinking. The blame game, however, results in what we describe as Below the Line actions and thinking. As you might imagine, when individuals consistently engage in these two very different modes of thinking and acting, they create different organizational cultures, which perform at strikingly different levels.

We have found that people who consistently adhere to the Steps to Accountability almost always think and act in an accountable manner. By the same token, people who fail to take these steps get stuck in the blame game, feeling victimized by circumstances that seem outside their control. They fail to move forward in their quest for results.

We should point out that it is not wrong to go Below the Line. We all do. It's human nature. In fact, we can all occasionally benefit from venting our frustrations about the obstacles that block our paths or sound off about the situations that seem to spin out of our control. However, if we remain stuck Below the Line, we become more focused on what we cannot do rather than on what we can do. In that case, we set our sights on the obstacles we face, not the actions we can take to get past those obstacles and achieve the results we want. People who are habitually Below the Line do not get results. Instead, they grow increasingly frustrated and paralyzed. They almost never feel fulfilled by their work. Their organizations, their teams, and their own careers falter.

People who live Above the Line accept the fact that they are, and must be, part of the solution. They focus on what they can do rather than on what they cannot do to get results. They look for creative ways to deal with obstacles, which they view as opportunities to make great things happen rather than as excuses for failure. Above the Line, people move forward, get results, and feel satisfied in their work. They, their teams, and their organizations prosper. Simply put, the more time you spend Above the Line, the greater will be your results. And the more time an organization spends Above the Line, the greater will be its results.

Above the Line accountability lays the foundation for a Culture of Accountability, in which people take accountability to think and act in the manner necessary to achieve organizational results. No other culture works as well to ensure success. Look closely at any consistently high-performing organization, and you will find a lot of people who have mastered this fundamental core competency. By the same token, examine an organization that continually underperforms, and you'll find people languishing Below the Line. People unfamiliar with our positive approach to accountability often misunderstand or misapply accountability in their organizations. Consider the last time you heard someone ask, "Who's accountable for that?" Was it said in an effort to determine whom to reward for getting good results? Probably not. People from all over the world tell us in our training workshops that accountability is something that happens to them when things have gone wrong. To them, accountability is more about punishment than empowerment. However, most everyone agrees that greater accountability, when understood and applied correctly, can and will improve an organization's results in dramatic ways.

A Culture of Accountability exists when people in every corner of the organization make the personal choice to take the Steps to Accountability. Each step builds on the previous one and involves best practices that typify what taking that step truly requires.

▶ **See It** means moving Above the Line or staying there whenever a new challenge arises. When you See It, you relentlessly obtain the perspectives of others, communicate openly and candidly, ask for and offer feedback, and hear the hard things that allow you to see reality. These best practices apply up and down the hierarchy in the organization, from boss to subordinate, from peer to peer, from function to function, and among peers. They help you courageously acknowledge reality.

▶ **Own It** means being personally invested, learning from both successes and failures, aligning your work with desired company results, and acting on the feedback you receive. When you Own It, you align yourself with the mission and priorities of the organization and accept them as your own. Ownership depends on linking where you are with what you have done, and where you want to be with what you are going to do. The Own It step lies at the heart of true accountability.

▶ **Solve It** requires persistent effort as you encounter obstacles that stand in the way of achieving results. When you take this step, you constantly ask the question "What else can I do?" to achieve results, overcome obstacles, and make progress. Solve

It includes overcoming cross-functional boundaries, creatively dealing with obstacles, and taking necessary risks. You cannot skip this step.

▶ **Do It,** the final step in the process, represents the natural culmination of the first three steps: Once you See It, Own It, and Solve It, you must get out there and Do It. That means doing what you say you will do, focusing on top priorities, staying Above the Line by not blaming others, and sustaining an environment of trust. You can take all three previous steps, but to stay Above the Line and achieve the result, you must take the crucial fourth and final step and Do It.

If everyone takes the Steps to Accountability, the entire organization moves away from the mistaken idea that accountability means "getting caught failing" and toward a more positive approach that empowers people to begin "starring in the solution." We could analyze several other characteristics of a Culture of Accountability, but at this stage we suggest you keep it simple. In a Culture of Accountability, people step forward and work hard to solve problems and get results. They do it willingly, not because some higher authority has commanded them to do it and not because they fear that not doing it will get them in trouble. They do it because their company's managers and leaders have used the Results Pyramid in a conscious and deliberate campaign to create the best possible results-oriented culture. We have seen it happen countless times over the past twenty years.

USING THE RESULTS PYRAMID TO ACCELERATE THE CHANGE IN CULTURE

In a world where being first means everything, accelerating the change process has become essential to getting business results. Believe it or not, you can create culture change in time to improve your organization's current key business results. *Change the Culture,*

Change the Game shows you precisely how to do that. Specifically, this book will equip you with the tools you need to do it surely and swiftly. Depending on the nature of your company's current culture, this process may entail anything from a few slight shifts to a complete cultural overhaul.

Do you need to make some shifts in the way people think and act in your culture? Most companies do. These shifts may be necessary because of a need for improved performance or in anticipation of, or sometimes in reaction to, a change in the business environment. Whatever the case, the Results Pyramid model will help you clearly understand and communicate what you need to do each time you need to effect change. The diagram below depicts the needed shift in the results, from R^1, the current results, to R^2, the desired results. R^2 may differ from R^1 because the new numbers are bigger, the economy is tougher, the competition has increased, the market has changed, or any number of other conditions that have set the bar higher. Remember, by definition, your culture produces your results. You can't expect the current culture, C^1, to produce R^2 results. It simply won't work.

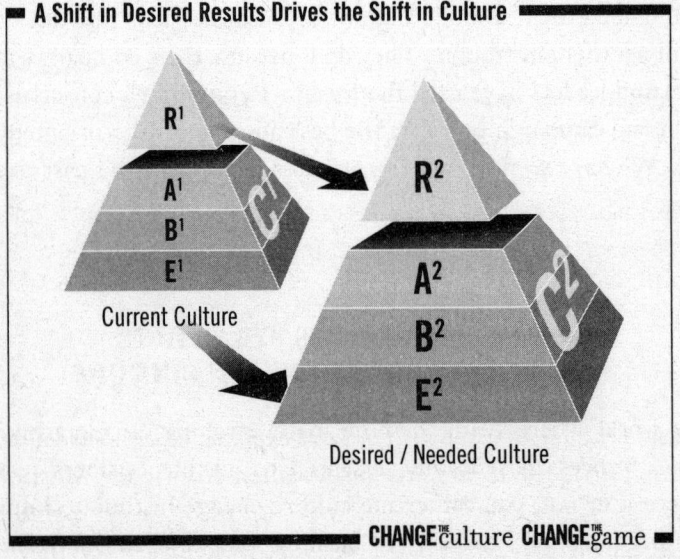

A Shift in Desired Results Drives the Shift in Culture

Current Culture

Desired / Needed Culture

CHANGE the culture CHANGE the game

We should emphasize that in most cases, C^1, the current culture, is not a bad culture. It's simply a culture that won't produce R^2. C^2, the new culture, always builds on the strengths of C^1. Always. However, to achieve R^2, some shifts in the culture will be required to motivate people to think and act in the manner necessary to achieve the new, desired results. More often than not, this does not mean a *total transformation* of your culture; instead, it simply means a *transition*, a more modest cultural shift. Keep in mind the fact that trying to extract R^2 from C^1 doesn't work. You can't expect the old culture to magically abandon its powerful, persistent, existing attributes and produce new results. That just won't happen. Not ever. To achieve new R^2 results, you must create the new C^2 culture that will produce those results. You do this by defining the needed shifts in the way people think (the new B^2 beliefs) and act (the new A^2 actions), which will then provide the new experiences (E^2) that will help them adopt those desired beliefs and actions.

Culture provides leaders with a powerful tool that produces results. Its power also stems from the fact that it persists and outlives our own personal influence. One CEO said it best when he told his senior management team, "Here's when I saw that culture was real. Early in my career, I spent some time in our Italian affiliate. After a period of time, I left for a new assignment in another country and lost touch with the organization. Five years later, I came back to Italy and didn't see one familiar face on the team: There had been 100 percent turnover. Yet the culture was exactly the same in that company. Nothing in the culture had changed, even though all the people were different!" It's so true. You can change all of the people and leave the culture essentially intact.

WORKING WITH THE ENTIRE PYRAMID

The power and persistence of culture explains why the usual tactics that managers use to improve results often don't work. Most of the usual fixes, from new people and new technology to new strategies and new structures, work only at the level of actions, when they work at all. Too often, leaders attempt to change the way people act without changing the way they think (i.e., their beliefs). As a result, they get compliance, but not commitment; involvement, but not investment; and progress, but not lasting performance.

The diagram below illustrates the barrier that arises when you set about improving performance and make the all-too-common mistake of focusing your attention on just the top of the pyramid: actions and results. By working with just these top two layers, you ignore the fact that people think and that there are reasons why people think the way they do; you leave unchanged the two elements that most fundamentally affect performance: experiences and beliefs.

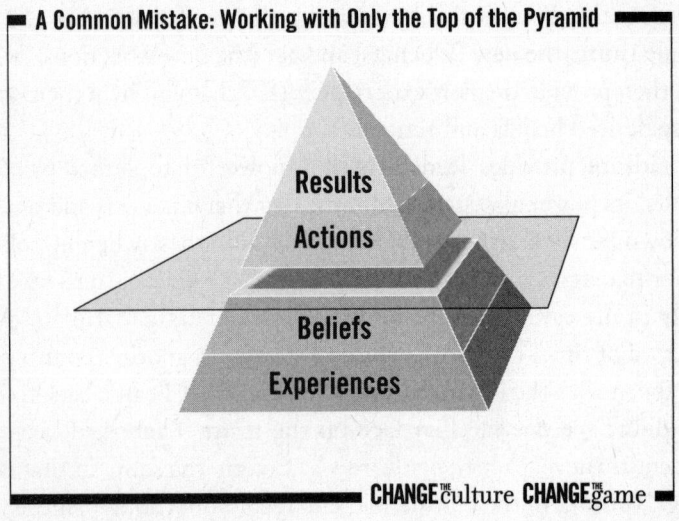

A Common Mistake: Working with Only the Top of the Pyramid

Results
Actions
Beliefs
Experiences

CHANGE the culture CHANGE the game

Working with the bottom of the pyramid causes more significant, long-lasting change, but it also takes more effort. To accelerate culture change, leaders must work with both the top and the bottom of the pyramid. We've found that leaders tend to work with the top of the pyramid because it looks easier to manage. They assume that because actions and results are more concrete and more observable, they can work with them more easily. However, those who have learned how to work with beliefs and experiences know that they are just as concrete and just as observable. While everyone can learn to do it, it does require a strong dose of courage to obtain the feedback necessary to unearth what people really believe and to create the experiences required to affect their actions.

As we mentioned earlier, we find it useful to think of accelerating culture change in terms of two distinct steps: implementation and integration. During the first phase of implementation, you deconstruct the culture. The management team becomes fully aware of the strengths and weaknesses of C^1. Together they examine the experiences (E^1), beliefs (B^1), and actions (A^1) that constitute the culture and carefully consider what they need to shift.

During the next phase of implementation, they reconstruct the culture. Now the team considers the current business environment and defines the organization's R^2. They also determine the experiences (E^2), beliefs (B^2), and actions (A^2) that constitute C^2.

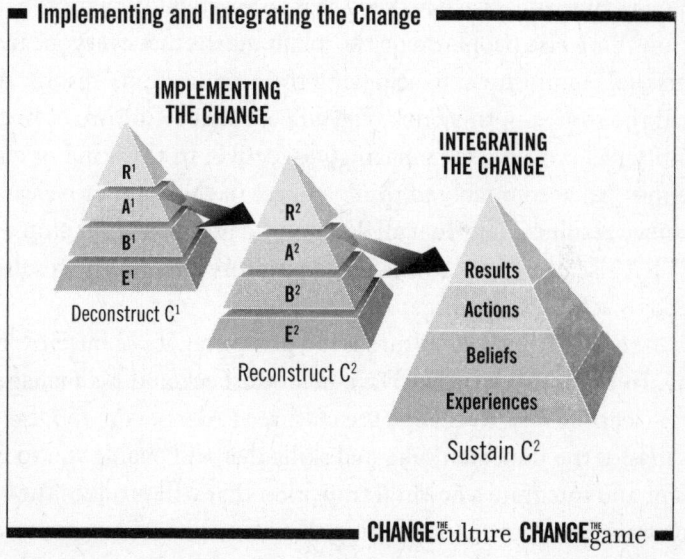

Implementing and Integrating the Change

IMPLEMENTING
THE CHANGE

INTEGRATING
THE CHANGE

R^1
A^1
B^1
E^1
Deconstruct C^1

R^2
A^2
B^2
E^2
Reconstruct C^2

Results
Actions
Beliefs
Experiences
Sustain C^2

CHANGE the culture CHANGE the game

The next step is to integrate the culture change into the current organizational systems and processes, thereby sustaining the C^2 shifts. At this point, the team applies the Culture Management Tools that we describe later in the book, tools that accelerate and reinforce the desired shifts. With a little training, the leadership of the organization can become quite adept at creating E^2 experiences that foster and reinforce desired B^2 beliefs. During this step, leaders monitor the culture to maintain a focus on results and on the actions and beliefs required to attain those results.

Ultimately, you must involve everyone in the organization in the process of changing and sustaining the culture. Once you gain momentum, you will find that the culture change becomes, to a certain degree, self-reinforcing. In and of themselves, better results (R^2) become a foundational experience that reinforces the belief that the effort to change culture matters and ranks as a top priority deserving everyone's continued attention.

BUILDING A CULTURE OF ACCOUNTABILITY

In our experience, we have seen that accountability matters as much as anything else people do on the job. It means that everyone makes a personal commitment to achieving the organization's results. As you read the stories in this book, you will see that a Culture of Accountability has proven itself amazingly effective. In this kind of culture, people feel accountable to think and act in the manner necessary to achieve results. They do it all day, every day. They never stop asking, "What else can I do?" to change the culture and get the results they need to achieve as an organization.

Creating the right culture is not an option; it is a business necessity. In the same way that Dave Schlotterbeck and his management team learned how to change the culture at Alaris, you, too, can learn to master the understanding and skills that will enable you to implement and integrate a cultural transition that will produce the results you want to achieve. Accelerating that transition will create competitive advantage, the kind of advantage that can change the game. To begin this process, we will start by working with the top of the pyramid to understand how defining results sets the stage for the culture change.

CHAPTER 2

Defining the Results
That Guide the Change

BUILDING A CULTURE of Accountability begins at the top of the Results Pyramid. That's why the first step in *Change the Culture, Change the Game* involves clearly stating the R^2 results you want to achieve. Frankly, it makes no sense to initiate any culture building activity or process unless you intend to increase the capability of the organization to deliver results.

The most compelling reason to work on your culture? Culture produces results.

"Opthometrics," a client and a respected optical retailer, provides convincing evidence that our assertion is true. Following several years of solid business results, a serious downturn in the economy posed a challenge to Opthometrics. Although the company had put initiatives in place to improve results, the numbers were not where Opthometrics wanted them to be. Early in the process, Opthometrics brought in two leaders known for their outstanding field management, both of whom believed that in order to improve the results, they needed to go to work on the culture.

That effort started with the Brand Leadership Team getting aligned around R^2 in several areas of operational performance. The current business model, R^1, was not delivering the desired business results and needed to change. Testing the premise that culture produces results, Opthometrics conducted a pilot in 5 percent of its stores, applying the principles and practices presented in *Change the Culture, Change the Game.*

There were plenty of skeptics whom the team needed to convince that changing culture would indeed change results. Everyone agreed to a pilot test with a clear definition of success that would make the conclusions perfectly clear. Bottom line, the pilot would need to show a significant impact on the business before the company could make a go-forward decision to launch the culture change effort worldwide in all of its retail stores. The team agreed that anything less than a 2 percent improvement in the pilot stores would trigger a no-go decision. Improvement that fell in the 2-to-5 point range would indicate the need for further evaluation. But improvement of 5 percent or more would support an automatic go and full-scale launch of the change effort. With the success criteria firmly established, they spelled out precisely how they would evaluate any performance improvements. They were not going to take any chance on investing their time and resources on culture unless the pilot met these standards of success.

After the first two months, results were well above 5 percent. The outcome was unequivocal: Changing the culture significantly increased the retail brand's ability to get the desired R^2 results. At Opthometrics, the culture began to change quickly as people began thinking and acting differently about how to do their daily work in the pilot stores. Not surprisingly, based on the results of the pilot, the client launched a company-wide effort to change the culture.

GETTING ALIGNED AROUND THE KEY R^2 RESULTS

Any organization that is serious about accelerating culture change can gain similar benefits by gaining alignment around the key R^2 results. Because the key R^2 results drive the activity, energy, and effort of the company, you cannot assume alignment around those results; you must purposely create and then consciously maintain it throughout the organization.

Would it surprise you to learn that nine out of ten management teams cannot describe with complete alignment the key results their organizations need to achieve? For instance, one company we worked with, a growing regional fast-food chain in the southwestern United States, the "Fast Grill," was planning to launch a massive nationwide expansion and needed to improve its profit margin in order to do that. In a planning meeting, we asked the Grill's top management staff, "What are the three key results you most need to achieve as an organization?" Everyone on the team replied, "Profit margin." At first it seemed as if they were aligned around this result. But any appearance of alignment quickly disappeared with the answer to the next question, "What's the number?" One executive called out, "5.5 percent." Another immediately disagreed, chiming in with "3.5 percent." Then another quickly reacted with a bit of exasperation, "I thought we agreed it was 7.5 percent."

We turned to the CEO, who was intently listening to this discussion, thinking that she could settle this matter and clarify the number. When we asked her for the number, she responded adeptly, saying, "It's somewhere between 3.5 and 7.5 percent." Ignoring the laughter, she continued, "Let me explain: 3.5 percent is the number we told corporate we could hit, 5.5 percent is the number we think we will hit, and 7.5 percent is our stretch goal." Believe it or not, this management team is not alone. Confusion about results is all too common in most organizations.

The Fast Grill team's confusion left the door open to poor execution, inviting Below the Line behavior, which undermines the foundation on which an effective culture change depends. Confusion licenses people to maintain the status quo and to dismiss their accountability to internalize the need for change. Confusion kills the momentum of any culture change effort because no one feels confident about which direction to move. When people fall Below the Line during a time of culture change, they fail to look at what else they can do to improve company performance and deliver results. Often, a move Below the Line not only impedes progress, it stops culture change dead in its tracks.

When we spoke privately with the Fast Grill's president, she told us that the parent company had clearly communicated the result the

Grill needed to achieve. In fact, corporate had told her that if the chain did not achieve the specified target, they might sell it. Corporate had also emphasized the fact that similar restaurant chains in the parent company's portfolio were achieving the expected return. Because the CEO knew that the team would view the corporate expectations as unrealistic, she doubted that her team members would align themselves around that target. When we asked, "What's the margin that you must deliver?" she replied, "5.5 percent." Although they had been missing the number, she acknowledged that they needed to hit it, and soon. She also agreed that if they did not change the way people thought and acted regarding hitting the margin, from top management on down and throughout every restaurant, they could not possibly deliver the 5.5 percent.

Over the next several hours, we worked with the senior team people to get them aligned around this key R^2 result and to determine the shifts in culture they would need to make in order to achieve it. First, they determined to stop sending their organization mixed messages and to start communicating the same key results to everyone in a compelling way. They committed to ensure that all employees could connect the dots between their daily work and the R^2 they needed to achieve.

Within months, a check on the alignment in the company proved that people at every level of the organization and within every restaurant understood and embraced R^2. A random visit to a restaurant would also reveal that even people busing tables understood the margin goals. When asked what their job was, they would respond, "My job is to achieve a 5.5 percent profit margin, and here's how I do it: The faster I clean and set a table, the more people we seat per hour. The more people we seat, the greater our contribution. The greater our contribution, the better our margin. That's what I do." Powerful, impactful, and clearly conveyed, this answer represented the shift in culture that Fast Grill needed.

With that level of clarity and alignment around the few key results that make up R^2, the Fast Grill enacted a cultural transition that literally changed the game for them. Within eighteen months, this organization realized a 200 percent increase in profit margin and delivered on 7.5 percent. They went on to launch their national expansion and became one of the top brands in their category by most measures. Ultimately, they were purchased by one of the top casual dining restaurant companies in the world, an organization known in the industry as the "mutual fund of casual dining," with a portfolio of restaurants successful at generating positive cash flow and profits.

DEFINING RESULTS THAT GET RESULTS

Before we go any further, one point warrants elaboration. We use the term *result*, rather than *goal* because *result* implies that either you will achieve something or that you have already achieved it. In contrast, *goal* suggests that you would like to have something happen, but might not accomplish it. A goal tends to be hopeful and directional, but not absolute.

When it comes to getting results, the story of Little Round Top from the Civil War battle of Gettysburg comes to mind. As the Confederate forces rushed to take the heights behind the town of Gettysburg on the second day of the historic three-day battle, the Union troops moved into position on a strategic hill known as Little Round Top. From this summit, the Confederate forces would have enjoyed the advantage of a clear field of artillery fire upon the entire Union line. It fell to Colonel Joshua Lawrence Chamberlain, of the Twentieth Maine Infantry, to protect this key defensive position and the flank of the Union army.

Having received orders to "hold this position at all costs," a clear key result, Colonel Chamberlain and his men repelled numerous attacks as the Confederate troops sought to weaken the flank and capture the summit. Wave after wave of intense fire and aggressive attempts to break the Union line were almost overwhelming. Facing the seemingly impossible task of holding his position with only half the strength of his initial force and little ammunition, Colonel Chamberlain, a former college professor from Bangor Theological Seminary, as a last resort, called for a bayonet charge. That bold tactic broke the Confederate line and protected the Union flank. Chamberlain understood and accepted the clearly defined result given him: "Hold this position at all costs." Clear results led to clear action. Retreat was not an option.

Management teams often fail to convey what they really mean in terms of R^2 results. In one noteworthy case, the leadership of an insurance company in Mexico ("Unido") identified the need to increase business production for its agents out in the field by developing a software program that would streamline the application process and yield a 50 percent increase in production.

The company needed to weed the inefficiencies out of its system to make it more competitive in the marketplace. Unido launched the new system with a great deal of fanfare. After all, they had made a huge investment of both time and money in the project; in fact, it was the single greatest capital commitment the company had ever made.

During a postproduction meeting, the IT department proudly proclaimed the new system effective, stable, and fully capable of supporting 35 percent production increases. What a resounding success! Or was it? At the same time, the Sales Management team, the primary end user of the system, declared the system a failure that fell short of hitting the intended result of 50 percent production increases. Believe it or not, the leadership team had not told the IT department about the intended 50 percent result. Essentially, the IT team had spent twelve months developing an application designed to underdeliver. Amazingly, we hear stories like this all the time, and they underscore the need to make a conscious and deliberate effort to define results in a way that helps produce results. That is what clarifying and communicating R^2 is all about.

WHEN DOES A NEW RESULT REQUIRE A SIGNIFICANT CULTURE SHIFT?

By definition, a result is an R^2 result when the current culture, C^1, will not produce the thoughts and actions throughout the organization critical to achieving it. Achieving R^2 will, by definition, require a culture change to C^2. That makes it essential that you determine in advance if your desired results really are R^2. To help you do this, we suggest using four criteria:

- Difficulty

- Direction

- Deployment

- Development

1. *Difficulty:* If the desired result will take more effort to achieve than past results, then you probably have set your sights on R^2, which more than likely will require that you make significant shifts in at least some aspects of your organizational culture. This increased difficulty may result from tougher objectives, similar objectives in a tougher business environment, or tougher objectives in a tougher environment. When the business environment changes, it usually becomes more difficult to maintain results, let alone improve them. Environmental changes, including all those listed in the box on page 36, could undermine almost any organization's ability to achieve results. They can make a great deal of difference when it comes to viewing a desired result as either R^1 or R^2.

2. *Direction:* If the desired results signal a significant change in direction for the organization, then this also indicates an R^2 and may necessitate a major cultural change. Changing direction can include introducing new products, entering new markets or exiting old ones, applying new technology, acquiring new companies, and implementing new strategies. Reacting quickly to market opportunities can bring about a sudden change in direction, the speed of which may, in and of itself, convert an R^1 into an R^2.

3. *Deployment:* Will the desired results require a large-scale deployment or redeployment of people or other resources? If so, this may demand a serious change in at least part of the culture. A redeployment

■ Common Changes in the Business Environment ■

1	Continued pressure on price
2	Industry consolidations among competitors and customers
3	Competitors improving and moving more quickly
4	Intensifying customer focus on value
5	Integration of the supply chain
6	Shorter, less predictable product life cycles
7	Rapid rate of technological change
8	Increasing importance of innovation
9	More mobile work force
10	New workplace issues and employee expectations
11	Globalization
12	European Union and other trade blocs changing the marketing and competitive landscape
13	Increasing regulatory pressure
14	Greater need for partnerships and alliances

■ CHANGEthe**culture CHANGE**the**game ■**

of resources from one part of the organization to another or from one area of focus to another often requires a new way of thinking about how to get things done. A major deployment of assets into the organization almost always requires a shift in the way people think and act in order to ensure the success of the venture, triggering an R^2 result.

4. *Development*: If the desired result demands that the organization develop a new capability or core competency, then you quite likely face an R^2. Developing new competencies either on the people side, with the capability of leaders or the expertise of personnel, or on the organizational side, with systems and structure, requires a significant change in mind-set that justifies a major culture shift.

Of course, the presence of any one of these variables may suggest that you should consider your desired results an R^2, necessitating a shift from C^1 to C^2. However, when you determine the presence of a number of these variables, the combination not only conclusively defines an R^2, but it also demands that the culture change in order to produce it.

At this point, you might find it helpful to examine the desired results your own organization needs to achieve. Are they R^1 or R^2? First, use the table below to list the top three results you need to achieve as an organization. These would be the three most important results that you will be held accountable to achieve.

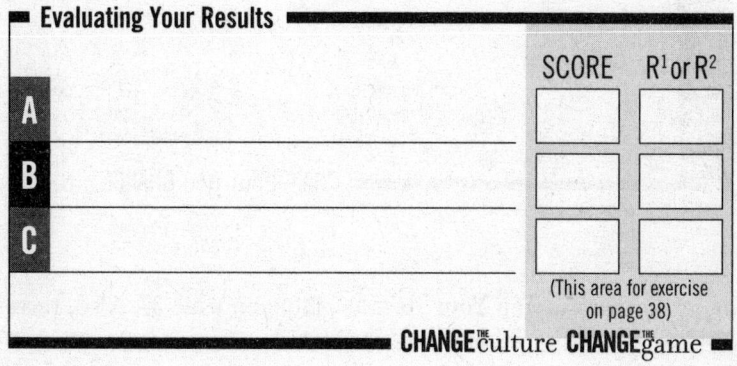

Evaluating Your Results

		SCORE	R^1 or R^2
A			
B			
C			

(This area for exercise on page 38)

CHANGE^{THE}culture CHANGE^{THE}game

Now use the grid below, "Rating Your R^2 Results," to analyze the nature of those results with respect to yourself, your team, or your organization. Would you label any or all of them R^1? R^2? Use the scale to rank the significance of the shift by rating your desired results against the four variables. Place the A, B, or C results from the preceding table, "Evaluating Your Results," on the appropriate 1-to-10 ranking for each of the four criteria below.

Use the breakdowns given below as your guide to add the points from each category (Difficulty, Direction, Deployment, and Development) together for a total score for each desired result (A, B, or C), and place that total score for each of those results in the Score

▬ Rating Your R^2 Results ▬

1	**DIFFICULTY**	1 2 3 4 5 6 7 8 9 10
		No real change in difficulty Significantly higher than past results

2	**DIRECTION**	1 2 3 4 5 6 7 8 9 10
		Same direction Significantly different direction

3	**DEPLOYMENT**	1 2 3 4 5 6 7 8 9 10
		No major deployment required Significant redeployment or deployment of people and/or resources required

4	**DEVELOPMENT**	1 2 3 4 5 6 7 8 9 10
		Current organizational capabilities will do the job Processes, systems, skills, and/or structure must change significantly

CHANGE the **culture CHANGE** the **game** ▬

box of the "Evaluating Your Results" table on page 37. Also, record whether the result, based on that total score, is classified as R^1 or R^2.

A score of 28 to 40 represents a clear R^2. Your culture may need to shift dramatically to achieve it.

A score of 16 to 27 indicates that this desired result is probably an R^2, and will most likely require a serious culture change effort to bring it about.

A score of 4 to 15 signals that the desired result is probably R^1, but it may require a more isolated and tactical shift, as opposed to an overarching one for the entire organization.

You may find it particularly useful to conduct this analysis with feedback from your group or team, which may yield a common view on whether the results you need to achieve are R^2 and whether achieving them will require a significant change in culture. On the other hand, you may unearth diverging views about the organizational challenges your desired results pose. In either case, an open discussion leading to alignment on this point may pay big dividends in terms of your ability to ensure success.

ACCELERATING CULTURE CHANGE: BEGIN WITH RESULTS

In most cases, time is of the essence when it comes to culture change, especially when management teams feel they are behind the curve and wish they had started the initiative earlier. Even so, you can accelerate the culture change, as we have shown, and make a timely impact on R^2. Consider the three essential steps to implementing the first tier of the Results Pyramid and forming R^2 to accelerate a change in the culture:

1. Define R^2.

2. Introduce R^2 throughout the organization.

3. Create accountability to achieve R^2.

Let's examine each of these steps.

Step 1: Define R^2

When it comes to results, remember that people will do what you ask them to do. So you'd better think hard about what you ask. For instance, "Netco," a global Fortune 500 company, had established its operating income results, R^2, for its European operations. The number was aggressive and raised the bar on performance throughout Europe. The president of overall European operations, "Frederic," understood the number the whole group needed to hit and had communicated it to his team of general managers. However, the old C^1 culture fostered the mind-set that each national affiliate head was rewarded solely on achieving his or her own country revenue

numbers, not the European group number, for which Frederic himself was responsible.

The realization that Netco lacked sufficient joint accountability suddenly dawned on Frederic when the year-end projections for
currency transactions revealed a projected $30 million operating-
income shortfall for the group. Frederic called a meeting with the
country GMs and told them about the projected shortfall, caused by
unforeseen losses on foreign-exchange transactions. When he asked
the group to search for every franc, mark, lira, and pound they could
find to help cover the gap, his request was met with a predictable
lukewarm C^1 response. The GMs figured the currency-exchange
problem fell beyond the realm of their personal accountability. In
retrospect, Frederic could see that because he had failed to define R^2
sufficiently, the group remained stuck in C^1.

As Frederic queried each country's general manager in turn, he
could see that they were single-mindedly focused on their individual
results. That focus caused a form of sandbagging known in the company as the old-gray-fox syndrome, by which the general managers
cunningly guarded their revenues to ensure they hit their individual
numbers not only in the current year, but in the coming year as well.
That was pure C^1 thinking and behavior, and it was clearly standing
in the way of achieving R^2 results. Frederic asked the group members to go back and work on the problem and see if they could find
a solution.

At a second meeting with the GMs, Frederic went around the
table, asking them all one by one what they could do to reduce the
shortfall. Not enough, it turned out. Their combined contributions
would only go halfway toward eliminating it. Frederic knew the
business well enough to realize that the GMs could, in fact, contribute more to the cause. As he pressed the point, they grew vocal: "If I
sacrifice now, will senior management remember what I did? What if
I fail to hit my numbers next year?"

A robust discussion ensued around the R^2 and why they needed
to achieve it, not just for their individual sakes, but also for the sake
of the European group. In the end, the team accepted the reality
that the group as a whole needed to perform or risk losing resources

and credibility within the larger organization. In an important break with C^1, they agreed to create a "team memory" of individual contributions made toward overcoming the shortfall.

To everyone's surprise, following a short break in the meeting, one of the affiliate heads who had originally resisted making a contribution to the group effort announced that he had "found" $5 million he could kick in to reduce the shortfall. Others rapidly followed suit. Finally, the group had embraced R^2, but not until C^2, the new culture, began to take root. Going forward, joint accountability for R^2 generated unprecedented teamwork among the affiliates to assume ownership for achieving both individual and group results.

Some managers avoid establishing a clear R^2 because they believe that murky objectives protect them from the risk of failure. Actually, murky results *create* failure, primarily by prohibiting alignment. Nothing creates accountability and alignment more surely than a clear statement of the results you want to achieve. People know when their organization lacks focus. Without a clear organizational result, they naturally pursue their own individual agendas, not the company's. When that happens, they define success in their own professional or personal terms ("As long as I hit my quota, I'll be fine"), leaving to chance the attainment of organizational results.

Step 2:
Introduce R^2 Throughout the Organization

To accelerate culture change, everyone in the organization needs to focus on achieving R^2. Culture changes one person at a time, and that process begins with getting each and every person in the culture aligned with R^2. Only when everyone understands a clearly communicated R^2 can they align the way they need to think (B^2) and act (A^2) to produce the desired result. A lack of this alignment makes everything harder, as shown in the diagram below. Implementations don't go as smoothly, cross-functional teams don't get along as well, communication seems less effective, and desired results become harder and harder to produce.

Conversely, the culture becomes aligned when people's actions,

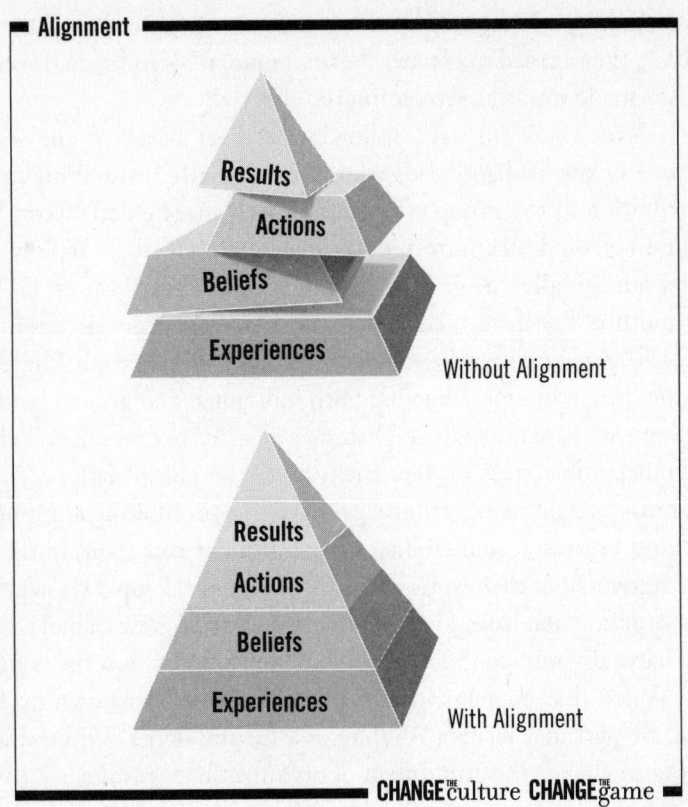

beliefs, and experiences align with R^2. This diagram suggests that a more powerfully aligned culture will more effectively, efficiently, and consistently focus on results. The more consistently people do focus on results, the more likely they will be to create the C^2 culture that will produce those results.

Effective leaders manage in ways that get a culture aligned with R^2, and then they keep it aligned. They say and do things to create experiences that generate or reinforce beliefs that motivate actions that produce the results. By the same token, they avoid saying and doing things that put the culture out of alignment. Managing a culture is a process, not an event; it never ends, even after you have successfully integrated R^2 throughout the entire organization.

Step 3:
Create Accountability to Achieve R^2

In a workshop setting, we often ask participants to define their jobs. Invariably, we hear a recital of job titles, such as quality supervisor, general manager, tax analyst, VP of manufacturing, or senior vice president of sales. The problem with these answers is that they merely identify where people sit in the organization, which has a huge impact on how people think about their jobs. That way of thinking places more emphasis on doing the job than on what is needed to achieve results. In contrast, when you effectively create accountability to achieve R^2, people start to see their purposes and roles differently, defining their jobs in terms of the results they need to achieve rather than their job descriptions.

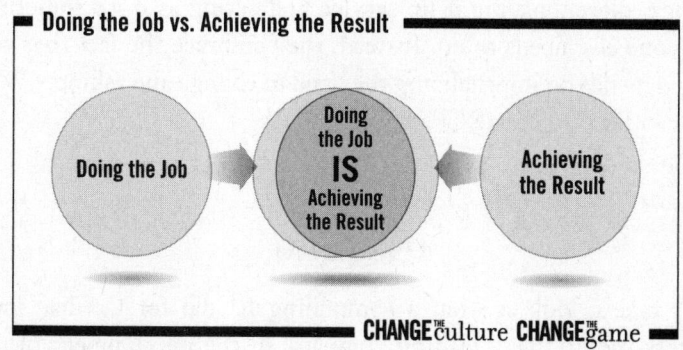

Closing the gap between doing the job and achieving the result, as shown in the above diagram, is essential to making R^2 a vital part of everyone's job in the organization.

THE PROCESS OF CREATING ACCOUNTABILITY FOR R^2

You cannot create accountability for R^2 unless you also recognize your accountability for R^1. After all, R^1 resulted from the collective experiences, beliefs, and actions of people in the organization. Taking accountability for R^1, good or bad, is an important step to creating accountability for R^2. The ability to make the connection between your R^1 results and what you have or have not done to produce them establishes the foundation of ownership you will need to get real about the shifts that need to occur. The act of claiming accountability for current and past results creates a powerful, positive experience for everyone in a company because it reinforces the idea that "If we are responsible for where we are, we can also be responsible for where we want to go."

This level of personal and organizational accountability lays an important foundation that will make or break your culture change effort. Only then can the leadership enable everyone to see and own R^2. The foundation of accountability resets the ground rules during the change effort. No longer can people externalize the need to change, merely paying it lip service and acting as if it's something everyone else needs to do. Instead, they embrace the fact that winning depends on internalizing the need to change and asking, "What else can I do" to create C^2 and achieve R^2.

R^2 IN ACTION

Let's take a look at what a compelling R^2 did for Cardiac Pacemakers Inc. (CPI), a leading company in the development of cardiovascular technology. Shortly following its acquisition by one of the top pharmaceutical companies in the world, Jay Graf became president of CPI and invited us to help him bring about changes in CPI's culture. In our first meeting, Jay described CPI as an organization "going ninety miles per hour on an icy road, headed toward a cliff." The company was experiencing historic sales growth, setting monthly performance records, and constantly celebrating its victories in the market, but despite all that success, Jay felt people at CPI were failing to see that their top two formidable competitors were poised to introduce technology that would leapfrog their own within two short years, when CPI's own patents on its top-selling products would expire. Without the next new product, sales growth at CPI would indeed drop off a cliff. CPI's acquired technology was fueling its growth, but the company had nothing in the product development pipeline to take its place.

What should Jay do? Upcoming acquisition opportunities were not proving fruitful. The hope of licensing new technology for the next new product was, as Jay described it, like "the heroin fix of the next promising acquisition." The prospect of internal new-product development looked bleak as well. CPI had not produced a major new product in years, and Jay's own staff believed that they couldn't "develop their way out of a paper bag." The company's product development process continually slipped behind schedule by three weeks every month, which, according to Jay, was just "another way of saying we got about twelve real weeks of work done every year." He concluded, "We took four steps forward and three steps back."

Jay believed that doing the hard work of building a first-rate, on-time, product development process would most assuredly turn the company around. Given the prevailing beliefs at CPI, such a turn-around would require a significant cultural transition. Without it, they could not hope to achieve R^2. And with time running out, they desperately needed to accelerate the transition.

As we worked with Jay and his team, they came to recognize the need to place the results, both R^1 and R^2, in front of the organization in a clear and compelling way. Everyone, from the board of directors to the frontline assembly workers, acknowledged the reality of R^1: Their inability to develop their own new products had resulted in a product development department where, after years of dismal performance, people lacked confidence.

In a series of town hall meetings and formal training sessions, Jay and his team described what the shift from R^1 to R^2 would look like. While the dialogue within the organization convinced people of the need to change the game, many voiced skepticism about the organization's ability to become the developer of the new products that Jay envisioned. History argued for pessimism. In spite of this, Jay and his team implemented their culture change effort by working with the first tier of the Results Pyramid and applying the three steps to forming R^2 presented earlier:

1. Define R^2.

2. Introduce R^2 throughout the organization.

3. Create accountability to achieve R^2.

The diagram below shows how Jay and his team described the shift from R^1 to R^2. Continued dialogue within the organization proved productive as people began to take accountability for what wasn't working and for what they needed to do to fix it.

The Shift in Results at Cardiac Pacemakers Inc.

R^1 RESULTS		R^2 RESULTS
Missing the market	TO	Leading the market
Few new products	TO	Many new products
Reliance on acquired technology	TO	Reliance on product development
Missing schedule	TO	Hitting / meeting schedule
4-year development cycle	TO	18-month development cycle

CHANGEᵗʰᵉculture CHANGEᵗʰᵉgame

Based on their determination to achieve R^2, the acknowledgment of the management team was crucial: They took accountability for having produced R^1. With management stepping forward, the rest of the company felt empowered to jump on board.

Describing the shift from R^1 to R^2 that your organization must make, even for changes less radical or less encompassing than those needed at CPI, helps everyone grasp the nature of the undertaking. Charting the necessary shift in results always reveals the need to shift the way people think and act in order to achieve R^2. You might want to take a minute to describe the shift in results that your organization needs to make by building from the analysis of your desired organizational results that you completed earlier in this chapter. List your R^1 results and the accompanying shift to R^2 that will be necessary to your success as an organization.

Are the shifts from R^1 to R^2 for your organization compelling?

Identifying Your Results Shift

	R^1 RESULTS		R^2 RESULTS
A		TO	
B		TO	
C		TO	

CHANGE the culture CHANGE the game

Do they cause you any amount of angst as you contemplate what it will take to make them happen?

In light of your own analysis, you may well wonder what sort of results CPI achieved. Did they accomplish R^2? Yes, and more. CPI became a primary driver of success within Guidant Corporation, considered one of Wall Street's most successful split-offs ever. CPI is now a part of the Boston Scientific Cardiac Rhythm Management Group.

CPI created "a new, product-development machine," as others in the industry described it, which produced fourteen new products in fourteen months. CPI's annual sales doubled, while the stock price increased ninefold. The company has become a worldwide market leader in a number of its product lines.

The speed of the cultural transition created significant competitive advantage for CPI and essentially changed the game for both itself and others in the industry. Clearly defining the shift from R^1 to R^2 allowed its leaders to speed up the change in culture and thereby speed up results.

IMPLEMENTING THE CULTURE CHANGE

As we progress through Part One of this book, we will show you how to apply and build upon each step of the Results Pyramid to accelerate a change in your own organizational culture. Developing the leadership competency to accelerate culture change is an essential skill for every leader today. Organizations whose leaders know how to optimize their organizational culture to produce R^2 create competitive advantage in a way that others will not. Compelling evidence proves that culture produces results and that the right culture produces the right results.

It bears repeating: Your culture produces your results. If you need a change in results, then you need a change in culture. Your culture is always working, and it's either working for you or against you. Enlightened leaders know that *either you will manage your culture, or it will manage you*. The R^2 that you define, when you do it right, will drive the discussion about what needs to change in the culture (the way people think and act). Getting everyone aligned around R^2 does not happen easily. It requires dialogue, engagement, debate, and leadership. However, when everyone buys into R^2, you are well on your way to accelerating the needed cultural transition. In the next chapter, we'll show you how to keep acceleration on track by identifying the actions you need to stop, start, or continue doing.

CHAPTER 3

Taking Action
That Produces Results

TWO THOUSAND FIVE HUNDRED YEARS AGO, Heraclitus, the Greek philosopher known for his wisdom on the subject of change, could have been describing today's ever evolving world when he wrote, "You could not step twice into the same river." More than ever before, today's leaders and managers must deal with the constancy of change in the business environment. The pressure mounts. As changes continue to come with full force and with little reprieve, it is essential to learn how to get both your people and your organization's culture to respond to change in a way that generates business results.

The word *change* means, "to make or become different." Thus, when it comes to changing your culture, you must determine to get everyone in the organization acting differently and taking A^2 actions each and every day. Clearly, you need to do more than just get people acting differently; you need to get them doing the right thing at the right time in a way that produces R^2 results. You cannot accomplish a successful cultural transition without that sort of targeted, directed, and focused change.

The single most important change in actions that needs to occur during a time of cultural transition is the shift to greater accountability. In our first book, *The Oz Principle: Getting Results Through Individual and Organizational Accountability*, we make the case that corporations today suffer from a crisis of accountability. To address the crisis, leaders and managers too often fall back on the power of their positions and the authority of their assignments, *expecting* accountability from others rather than engaging it.

Fundamental to every organizational process and system, accountability defines the foundation of all working relationships. It is the "nerve center" running throughout the organization, and it drives the smooth and effective functioning of everything that happens. However, too many leaders and managers build their accountability systems on outdated command-and-control structures and methodologies. Naively, they expect to drive accountability through the organization, ignoring the fact that they often leave people feeling bruised and battered rather than motivated and engaged.

In today's environment, business moves so rapidly and information comes so quickly that you need responsive systems that propel people to become invested, proactive, resourceful, accurate, quick, and creative. Accountability is the low-hanging fruit when it comes to optimizing organizational performance. Getting employees to invest fully in achieving results is critical to accelerating a shift in culture. Yes, you can change your culture quickly, but you cannot accelerate the speed of cultural change until you get people to abandon the external focus implied by such questions as "What else can you do?" and "Who else can I blame?" Speeding up the cultural change means getting everyone to internalize the need for change and ask, "What else can I do to demonstrate actions more consistent with A^2?" and "What else can I do to achieve R^2 results?" Helping employees fully engage with a keen sense of investment and ownership is critical to accelerating the culture shift. Bear in mind that culture changes one person at a time. When people throughout the organization begin to own and feel accountable for the change they personally need to make, real change begins to occur—fast!

Accountability, done effectively, is a skill you can develop just like any other skill, and while it is not a difficult skill to acquire and hone, it does require a high degree of conscious effort. When you do it right, you'll also find it the fastest way to improve morale.

A Conference Board survey of American workers revealed that over half the American workforce does not feel engaged at all. The results of this survey reported job satisfaction at 45 percent, its lowest level since 1987. In addition, 64 percent of employees under age twenty-five express dissatisfaction with their jobs. Getting people engaged in their work so that they invest in and take personal ownership of the results of the organization can turn these numbers around. That's what accountability is all about. And that's why getting people to take personal ownership is the most important A^1-to-A^2 shift an organization intent on culture change can make.

What does this shift to greater accountability look like? "Opthometrics," the client we introduced in chapter 2, provides a good example. "Judy" and her store team had been missing plan. They kept hearing that they could "find plan in the store." That simply meant that a greater effort with customers who visited their store would yield the desired sales. But the result was not coming easily. After some tough feedback from her supervisor and some deep soul-searching, Judy shifted her focus from actions (A^1) that were allowing people to make excuses for failing to meet plan to actions (A^2) that were embodied in the statement "Customers do not walk away without finding something they need."

When Judy asked each associate in the store why people left without making a purchase, she discovered that they just let customers leave because they had not engaged them sufficiently to address the usual objections: "Just looking," "Too expensive," "Left my prescription at home," and "Haven't had an eye exam." Creating a new sense of accountability and engagement for getting the result, Judy refocused the actions people were taking from A^1 to A^2. This meant getting the associates to respond personally to the question, "What else could we have done to help those people become our customers?" To further stimulate their thinking, Judy began quizzing her people: "When a potential customer says, 'Oh, I'm just looking,' do we still insist on showing her our product and the layout of the store, or do we say, 'OK, if you need anything, I'll be over here?' When people tell us, 'That's too expensive,' do we ask them where they found the same products or services for less or why they thought the price was too high? When someone claims, 'I left my prescription at home,' do we respond, 'No problem, we can call your doctor's office and get it for you'? Or when anyone says, 'I've not had an eye exam,' do we take them next door to our optometrist, who can examine their eyes immediately?" The responses to her questions led Judy to conclude that no one was doing these things. Their A^1 actions could not possibly produce R^2 results.

Focused on moving to A^2, Judy and her associates began to take greater accountability by asking what else they could do to See It, Own It, Solve It, and Do It. They immediately began to focus on turning walk-in traffic into customers by asking the right questions, calling customers' eye doctors for prescriptions, and encouraging on-site eye exams. As they took greater accountability for the results of the store, Judy's team even began to engage their customers' friends who accompanied them to the store. The result: The fourth quarter was over plan. Indeed, they "found plan in the store" by taking greater accountability. Unless you make that kind of accountability integral to the shift from A^1 to A^2, you will not only find it harder to form the C^2 culture, but you will not be able to make the shift as quickly as you'd like.

Here's an example of how our clients usually describe the actual shift in accountability from A^1 to A^2:

The Shift in Accountability: A^1 to A^2 Actions

A^1 ACTIONS		A^2 ACTIONS
People externalize the need for change	TO	People internalize the changes they need to make
People wait to be told what to do	TO	People take the initiative to figure out what they need to do
People institutionalize *Below the Line* excuses as accepted reasons not to move forward	TO	People stop making excuses and start asking, "What else can I do?"
People don't get engaged and don't show full ownership	TO	People personally invest in making things happen
People focus on identifying problems	TO	People focus on finding solutions

CHANGEtheculture CHANGEthegame

To make it perfectly clear, it really doesn't matter how many other ways the culture needs to shift; if you don't shift the way people take accountability, you won't create the other shifts you need to make either. Without a doubt, accountability provides the primary ingredient for accelerating culture change.

THE THREE LEVELS OF CHANGE

We use a simple model to show the three different levels of organizational change. In the Input/Output Change Model, an impetus to change (the input) causes one of three kinds of change (the output) to occur: temporary, transitional, or transformational.

A Level One Change is a temporary change, in which you make small, incremental modifications to existing patterns but do not maintain them over time. For example, you might acquire a new skill in a training workshop, practice it for a while, and then, for one

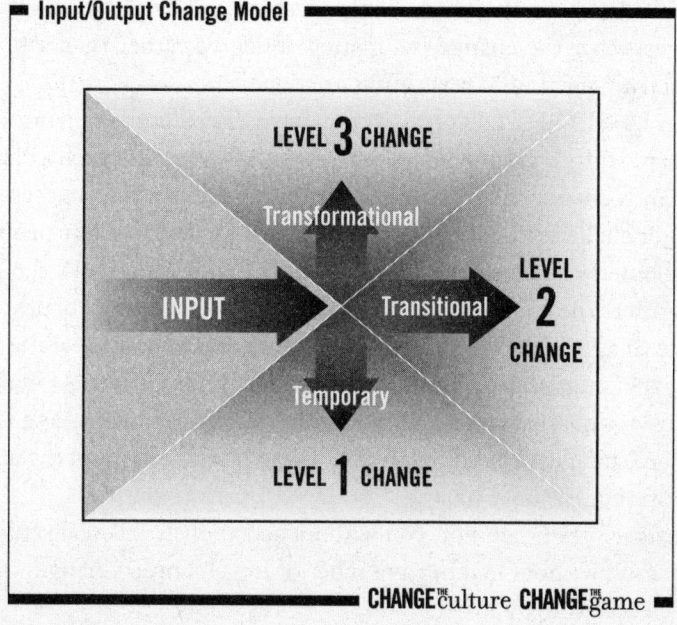

Input/Output Change Model

LEVEL **3** CHANGE

Transformational

INPUT — Transitional — LEVEL **2** CHANGE

Temporary

LEVEL **1** CHANGE

CHANGE the culture CHANGE the game

reason or another, abandon it a short time later. One top leader of a major client corporation enthusiastically implemented the skill of seeking personal feedback from the people with whom he worked, shortly after learning about it in a workshop. Everyone around him was delighted with the resulting dialogue and his interest in their viewpoints. However, a few weeks later during a follow-up call, we found that he had stopped the practice. When we asked him why, he could offer no good reason. He had just stopped doing it.

A Level Two Change is a transitional one, in which you make small, incremental modifications to existing patterns and consistently apply them over time. We saw this happen at a hospital that needed a transition in the way people approached shift work. In the past, the organization's A^1 actions included emphasis on tackling issues raised predominantly during the normal workday from nine to five, Monday through Friday. Now, with a desire to improve patient care around the clock, they needed to shift their focus to emphasize quality without prioritizing the "prime time" hours over other times. Shifting the emphasis did not require a major remake of the culture, but it did entail an important change in the way people thought and acted relative to the needs of the customer. The word *transitional* suggests that the change is a matter of degree rather than a fundamental change in the way things are done.

A Level Three Change is a transformational one requiring a significant shift in the way people think and act. Because such a change demands entirely new patterns of thinking and acting, it poses a far greater challenge than either Level One or Level Two. The people at Opthometrics needed to make a Level Three Change. It's the level that offers the biggest potential payoff and, when done properly, will make the greatest difference in performance. In the case of the hospital that engaged in a Level Two Change, their shift to A^2 in order to provide quality care around the clock might also qualify as a Level Three Change, depending on the degree of difficulty and the actual importance of the shift.

More often than not, you will not accomplish full-scale cultural transition without making a number of Level Three Changes in the way people think and act.

ALL BEHAVIOR IS REWARDED, EVEN A¹ BEHAVIOR

Sometimes A^1 actions defy comprehension, appearing extremely counterproductive and even illogical. Usually, everyone in the organization knows these actions need to change. During countless hours of interviewing and surveying thousands of people over the last two decades, we have heard people describe, without batting an eye, both the effective and ineffective ways people operate in their organizations. With ease, they describe in some detail what people do that impedes results and what they do that fosters achievements. From time to time, leaders in these organizations ask us, "If people are so clear about the things that we need to do differently to be more effective, then why don't they just do it? How do you explain the disconnect?"

Understanding why people do what they do is an important part of the process of accelerating the shift to A^2. Years ago, an experienced instructor of a local parenting group began his class by telling his students, "If you only remember one thing from this class, remember this: All behavior is rewarded." Over the years, we have pondered and applied this statement many times and in many different situations. It has resonated with everyone with whom we have shared the insight. Indeed, the principle has proven to be invaluable as we consult with our clients and address the question of why people do what they do. Often you can explain why people act the way they do after you discover their beliefs concerning the expected positive or negative consequences of their behavior. If you want to understand why someone is doing something, you must discover their beliefs about what they think will occur as a result of either taking or not taking a particular action.

This hit home years ago with one of the authors during a family vacation at a cabin in the mountains. With the arrival of some family friends, everyone settled into a competitive game of Chinese checkers. As you may recall, the winner of the game is the first player to move all ten of his or her marbles from their starting position to the other side of the board. The game that day included four adults and the author's ten-year-old son. The game progressed nicely for over an hour. Then, to everyone's surprise, the young boy did something entirely unexpected. Through a series of moves, he positioned one of his marbles in each player's final position. Everyone looked on in astonishment. In just a few moves, he had made it impossible for the game to continue.

With some disdain, his father asked him to collect his marbles and kicked him out of the game. After the adults finished the game, the father asked his son why he did what he did. He said he found the game fun and interesting at the beginning when he would jump several marbles at a time to progress across the board. When he did that, everyone would ooh and aah and praise his move. However, as the game progressed and it became more difficult to make such satisfying jumps, he lost interest and set it up so no one could win. Pretty smart young man! As he described his strategy, it suddenly became clear that at some point the son had stopped playing to win and had started playing not to lose, changing the game entirely. His behavior reflected his belief that if he arranged his marbles in a way that prevented everyone else from winning, he would not lose.

It happens in business all the time. During a time of organizational transition, we frequently see people at every level playing not to lose rather than playing to win. The perceived personal risk inherent in successfully executing A^2 can motivate defensive behavior when people worry more about protecting themselves than creating C^2. Again, laying the foundation of accountability and then effectively implementing the competencies associated with managing cultural transition presented in this book will help you check this defensive behavior and get people playing to win.

Effective managers recognize that people pay attention to all the signals the organization's culture sends about how to act. They understand that action—focused action, doing-the-right-things-at-the-right-time kind of action—produces results. You can't pay attention to the culture of an organization without paying attention to actions. But you must also understand that actions are influenced by the beliefs people hold and the experiences people cite (the bottom of the pyramid) as they seek to justify their behavior.

GOING THROUGH THE MOTIONS

Ernest Hemingway once wrote, "Never mistake motion for action." Mere motion accomplishes nothing and can prove more exhausting than action. Energy expended without achieving the result can wear you out, both emotionally and physically. When it comes to culture change, we've seen far too many organizations just go through the motions, wasting time doing things that never yield any real change and progress.

In fact, we've compiled a list of some common practices that often fail to have the intended impact when it comes to promoting cultural change. Have you ever experienced any of these?

Top 7 Ineffective Change Practices

1. Distribute the corporate values statement.

2. Restructure or reorganize.

3. Hire or fire someone.

4. Change the reward system.

5. Form a team and isolate it from the culture.

6. Promote someone.

7. Rewrite policy.

Used in isolation, these widely used practices often fail to produce the desired result of shifting the culture and getting people to act differently. Flailing about with low-impact efforts misdirects energy, wastes time, misses the mark, and breeds frustration.

You cannot effectively and quickly shift culture without influencing people to take the right A^2 actions, but you cannot merely announce what you want people to do differently and then sit back and expect them to do it. That would be like telling teenagers to change their attitudes and behave differently. What are the chances that would work? Nor can you induce change with the traditional practices we listed above that organizations so often use in a vain attempt to trigger a new way of thinking in their people. How many leadership teams have ended up disappointed with a restructure because it only resulted in a repeat of past performance? How often has "new blood" become part of the culture so quickly that, rather than change it, the culture has actually changed them? Our own experience has shown that you can change where people sit in the organization, but that probably will not change the way they think. Going through the motions of the traditional practices on the list will often produce activity, while failing to deliver results. Rather than employ these traditional practices, you want to apply methodologies that make a fundamental difference in how people act. That begins with the A^1 to A^2 analysis.

STOP, START, CONTINUE

Accelerating a shift in the way people act requires a clear understanding of what you need to stop doing, what you need to start doing, and what you need to keep doing. Here's an example of the Stop/Start/Continue analysis from "Shopright," a retail food and drug chain.

To generate the list shown on page 59, three levels of Shopright's management engaged in an open, candid dialogue regarding the needed shift to a new culture. Their Stop/Start/Continue analysis began to describe the shift from A^1 to A^2 within the context of R^2. Only within the context of R^2 can you define the A^2 actions you need to take.

Let's apply this analysis to your own organization or team. First, pick the top three R^2 results you need to achieve. Use the diagram on page 60 to record your responses.

Now list the A^1 actions that get in the way of achieving R^2. These are actions people should stop doing. Be as honest as you can about what doesn't work. Bear in mind Winston Churchill's observation: "However beautiful the strategy, you should occasionally look at the results." Honestly evaluating what is and is not working will help you answer the question "What actions should our people stop because they just don't get results?"

Stop/Start/Continue: "Shopright"

R^2 RESULTS	THE SHIFT IN ACTIONS

R^2 RESULTS

Greater store-level ownership for sales in order to hit store sales budgets and achieve regional sales budgets.

Labor costs held to the budgeted level

THE SHIFT IN ACTIONS

A^1 to STOP

- Changing the targets when obstacles present themselves
- "Open door" policy for regional managers only
- Switching from program to program too quickly *("We don't stick with any one initiative long enough.")*
- Blaming and finger pointing
- Managing by fear and negative reproaches
- Drifting from our original corporate philosophy *("We are family owned and operated.")*
- Making all the decisions in the office of the CEO

A^2 to START

- Communicating the regional budget to *all* employees
- Creating ownership for individual store budgets, first at the store manager level and then throughout the entire store
- Increasing the focus on ROI/shareholder value
- Enabling people to make fast decisions
- Confronting poor performance and providing feedback
- Paying greater attention to customers; see stores through customers' eyes
- Low-cost operating and buying methods
- Taking individual accountability for the store sales budgets by constantly asking, "What else can I do to achieve the budget?"

A^1 to CONTINUE

- "Open door" policy below regional manager level
- Stock ownership (most employees are shareholders)
- Fostering strong work ethic and pride in the company
- Having a strong backstage/warehouse/distribution operation

CHANGE^{THE}culture CHANGE^{THE}game

Then think of the A^2 actions people don't take but should. What do they need to start doing in order to achieve the R^2 you listed?

Finally, determine what key A^1 actions you want people to

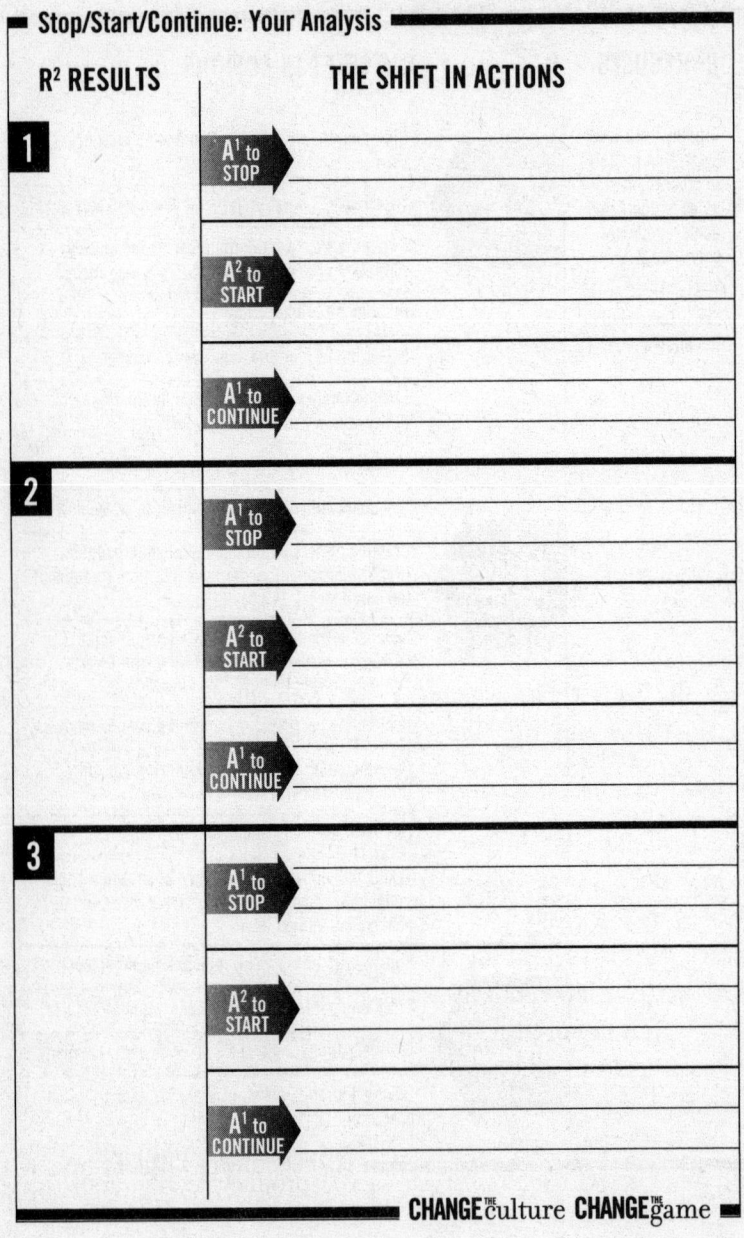

Stop/Start/Continue: Your Analysis

R² RESULTS   **THE SHIFT IN ACTIONS**

1

A¹ to STOP

A² to START

A¹ to CONTINUE

2

A¹ to STOP

A² to START

A¹ to CONTINUE

3

A¹ to STOP

A² to START

A¹ to CONTINUE

CHANGE the culture CHANGE the game

continue doing. These are the strengths of C^1 that will continue to help you achieve R^2. They provide the foundation upon which you will build C^2.

Consider what would happen if you could quickly discontinue the A^1 actions and replace them with the A^2 actions you listed in your Stop/Start/Continue analysis. How would these actions affect your organization's or your team's ability to achieve the three R^2 results you listed? Can you expect to achieve R^2 if you fail to create A^2? If you expect to make a strong start toward a successful culture shift, then you must hold yourself accountable to acknowledge reality throughout this exercise. At the same time, you will find it quite helpful to get candid feedback from team members about what they think the organization should stop, start, or continue doing.

A WORD OF CAUTION

You should watch out for the three classic mistakes leaders often make during a time of cultural transition, mistakes that can cost valuable time and sabotage even the best intentions. The first of these mistakes occurs when management teams attempt to prescribe A^2; the second stems from not supporting early A^2 adopters; and the third happens when management focuses only on the Actions level of the Results Pyramid.

Prescribing what A^2 looks like for the rest of the organization usually does not work. While pinpointing what people should stop, start, and continue doing is a good beginning, it won't accomplish much if it does not provide context for management's most important job: creating an environment in which people at all levels ask themselves, "What should I stop, start, and continue doing in order to create C^2 and achieve R^2?" In the right environment, people will come up with quick, creative, and productive answers to that question.

By involving everyone in the Stop/Start/Continue analysis, you create ownership for A^2 and a more accurate list of what needs to change. Who could better answer the question about results-producing behaviors than those who live with A^1 every day? When you involve the organization in defining actions, you increase its capability both to manage and to accelerate the culture change. Of course, when we talk about the shift to A^2, we are talking about either a Level Two or Level Three Change, a lasting and fundamental change in the way people do business on a daily basis, not just a cosmetic shift in which people merely pay lip service to a new way of doing things.

Another classic mistake that often hampers a cultural transition is a lack of support for early A^2 adopters. At first, A^2 runs counter to the C^1 culture. While the champions of the cultural transition may recognize A^2 when they see it, many others will not. They may even think that the people who adopt A^2 don't fit in the organization. Helping people recognize A^2 when they see it, and championing those who adopt A^2, will position others to support the cultural transition and speed up progress. Eventually, as the "middle masses" join ranks with the early adopters, the whole organization will begin institutionalizing A^2 as the "way we do things around here." Ultimately, the C^2 culture will motivate, remind, signal, suggest, dictate, and reinforce A^2.

The third classic mistake occurs when you focus only on the Actions level of the Results Pyramid. Eventually, a narrow focus on behavior tends to express itself in more punitive and prescriptive ways. Accelerating culture change demands that you work with all levels of the pyramid both simultaneously and sequentially. It's just not enough to work only on what people do; you must also address how they think. Single-mindedly focusing on actions will tend to create the wrong kind of accountability, the kind that drives people Below the Line, where they wait for orders. That kind of accountability significantly diminishes the morale of the organization.

Culture consists of both what people think and what they do. Our experience successfully working with culture change over the last two decades as leadership and management consultants has continually reinforced this central idea: If you change the way people think, you will change the way they act. In the next chapter, we will closely examine the Beliefs level of the Results Pyramid and show you how to work with people's beliefs in conjunction with their Actions.

We all know that no one can change human behavior overnight. There will always be early and late adopters, and even some who simply cannot implement more than a temporary and counterproductive Level One Change. Even those who fully embrace the need to act differently can backslide from time to time, particularly during the early stages of the change process, when the pressures of C^1 continue to exert themselves on the organization. Because C^1 has a high degree of "stickiness," some features of the old culture will almost always persist, even when you are making great progress in your efforts to shift the culture completely. For now, rest assured that the more you use the right tools and the more effectively you use them (the subjects of chapters 6 and 7), the more surely and completely your organization will adopt A^2 actions critical to the shift in culture.

MAKING THE SHIFT FROM A^1 TO A^2

"Emiliano's" restaurants, a leading brand of "Norcross Global," one of *Fortune* magazine's Most Admired Food Services Companies, experienced the positive impact on their R^2 when they succeeded in getting people to focus on taking the right A^2 actions. With the entire restaurant category mired in the deadening effects of a slogging economy, Emiliano's management had fallen into the classic trap of trying to improve results by focusing solely on what people do. While that seems to work in some cases, it never works when what you need is a fundamental shift in culture in order to produce R^2.

Emiliano's leadership recognized that the harder they pushed on actions, the worse it got. The work environment had become a "culture of activity" saddled with lots of measures, lists, and graphs. Posters listing the twenty activities that workers needed to perform between shifts hung in the back room of each restaurant. This list ("the nonnegotiables"), along with the names of anyone who missed fulfilling them, signaled that the organization had gone into information overload, with an almost obsessive focus on what people were doing.

The COO reported that he began hearing the same story repeated over and over again, to the point that he knew exactly how people were feeling. Standing next to a team member at the back-room board, an Emiliano's manager asked him if he knew what he was looking at. The fellow offered a classic response: "I have no idea. I'm only looking to make sure my name's not up here." C[1] had turned into a "tell me what to do" environment where management implemented accountability with external measures focused solely on activity as a solution. People were beginning to feel badgered by management as the focus on compliance increased and the threat of losing their jobs hung constantly over their heads.

At one point, results deteriorated so much that management, in an effort to motivate compliance with the non-negotiables, estab-lished a more prescriptive approach to reporting, goal setting, and communicating through a creative merit system. Basically, if peo-ple met the metrics, they would win first priority in selecting the shift they wanted to work. Rather than motivating the workforce, however, this approach pitted people against one another, creating a strong sense of competition and undermining any sense of team. Women who had planned their schedules to accommodate their families would complain, "I lost my schedule last week." An already competitive culture had become competitive to a fault.

In the restaurant business, the little things matter: A single point higher in food costs can make a huge impact on performance. A decline of just 10 basis points can translate into a loss of $2 mil-lion. Over a month, these kinds of numbers can ruin an entire P&L. Emiliano's management tried to control these costs by managing such details as requiring preportioning (measuring food ingredients before they're needed, assuring more exact quantities than a worker might use in the heat of the kitchen). However, they soon recog-nized that their "management by edict" approach, the most com-monly used leadership practice in any business anytime new results are needed, was producing a "culture of activity" rather than the results they were looking for. People were working by checklist and mandate, falling short of implementing the true intent of these prac-tices and lacking the personal ownership they really needed to get it right in the restaurants.

Emiliano's management faced a tremendous challenge. They

needed to get everyone throughout their worldwide chain of restaurants to not just implement activities that were presented to them, but to take ownership for creatively and intelligently replicating the best practices without mandate or force. They had made activity the objective, when what they really wanted was better results within the unique customer environment of each restaurant. At this point, the focus on activity, the A^1 actions they most needed to shift, permeated the entire organization, including the management team. Regional directors performed regular visits, quickly moving down their checklists but not really scratching the surface of how to improve operations in the restaurants. Their visits needed to go beyond the checklist to gain an intimate understanding of what was really happening in the restaurant and then engage the people who could really make a difference in the open conversations that would help improve profitability. That's what A^2 looked like for them—a shift in focus from activity-based to results-based management practices. Without it, R^2 would never occur.

Ultimately, the Emiliano's management team acknowledged that telling people how they needed to act in every situation was not working for them and that in order to achieve R^2, they would need to take an entirely different approach and make the shift to results-based management practices. At this point, they enlisted Partners In Leadership to help them learn what they needed to do as leaders to enroll people in the culture change effort and create an environment where employees at every level understood R^2 and experienced the A^1 to A^2 Stop/Start/Continue analysis for themselves.

This new focus led to a more collaborative development of A^2 actions that were more results-based than activities-based, creating ownership and accountability for making sure people did the right things at the right times in the restaurants. The management team stopped relying on ineffective "tell me what to do" change practices and started using the engagement-oriented change methodologies described throughout this book. Not only did they stop overprescribing the actions people should take; they began supporting and praising the early adopters of the C^2 culture who were exemplifying the A^2 actions they wanted people to implement. The list of non-negotiables came down. The merit system on scheduling took a new direction. Regional directors began engaging people to solve problems during their visits to restaurants. A^2 actions began to take shape without compulsion throughout the organization. The result? In an industry in which companies had been hit hard by the recession, Emiliano's began to realize their R^2 objective, hitting their plan on sales, beating their plan on profits, and blowing away their turnover goals. Wall Street rewarded their efforts with a healthy increase in stock price.

BUILDING THE PYRAMID

Understanding what needs to shift in the actions people take is an important first step toward accelerating culture change. Once you determine the shifts in behavior from A^1 to A^2, you can begin traveling a clear path to where your organization needs to go. Creating a clear picture of what C^2 looks like in terms of what people need to do differently is a key to accelerating change. Doing this collaboratively in an environment of heightened personal accountability speeds up the process and provides the foundation that will ensure a successful journey. Abandoning the sole reliance on traditional and ineffective change practices, focusing instead on approaches that truly engage the workforce in embracing personal change, greatly enhances the prospects for success.

But we need to make one point perfectly clear before leaving this chapter: Nothing, absolutely nothing, gets people to change the way they act faster than getting them to change the way they think. When you work only with the top of the pyramid, Results and Actions, you limit your ability to accelerate the shift to C^2 and minimize the chances that A^2 will become part of the way people do things in the organization. Beliefs, more than anything else, will motivate necessary behavioral shifts, so you must help people adopt the beliefs that will yield the actions needed to produce R^2. Next we will describe how you can accelerate the shift to a new culture by identifying and creating beliefs that motivate the right kind of actions to achieve desired results.

CHAPTER 4

Identifying the Beliefs
That Generate the Right Actions

DURING TIMES OF CHANGE, managers and leaders often focus their efforts exclusively on the top two levels of the Results Pyramid. Our clients quickly learn, however, that they can greatly enhance their success at accelerating a change in culture when they expand their focus to work with the seemingly less tangible Beliefs level at the bottom of the pyramid. There is a simple yet powerful relationship between the beliefs people within the organization hold and the actions they take. Their beliefs about how work should get done directly affects what they do. If you change people's beliefs about how they should do their daily work (B^1) and help them adopt the new beliefs (B^2) you want them to hold, you will produce the actions (A^2) you want them to take. When leaders work with this deeper, more lasting aspect of behavior, they tap into the most fundamental accelerator of effective culture change.

The need to change culture often arises whether we are ready for it or not. Consider the profound change that occurred in the wireless communications industry when the business model changed almost overnight with the introduction of the innovative iPhone by Apple. Apple founder Steve Jobs had tasked two hundred top Apple engineers to create the iPhone. Stressful deadlines resulted in screaming matches between co-workers and among exhausted engineers, who, according to a *Wired* magazine article, "frazzled from all-night coding sessions, quit, only to rejoin days later after catching up on their sleep." In one case, "a product manager slammed the door to her office so hard that the handle bent and locked her in; it took colleagues more than an hour and some well-placed whacks with an aluminum bat to free her."

The new product required a monumental effort, but a little over a year after its introduction, the iPhone accounted for 39 percent of Apple's revenues and was the single largest contributor to Apple's bottom line. Steve Jobs changed the game by getting the big players in the staid wireless industry to agree to a new business model, one that shifted beliefs about handsets. Until then, the industry had defined them as "cheap, disposable lures, massively subsidized to snare subscribers and lock them into using the carriers' proprietary services," as *Wired* put it. After making this strategic shift in beliefs, major players began using smartphones to differentiate their offerings and win customers. As this new business model moves forward and continues to morph, wireless providers will need to help the people in their organizations make corresponding shifts in their beliefs about how they conduct their daily business. Those who make these operational shifts happen quickly and effectively will create competitive advantage.

In another case, the human resources network of SSM Health Care, which owns and operates six hospitals in St. Louis, determined to change the company's image among its customers and its own team members. At the outset, team leaders made the desired shift from B^1 to B^2 beliefs perfectly clear: Stop thinking like a traditional support function with a transactional focus (B^1), and start thinking like a business partner with a more strategic focus (B^2). HR wanted to partner more fully with the business units throughout the network and help them achieve their business results.

Once people throughout HR adopted new beliefs about their roles, the change happened so quickly that it astonished even us. They outsourced their employee recruitment division and created specialties in the benefits and compensation administration areas, so that the staff in the new HR service centers could offer those services as part of their function. With their remaining HR resources, they concentrated their efforts on converting their internal HR professionals into HR consultants. Soon they fielded a new team of twenty consultants, each guided by a single purpose: Support their business partners in achieving their key operating results. What began with a shift in one belief has culminated in an impressive HR network that operates today as a purpose-driven support function providing unprecedented value to its internal clients.

Every day, we hear similar stories from leaders and managers all over the world who are benefiting from working at the Beliefs level of the Results Pyramid. So why would any leadership or management team fail to focus its attention on that level? The answer to this question lies in five common misperceptions about working with beliefs.

Top Misconceptions About Working with Beliefs

1. Beliefs are too hard to discern; you can't read people's minds.

2. Beliefs are not observable; you can't measure progress.

3. Beliefs are more difficult to work with; you don't know what to do.

4. Beliefs take more time to change; you can motivate actions more quickly.

5. Beliefs cannot be mandated; you must convince people.

Without the right methodology and approach, you might assume you can manage actions more easily than beliefs. However, a sole focus on actions will often result in little more than frustration, a lot of counterproductive effort and a "tell me what to do" culture. While new plans, policies, and procedures deserve their proper place in organizations, they often fail to bring about lasting change, particularly during a time of cultural transition. By applying our best practices to implementing the Results Pyramid, you will avoid the traps associated with these common misconceptions and discover the practicality of working with beliefs. Once you master the Beliefs level of the pyramid and learn how to help people abandon unwanted B^1 beliefs and adopt desired B^2 beliefs, you will actually find that you can more quickly and easily accomplish the changes you want to make.

"Synergy," one of our clients, recently experienced the frustration that often accompanies a focus solely on actions. Seeking to motivate higher attendance at monthly company meetings, the company instituted a reward called the Wheel of Fortune, a device spun by an employee, randomly selected beforehand, to award someone a monetary prize for simply showing up at the meeting. However, rather than prompting people to attend the meeting, the Wheel of Fortune quickly became an entitlement from which people expected to benefit whether they showed up at the meeting or not. AWOL meeting participants would actually ask their bosses or best friends to go up and spin the wheel for them and retrieve their money if they won. Synergy's preoccupation with behavior did not change behavior. People still failed to attend meetings, but now a lucky absentee would pocket additional compensation.

When managers who work only with the top two levels of the pyramid fail to see desired changes in behavior, they generally opt for their one remaining solution: If you can't change the behavior, then you must change the results. "Changing the number" may seem like an obvious mistake, but it happens all the time. Although managers may regularly redefine their targets, this tactic will not help them solve their underlying problems, nor will it provide a long-term strategy for the viability of the organization.

Consider a shift in beliefs that you need to make in your own organization. First think of an R^2 result you currently want your organization to achieve but toward which you're not seeing satisfactory progress. Record it in the diagram below. Now identify at least one somewhat commonly shared belief that, if changed, would prove instrumental in achieving your R^2 result.

To what degree do you think people would act differently if they adopted, embraced, and felt motivated by this new belief? To what extent would this belief lead to improved results? What stands in the way of getting people to entertain this belief?

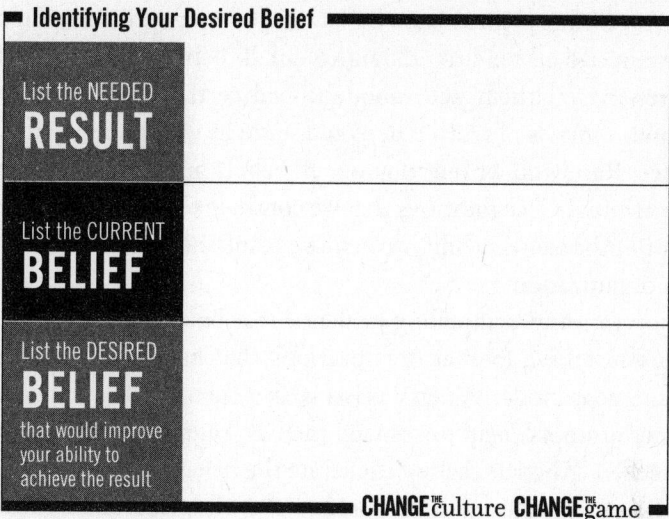

The beliefs people hold significantly influence what they do on a daily basis, and these beliefs will strongly resist change unless you deal with them directly. That explains why so few managers work with this level of the pyramid.

We have all seen that changing jobs can lead to a fairly immediate change in beliefs. We will never forget working with a plant management team that faced huge challenges as it tried to gain widespread support for its new safety objectives. One of the mechanics on the team, who had never regarded safety as his job, was promoted to the position of safety manager. You would not believe the immediate and striking 180-degree shift in his attitude and behavior. It happened so swiftly that his conversion to safety as an everyday priority became the talk of the plant, leading to praise from his now fellow managers and to disdain from his former team members. His remarkable passion for the topic seemed quite sincere. In most cases, however, changing where you sit in the organization does not change how you think. While new perspectives that accompany a change in position do occur, experience has shown that most often people bring their old ways of thinking, their B[1] beliefs, into a new job.

We call this phenomenon belief bias, a trait we all share. In most situations, we all tend to hold on to our B^1 beliefs, cherishing them and relying on them with unquestioned certainty as if they were delicious morsels of truth that would serve us well in every situation we face. Rarely do we question our B^1 beliefs; instead we fall prey to their habitual C^1 suggestions that we continue to behave in ways that do not optimize our ability to achieve results, either individually or as an organization.

You can find compelling evidence that beliefs can shift quickly when you take a look at organizations that have gone into crisis-management mode. When a crisis strikes, people's natural survival instinct prompts them to suspend their B^1 beliefs and quickly adopt the needed B^2 beliefs that will generate the behavior essential to solving the problem at hand. Unfortunately, when the crisis ends, the old B^1 belief bias usually returns with a vengeance, pulling everyone back to business, and the C^1 culture, as usual. Learning to work effectively with the bottom of the Results Pyramid to shift people's beliefs will not only counteract that tendency, it will accelerate the achievement of the C^2 culture and the R^2 results.

NOT ALL BELIEFS ARE EQUAL

Not all beliefs are equal in terms of strength and conviction. With this in mind, our methodology for accelerating culture change emphasizes that we do not focus on changing every kind of belief. As shown in the diagram below, there are real differences in the kind of beliefs we hold.

A Category 1 belief does not reflect a high degree of belief bias and does not influence people's actions in a dramatic way. When presented with new information, people fairly easily abandon this kind of belief. For instance, a sales representative may feel that the most effective presentation to a customer involves using the old marketing materials she knows by heart. A phone call with her supervisor, however, may convince her that the new marketing pieces will improve

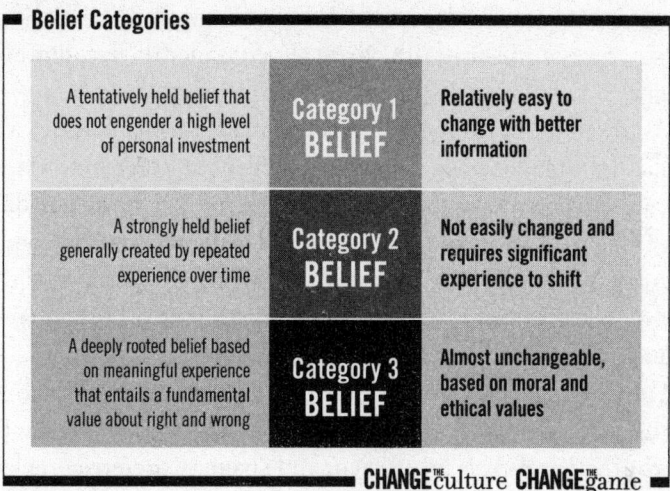

Belief Categories

A tentatively held belief that does not engender a high level of personal investment	**Category 1 BELIEF**	**Relatively easy to change with better information**
A strongly held belief generally created by repeated experience over time	**Category 2 BELIEF**	**Not easily changed and requires significant experience to shift**
A deeply rooted belief based on meaningful experience that entails a fundamental value about right and wrong	**Category 3 BELIEF**	**Almost unchangeable, based on moral and ethical values**

CHANGE THE culture CHANGE THE game

her ability to motivate the customer to make a buying decision. As a result, the rep quickly abandons the belief that the old materials work best and adopts the belief that the new materials will be more effective in helping her achieve her sales number.

A Category 2 belief, steeped in experience, is strongly held, fully embraced, and not easily abandoned. For instance, when people in an organization believe, "You can't say what you really think to management because they don't want to hear it," that is probably a Category 2 belief. This belief, developed over time, reflects a strong opinion based upon powerful personal experiences. You cannot easily shift this category of belief, because people see it as an accurate description of the truth and a strong guide to how they should behave.

A Category 3 belief resides at the very foundation of a person's values concerning moral, ethical, principled, right and wrong behavior. People hold such beliefs so deeply that they will abandon them only under extreme pressure and often not even then. For example, imagine someone believing strongly that intentionally falsifying information on a production report would be unethical, immoral, and against the law. That bedrock belief will not likely change unless a person faces a life-or-death threat. Even under duress, however, a Category 3 belief may defeat all efforts to alter it.

We often illustrate the significance of a Category 3 belief with a real-life example we observed during a client engagement. Management at a nuclear power plant sought to minimize downtime during outages planned to allow the company to make repairs and complete a maintenance inspection. Each day of downtime cost the company a million dollars in lost revenue. Management, with a keen interest in minimizing the loss, continually required shorter and shorter outages.

These shortened intervals led to more and more "Band-Aid" fixes to keep operations running. Many of the workers in the plant thought the Band-Aids insufficient and strongly preferred replacing some parts outright, which would require more time and expense for the repair. Plant employees held a Category 3 belief that was being challenged by management. Worried about their safety, workers saw the issue in terms of right and wrong. On the other hand, management deemed their demands safe, reasonable, and practical. In the absence of convincing evidence that would alter their opinions, the workers took the matter into their own hands and sabotaged a valve they felt they had bandaged once too often. This forced the plant to shut down for an additional four days while workers made the needed repairs.

When we talk about shifting beliefs to change the culture, we are usually talking about working with Category 1 and Category 2 beliefs that reflect "how we do things around here." While Category 1 beliefs can shift fairly easily, particularly when people are presented with better information, shifting a Category 2 belief requires greater skill and thought, particularly if you need to do it quickly. Changing Category 3 beliefs usually involves a higher degree of emotion and pain.

We see this whenever a particular shift involves a modification of the "social contract" between employees and employers. Such shifts may include reducing the workforce, changing the working hours, altering the rate of pay, or requiring retraining in new skills. Certain employees feel that such changes violate the rights to which they feel entitled. Leaders must appreciate how deeply and strongly people may hold a certain belief, because that will dictate how much effort, energy, and attention it will take to shift it.

CULTURAL BELIEFS: THE ROAD MAP FOR CULTURAL CHANGE

Category 1 and Category 2 beliefs are central to your organization's culture and are reinforced and transmitted daily in an efficient, almost naturally occurring, self-perpetuating process that requires minimal direction and limited nurturing. You can witness this process at work when a new employee takes a lunch break the first day on the job. As the lunchtime conversation unfolds with co-workers, the new employee will eventually ask, "How do things really work around here?" In essence, the person wants to know the prevailing Cultural Beliefs that dictate how to get work done in the organization: "What's important to management? What do I need to watch out for? Who do I need to watch out for? What do I need to make sure I do without fail? How do people get promoted? How do they get in trouble?" In response, co-workers answer these questions by sharing their beliefs about the organization's culture, beliefs that others in the organization most likely also share, beliefs that tend to constitute the prevailing and company-specific notions about the "rules of engagement."

This raises some fundamental questions that you need to answer: Are the B^1 beliefs that people are sharing the ones you want them to hold? Do these beliefs inspire movement toward C^2, or do they cause people to retrench into C^1? Will these specific beliefs lead the organization forward in its effort to deliver R^2 results, or not? If not, you have a significant cultural problem that needs solving. You can appreciate the seriousness of this problem when you consider how little it takes to assimilate new employees into the existing culture. Total enculturation often occurs quickly when the new employee goes to lunch the next day with another co-worker and hears the same beliefs repeated almost verbatim in answer to the question

"How do things really work around here?" With as few as two points of contact, new employees become complete adopters of the C^1 culture, embracing the prevailing B^1 beliefs and dashing any hopes their employer had of introducing new thinking to the job.

This brings us to the heart of the matter: Managing culture is all about getting the culture to work for you by fostering the beliefs you need people to hold and the actions you need them to take. What would you want people saying to new employees when they seek guidance about how things work in your organization? We advise management teams who seriously desire to accelerate their cultural shift to consider this new hire dialogue as they form their Cultural Beliefs statement. This statement will serve as a cultural road map for your journey from C^1 to C^2 and can provide the single greatest catalyst for change. When you effectively identify and implement B^2 beliefs, you accelerate culture change and create the kind of organizational capability that produces game-changing results.

IDENTIFYING B^2 BELIEFS

To effect a culture change and set the organization on a new course, leaders must identify, honestly and completely, two kinds of beliefs: B^1 beliefs that are hindering the company from achieving the targeted results and B^2 beliefs that would help the company move forward. This often calls for individual and collective soul-searching and completely open feedback about the true reality of the situation.

Look at it this way. People in organizations hold two kinds of beliefs: those that will help them achieve R^2 and those that won't. Obviously, you want to promulgate what you need and change what you don't. A company's leaders, with the help of other key people who might lend a hand, can identify these two sets of beliefs by answering two basic questions: What current beliefs will prevent us from achieving R^2, and what beliefs will propel us toward achieving R^2?

The first of these two questions leads to phase one of the implementation step of the culture change that we introduced in chapter 1: This step involves deconstructing C^1. Understanding the components of the current culture, including the existing broadly held beliefs, is essential to knowing what you need to shift in order to achieve R^2.

Let us stress that while certain B^1 beliefs are undesirable, they are not necessarily inaccurate. People may be entirely justified in holding certain beliefs. It's not a question of right or wrong; it's a question of effectiveness. Will the existing beliefs produce the A^2 actions needed to achieve the result? The exploration of what people currently believe should not be undertaken to invalidate existing perceptions but should instead represent a robust first step toward changing them for the better.

The second question in the B^1 to B^2 analysis spotlights missing beliefs that, if adopted, will help people achieve results. These beliefs motivate people to take A^2 actions. They define what someone would say in answer to the question "How do things really work around here?" Getting to the truth about what needs to change often requires an engagement with outside facilitators who can aid in this assessment phase.

Here's an example of one client organization's analysis of a B^1 belief and the resulting A^1 actions. Together, this belief and the accompanying actions characterize the elements of the C^1 culture that the management team determined would need to change.

Note the impact of this B^1 belief: a lack of candidness that slows

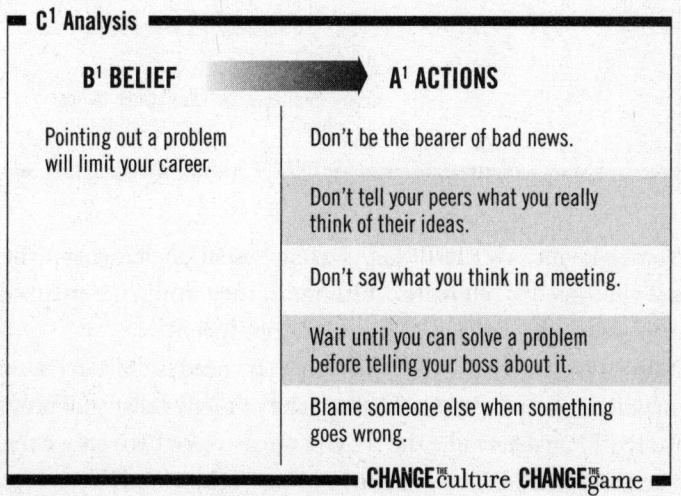

C^1 Analysis

B^1 BELIEF	A^1 ACTIONS
Pointing out a problem will limit your career.	Don't be the bearer of bad news.
	Don't tell your peers what you really think of their ideas.
	Don't say what you think in a meeting.
	Wait until you can solve a problem before telling your boss about it.
	Blame someone else when something goes wrong.

CHANGE^{THE}culture CHANGE^{THE}game

down decisions, stops the flow of information, makes it harder to move forward, and leads to an abundance of disappointing surprises.

People tell the truth about their beliefs concerning the organization all the time, confiding to their friends, their family, and even their peers on the job. However, when it comes to telling management, they often clam up. That's usually because C^1 exerts its power and makes the risk of speaking up intolerable. One way or another, you will need to get to the truth and understand what people really think. If the management team doesn't come to grips with this need, it will surely miss an opportunity to target B^2 beliefs in a way that will directly influence the actions needed to produce R^2.

Referring to our example, examine one of the B^2 beliefs that our client identified as a crucial element in the C^2 culture.

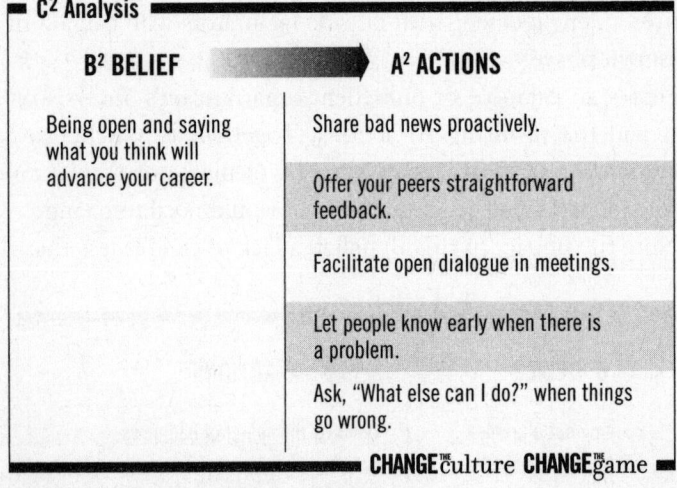

C^2 Analysis

B^2 BELIEF → **A^2 ACTIONS**

B^2 BELIEF	A^2 ACTIONS
Being open and saying what you think will advance your career.	Share bad news proactively.
	Offer your peers straightforward feedback.
	Facilitate open dialogue in meetings.
	Let people know early when there is a problem.
	Ask, "What else can I do?" when things go wrong.

CHANGE the culture CHANGE the game

Management saw the B^2 belief as an essential element in the C^2 culture they needed to create. Without it, they would never speed up the organizational processes enough to produce R^2.

Now consider some of the beliefs that you need to shift in your own organization, group, or team. Identify any of the B^1s that stall progress toward R^2. Then determine the B^2s you want to create to replace the B^1s you need to discard in order to move toward achieving R^2.

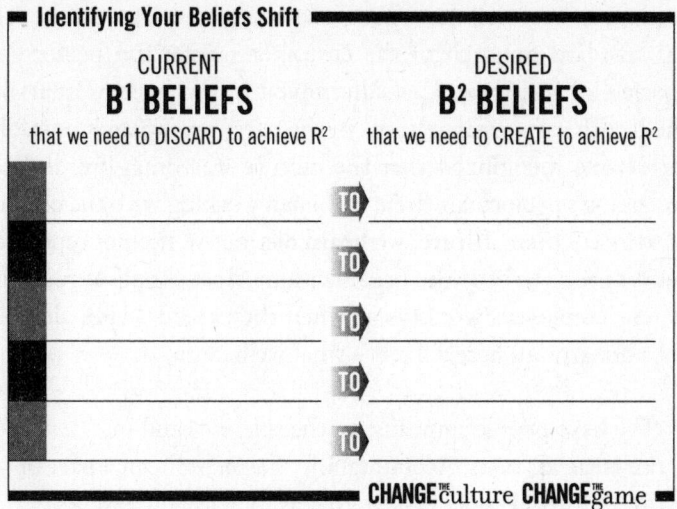

■ **Identifying Your Beliefs Shift** ■

CURRENT
B¹ BELIEFS
that we need to DISCARD to achieve R²

DESIRED
B² BELIEFS
that we need to CREATE to achieve R²

TO

TO

TO

TO

TO

■ **CHANGE**ᵗʰᵉculture **CHANGE**ᵗʰᵉgame ■

What will happen if you do not create these shifts in beliefs in your organization or team? On the other hand, what will happen if you create an environment in which people embrace these beliefs in a way that institutionalizes them as part of the new hire dialogue?

CULTURAL BELIEFS: A CASE IN POINT

With pressures from a declining economy in a state with a population shrinking faster than that of any other state, and with the state's industrial base in dire straits, the leaders of a regional health insurance provider, "Eastside HealthPlans," knew that they needed to make a major shift from R^1 to R^2, and they knew they needed to do it quickly.

For some time, the company had focused on customer satisfaction measures that were mandated and monitored by a multinational parent company that owned several other regional health care organizations. The parent's customer satisfaction program included several measurements of how timely and accurately Eastside enrolled new members, processed claims, and resolved inquiries. The measurements involved a "points earned" system that awarded points depending on how well the organization performed against the established standard for each of the customer satisfaction performance categories. At the time, Eastside ranked in the bottom quartile of all the health care organizations in the parent company's portfolio.

Everyone recognized that the culture was dragging down the organization's performance. As we began working with the executive team to assess their culture, we heard distinctive themes repeated by leaders at every level of the organization. Most people agreed about what new employees would hear when they asked, "How do things really work around here?" Here's what we heard:

- "We have people standing on the sidelines and in the bleacher seats. Accountability has *never* been a part of this culture. People believe that as long as you have a warm body, you will always have a job. Little urgency is required of anyone. People sit back and wait for direction to come, and then we accept and even reward mediocre performance."

- "We work in deep silos. Rarely does anyone reach out cross-functionally prior to making important decisions."

- "New ideas are rarely embraced due to a mind-set of 'We've always done it that way.' As a result, there's a perception that we are risk averse and are in love with the status quo. When really good ideas do surface, we always call them Phase 2 and put them on a list somewhere."

- "We have quiet meetings that lack passionate and honest dialogue. People say what they think after the meeting in the hallway but rarely in the meeting itself."

- "There is a lack of alignment and a lack of focus around clearly defined organizational results. We have no shared vision or goals."

- " 'It's not my job!' is an oft-repeated mantra within too many of our divisions. We throw problems over the fence."

This list of C^1 cultural characteristics that stood in the way of achieving R^2 revealed strong B^1 beliefs about how things were done at Eastside. Our experience has shown that this is not an uncommon list for organizations looking to make a change. Many leadership teams struggle with the fact that, while everyone tends to support the need for change, no one is quite sure how best to define it in a memorable and useful way. At Eastside, we helped senior leadership address this issue by creating alignment among the expanded leadership team around the key Cultural Beliefs needed throughout the organization. These B^2 beliefs would guide the needed A^2 actions and produce the desired R^2 results. Here's how their Cultural Beliefs statement characterized the needed C^2 culture:

Cultural Beliefs: "Eastside HealthPlans"	
Act Now	I commit each day to act with urgency to beat the competition.
Reach Out	I build partnerships across the enterprise to achieve outstanding corporate results.
Own It	I take accountability for our results and constantly ask, "What else can I do?"
Let's Talk	I seek, listen, and share to foster an open and honest exchange.
Be Radical	I implement innovative solutions for stakeholders as part of my daily work.
Embrace Lean	I beat the competition by maximizing efficiency and by being leaner, faster, better, every day.
Be Aligned	I align my daily actions with, and focus on, achieving our corporate results.

CHANGE THE culture CHANGE THE game

Just two years after initiating the Culture of Accountability Process and defining the Eastside Cultural Beliefs, the CEO stood before his leadership team and announced that for the first time since the parent company's customer satisfaction program began, they had earned the maximum possible 100 points, either meeting or exceeding the standard for all critical measurements. This achievement resulted in Eastside achieving the first-place ranking among all its sister companies for the first time ever. This transformation occurred in just two years and marked a significant change in the way employees throughout the company were thinking and acting with respect to the company's commitment to their customers.

Cultural Beliefs inform a way of thinking. They work in concert to create just the right balance among the beliefs. You can't articulate just one belief, promulgate that belief, and expect it to motivate the right actions. You need a set of beliefs that function together as a system. For instance, at Eastside, the leaders needed people to "Act Now!" with a sense of urgency, but they also wanted people to "Reach Out" and work cross-functionally across the organization. In addition, they needed people to "Own It" and take accountability to ask, "What else can I do?" and to implement "Let's Talk" by fostering an open and honest exchange of ideas and opinions. That's how Cultural Beliefs work: They form an interdependent system of how people in the organization need to think and act differently to achieve R^2. They are a set of beliefs that harmonize with one another and work together to guide A^2 actions.

CREATING THE CULTURAL BELIEFS STATEMENT

The B^2 shifts you select will form the basis of your Cultural Beliefs statement. Prioritizing the most important shifts and capturing them in your statement is an essential step in creating a successful cultural transition. Our research and experience reveal that the more consciously and deliberately you approach the task of identifying B^2 beliefs, the more effectively you can write your Cultural Beliefs statement.

You'll want to structure your own Cultural Beliefs statement to look much like the one Eastside fashioned for its culture. Of course, your list of B^2 beliefs will reflect your organization's unique needs. Remember, when it comes to culture, one size does not fit all. Every company must identify its own specific B^2 beliefs that will guide the actions needed to achieve its unique R^2 results.

It probably goes without saying that no one person should write a Cultural Beliefs statement. This pivotal statement should be the product of group interactions in which the management team, broadly defined, describes the key B^2 beliefs that the organization needs to create. You should avoid compiling a comprehensive listing of every possible belief you need people to hold, because that would dilute the list and distract everyone from the truly vital ones. Rather, your list must capture the missing beliefs that, if added, would propel your organization, department, group, or team toward R^2.

We recommend you begin each belief statement with the word *I*. Because culture changes one person at a time, every single leader, manager, and individual contributor needs to internalize the Cultural Beliefs. People need to read the belief as though it exists as a thought in their own minds, guiding their actions to A^2. Clients often ask, "Why not start each belief statement with *We*?" Our experience has taught us that the *I* is often lost in the *we*. The CEO of one large pharmaceutical company we worked with early in our career gave us a perfect example of this. He told us that when he joined the organization, he wanted to identify the extent of accountability throughout the company. As he searched, he could not find a single point of accountability for any decision made at any level. Every time he asked who made a particular decision, he heard the name of one of the teams. It appeared to the CEO that the culture consisted of an environment in which both no one and everyone were accountable at the same time. In exasperation he exclaimed, "Teams don't make decisions! Leaders do!" He did not seek to punish people if things went wrong, nor did he wish to disenfranchise team members in their collaborative effort to help the organization arrive at the right answer to problems. He simply wanted to speed up better decision making by allowing leaders to take on more authority and willingly accept accountability to get things done. Having this level of personal accountability for living the Cultural Beliefs that lie at the heart of C^2 is critical to accelerating the culture change. That's why we suggest establishing ownership for the Cultural Beliefs statement by opening each statement with *I*, thereby giving a pointed reminder that every single person must assume accountability for acting in accordance with each of the Cultural Beliefs.

Cultural Beliefs statements, particularly those crafted in a participative manner with an eye toward getting people to sign on, provide an extremely powerful tool for culture change. Try writing each statement in a way that will actualize C^2, while acknowledging the fact that the given belief has not yet fully taken hold.

Rely on the words people would actually use to answer the new employee's question, "How do things work around here?" Craft the statements in the first person and make them affirmative. Remember, the statements describe the way people need to think and act to achieve R^2. They describe your desired state, your C^2 culture.

Although managers draw the cultural road map, they cannot expect it to take hold if people cannot relate to it. As you draft your statements, keep in mind that you are addressing every employee throughout the entire organization. These B^2 belief statements will motivate different A^2 actions from people at every level. You should bear in mind that the statement cannot stand entirely on its own without the definition, interpretation, and explanation that give the words their most precise meaning. The beliefs should be written broadly enough to stimulate dialogue and discussion about how they apply to every job in every part of the organization. That's why you can't settle for merely tacking them up on the wall in the conference room or handing them out as a memo to every employee. Rather, you should introduce the statement using a process that will help people understand, buy into, and own each of the beliefs with all of the richness contained in its carefully selected words, a topic we will discuss in more detail in chapter 10, "Enrolling the Entire Organization in the Change."

THE POWER OF WORKING WITH BELIEFS

A good illustration of the power of working with beliefs comes from retailing giant Sears, Roebuck and Co., which has experienced ups and downs in performance over the years. This particular story, a favorite of ours, comes from a period in Sears's history when the company executed a major turnaround in performance. At the time, Chief Learning Officer Anthony Rucci, as reported in a *Fortune* magazine interview, voiced surprise at employees' misunderstanding of the company's business and goals. In meetings with workers, Rucci would ask, "How much profit do you suppose Sears keeps on every dollar of revenue?" The median response was forty-five cents after tax." At the time, their profit was 1.7¢ on the dollar. Rucci concluded, "We have an economic literacy problem here. That's management's fault." Rucci grew quite concerned over the fact that the beliefs employees held about the success of the company negatively influenced how they approached their jobs.

Rucci asked another question: "What do you think is the primary thing you get paid to do here?" Over half the people answered, "To protect the assets of the company." Employees held the belief that "protecting" the company was their number-one priority. Rather than helping the customer (a proactive posture), employees were monitoring the customer (a defensive posture). With this belief in place, actions followed, and so did results: some of the lowest customer-satisfaction scores in the retail industry.

It amazed Rucci to learn that the focus on financials had led people to lose sight of satisfying customers. Rucci realized that the company was driving performance by almost exclusively stressing the "hard" side of the business: "What gets measured, gets done." He knew the company needed to refocus on the customer. "We knew that unless we produced credible, auditable measurements in all three areas—shop, work, and invest—all the attention would gravitate to the financials, and we wouldn't get the traction we need on shop and work." To make the "soft" concepts more concrete, the company analyzed thirteen financial measures for 820 full-line department stores, millions of data points on customer satisfaction, and hundreds of thousands of employee-satisfaction data points. Their analysis told them "that employees' attitudes about the job and about the company are the two factors that predict their behavior in front of the customer, which in turn predicts the likelihood of customer retention and customers' recommending us to others, the two factors that, in turn, predict financial performance."

Using empirical data, Rucci demonstrated the fact that employee beliefs drive actions and results. He also substantiated the fact that a shift in employee satisfaction ratings (employees' beliefs and attitudes about the store and the company) by five measuring units (on their internal scale) in one quarter would translate to a two-unit increase in customer satisfaction scores the next quarter (the result of employees' actions based upon their new beliefs) and to revenue growth the following quarter that would beat their stores' national average by 0.5 percent. Sears's leaders believed so strongly in this relationship that they began to link 30 to 70 percent of the company's top two hundred executives' incentive compensation to nonfinancial performance measures.

Sears worked to shift its culture and change the way sales associates thought about their daily work in the stores. It drove the new key beliefs about financial literacy and about defining employees' jobs in terms of satisfying the customer throughout the entire organization. Management began by educating employees on the changes in the business environment that had occurred since the 1950s. For example, trend data showed that consumers had reduced their trips to shopping malls by over 66 percent. In response, one forklift operator in Detroit said, "Wait a minute! If people are going to the mall one third as often, and all our stores are in malls, why are we spending so much money remodeling those stores?" Rucci's reaction? "I'm sitting in the back of the room going hallelujah! You want people to know enough about the business to ask those kinds of questions."

The management team adopted many other new beliefs about how to bring about positive change throughout the organization, such as these three: "Access to information is what motivates change and improvement." "People in the stores have to participate in whatever goal-setting process you've set up; that's how you promote ownership." "When people get a chance to accomplish something themselves, they build self-esteem; they just come to life."

Rucci and his team recognized that changing beliefs leads to a change in action and results; they proved it to themselves statistically. Not coincidentally, a *Fortune* survey conducted not long after the company changed its culture showed that, at the time, Sears delivered the fifth-highest improvement among 206 companies in customer satisfaction and nearly doubled its margin, from 1.7¢ to 3.3¢. This gratifying bottom-line improvement and overall change in performance clearly depicts the impact and efficiency of working with the beliefs people hold.

BUILDING THE PYRAMID

Effective leaders understand that beliefs drive people's actions. Culture change involves getting people to adopt B^2 beliefs about "how things are done around here." An organization's Cultural Beliefs statement describes its Culture of Accountability. Recall that we have defined a Culture of Accountability as a culture (C^2) in which people take accountability to think and act (B^2 and A^2) in the manner necessary to achieve the needed result (R^2). Creating clarity around the key Cultural Beliefs that need to shift will help accelerate the transition to a new culture and increase the likelihood of delivering desired results.

The corporate communications department does not draft the Cultural Beliefs statement for public consumption. Rather, management assembles it, with input from employees, as a practical tool to create alignment and produce results at every level of the organization. In chapter 10 we will further examine the use of the Cultural Beliefs statement and address such issues as how to present the statement to the rest of the organization and how to use it to fully implement the culture change throughout the organization.

Responsibility for creating an environment in which people buy into and live the Cultural Beliefs falls on the broad shoulders of leadership. We firmly believe that few other leadership acts can contribute more to an organization's success.

You cannot bring about a change in beliefs simply by asking

people to do it, although that represents a good start. To foster the adoption of B^2 beliefs, management must create experiences that will convince people to change their beliefs and begin thinking differently about their daily work. This is perhaps leadership's greatest challenge and the crucial level of the pyramid that we will tackle in the next chapter.

CHAPTER 5

Providing Experiences
That Instill the Right Beliefs

THE EXPERIENCES THAT FORM the foundation of the Results Pyramid drive accelerated culture change. Whether you realize it or not, you provide experiences for everyone around you every day. Each interaction you have with others in the organization creates an experience that either fosters or undermines desired B^2 beliefs. Quite simply, the experiences you provide create the beliefs people hold.

Helping thousands of clients successfully accelerate culture change over the last two decades has convinced us that leaders must become highly proficient at creating the right E^2 experiences. Those who gain this proficiency will more likely achieve their R^2 results as they accelerate the shift from C^1 to C^2 and develop a Culture of Accountability. We feel confident that when you focus on the foundation of the Results Pyramid and provide the right experiences, people will change the way they think. If you change the way they think, then you can change the culture; and when you change the culture, you change the game.

THE RIGHT EXPERIENCES FORM THE DESIRED BELIEFS

A good example of using experiences to create beliefs comes from a privately owned ice cream chain, Amy's Ice Creams, headquartered in Austin, Texas. Leaders of this thirteen-unit chain purposely focus on creating experiences to manage their culture and produce results. Amy Simmons, owner of the chain, launched Amy's Ice Creams with the personal belief that in order to compete for customers under the heat of the East Texas sun, an ice cream shop must do more than simply offer mouthwatering refreshments. Amy distinguishes her creamy confectionery shops by delivering an experience with every scoop of ice cream she sells!

When an *Inc.* magazine cover story profiled the company, it described the employees of Amy's Ice Creams as performers. Customers waiting in line watch employees juggle their ice cream scoops, toss balls of ice cream around, and even dance on the freezer tops. Reporter John Case noted, "If there's a line out the door, they might pass out free samples—or offer free ice cream to any customer who will sing or dance or recite a poem or mimic a barnyard animal. They wear costumes. They bring props. They pop trivia questions. They create fun." In short, Amy's people create experiences for their customers and for their fellow employees. Like the culture of many other successful companies, the culture at Amy's Ice Creams didn't just evolve; a leader purposefully created it, and it grew one experience at a time, one person at a time. Case points out that Amy "had to get the right people and get them to behave in the right way. And because their behavior had to be inventive, unflagging, and self-initiated, she had to get them to know what the right way was without being told." In other words, the company could only create and sustain the Amy's Ice Creams way of thinking through experiences from which people learn for themselves the importance of displaying their utmost creativity. Once employees translated experiences into shared beliefs, no one needed to tell them what to do. They did it naturally, as an integral part of their jobs. Amy knew that she couldn't just tell her people what to do. She needed to create the experiences that nurtured the belief that everyone who worked for Amy's must work hard each and every day to invent the fun and games that characterized the Amy's culture.

To accomplish this, the company exposes all prospective employees to the "Amy's experience" before hiring them. Instead of an application form, each prospective employee receives a plain white paper bag to take home. The only requirement is to write one's name and contact information somewhere on the bag. The only other instruction: Do something with the bag, and bring it back in a week. According to Amy, "Those who just jot down a phone number will find that Amy's isn't really for them, but an applicant who produces something unusual from a white paper bag tends to be an amusing person who would fit in with our environment." In response, Amy's has seen it all: lavishly decorated bags, bags transformed into puppets, bags containing creative videos, and even a bag reduced to a pile of ashes. From the very start, experiences at Amy's Ice Creams reinforce the belief that "things are different here." Over and over, this simple experience, created right up front in the hiring process, has proven effective in defining, differentiating, and transmitting the Amy's culture, and it creatively demonstrates how experiences provide the foundation for desired beliefs. The results for this wild and crazy company? You probably guessed it. Amy's Ice Creams consistently dominates their local market.

Experiences create beliefs. The right experiences create the desired B^2 beliefs. To accelerate culture change, you should ask yourself this key question: What experiences do I need to provide in order to create the B^2 beliefs we need in the organization? Keep in mind that, for good or bad, you are already creating experiences (E^1) and beliefs (B^1) and a culture (C^1), and you will continue to do so, whether you do it consciously or not.

Providing experiences that foster the right beliefs can take more than a little imagination and effort. We like the apocryphal story about the steel company whose board hoped to shake up a moribund culture by hiring a new CEO. The CEO began his job determined to change the culture and improve productivity. The first belief he wanted to instill in his people was that there would be no tolerance for any slackers in the workforce. During his first tour of the facilities, he came upon an employee leaning against the wall in one of the offices where everyone else in the room was busy working.

Wanting people to see him as a firm and decisive boss, the CEO singled out the idle employee and asked, "How much money do you make a week?" The young man looked surprised, but responded, "Four hundred dollars a week. Why?" The CEO shot back, "Wait right here!" He quickly went back into his office and returned a few minutes later to hand the young man $1,600 in cash with a stern admonishment. "Here's four weeks' pay. Now *get out*, and don't come back." After the man walked away, the CEO beamed at the remaining workers, quite happy with the strong message he had just sent. He asked the onlookers, "Does anyone want to tell me what the heck that goofball did around here?" From the other side of the office, a small and somewhat reluctant voice called out over a cubicle wall, "He's the pizza delivery guy from Domino's."

Becoming conscious of the experiences you are creating and the impact those experiences have on what people believe is a competency every leader must possess or quickly develop. Understanding the impact of experiences is absolutely imperative to any successful effort to change the culture. Many leaders find that early in their change efforts, the experiences they create fail to influence prevailing beliefs in the way they had hoped they would. To avoid that happening to you, we suggest you take these four principles to heart:

Principle 1: People work to validate rather than invalidate their current beliefs by filtering new experiences through the lens of their current beliefs. We call this selective interpretation.

Principle 2: People often cling to old beliefs and only reluctantly surrender them, falling prey to what we refer to as belief bias. As with selective interpretation, people are generally unaware that they are doing this.

Principle 3: People frequently fail to take accountability for the beliefs they form, choosing instead to see those beliefs as natural and logical conclusions based upon their experiences.

Principle 4: Because the beliefs people hold do not readily change, the best indicator of future behavior is past behavior.

In some cases, as in the tale of the steel company's CEO, experiences can actually backfire, inspiring beliefs exactly opposite of those you sought to instill. Accelerating the transition to a Culture of

Accountability will occur only when you learn the importance of interpreting the experiences you create. In fact, everything depends on it.

EXPERIENCE TYPES

Leaders who do not understand the importance of interpreting the experiences they create seldom see desired B^2 beliefs adopted by people in their organizations. Therefore, you should always expect that most of the experiences you create will require careful interpretation. Otherwise, the bias toward holding on to B^1 beliefs will persist with full force and defeat your efforts to get people to see things anew.

Because everyone views the same experience with a different set of eyes, very few experiences will "stand on their own two feet." You need to prop them up with the right interpretation. Otherwise, you cannot expect people to understand precisely what you intended. Not all the experiences you create are equal. From our observation, the experiences leaders provide in an attempt to create B^2 beliefs fall into one of four experience types.

Experience Types

Type 1 EXPERIENCE	A meaningful event leading to immediate insight, needing no interpretation	**Clearly Understood**
Type 2 EXPERIENCE	An experience that needs to be interpreted in order to form the desired beliefs	
Type 3 EXPERIENCE	Experiences that will not affect prevailing beliefs because they are perceived as insignificant	
Type 4 EXPERIENCE	Experiences that will always be misinterpreted regardless of the amount or quality of the interpretation	**Completely Misunderstood**

CHANGE the culture CHANGE the game

We have built this model after observing many leaders who have both successfully and unsuccessfully attempted to provide E^2 experiences they hoped would create B^2 beliefs. Understanding the type of experience you are providing will help you calibrate the degree of interpretation required and decide whether you need to rethink the type of experiences you are providing in your effort to create B^2 beliefs. Consider the CEO from the steel company for a moment. What type of experience did he think he was creating? What type of experience did he really create? You could argue that he thought he was creating a Type 1 experience, but in fact he ended up creating a Type 4. We see this happen all the time. But it need not happen to you, provided you adopt an effective methodology for creating experiences that instill B^2 beliefs.

A Type 1 experience communicates a clear, meaningful event leading to immediate insight. It will foster the desired belief without any interpretation by management. For example, a memorable example of a Type 1 experience occurred during the Y2K fervor in the year 2000 when everyone worried that the "millennium bug" caused by a rollover problem due to the way programmers had dealt with dates prior to that time would crash computer-based systems worldwide. While experts widely debated the validity of the potential glitch, some major airlines grounded their planes on December 31, 1999, and January 1, 2000. However, the Chinese government, in an effort to send an unmistakable message, decreed that all airline executives from the People's Republic of China occupy seats on airborne aircraft at midnight, December 31, 1999, Greenwich Mean Time. This epitomized a clear Type 1 experience that needed no interpretation by the airline executives in China: Y2K compliance was non-negotiable. The airline executives would do whatever it took to achieve it. Every executive understood that their life depended on making sure the planes flew safely at midnight at the turn of the millennium!

Type 1 experiences are difficult to find, as most experiences will not be interpreted by everyone the same way. Even though the message sent by the Chinese government seems to have created a clear Type 1 for airline employees as well as the flying public, some executives may have actually interpreted the experience as a Type 4, feeling that their government was putting their own personal safety at risk. What may look like a Type 1 to you can look like a Type 4 to someone else. Keeping these distinctions in mind can help you more effectively recalibrate the experiences you provide as you work to move the culture change forward.

When you do manage to provide an experience that most people view as Type 1, you will powerfully influence people to adopt the targeted B^2 beliefs. In fact, when it comes to leading a culture change, nothing will serve you better than creating Type 1 experiences. Look for and seize every opportunity to do so.

A Type 2 experience requires careful interpretation before people will adopt the intended B^2 belief. As we said earlier, most of the experiences you provide will fall into this category, because most experiences do need interpretation at some level.

Just as "Beauty is in the eye of the beholder," we would suggest that beliefs are in the mind of the observer. In other words, determining which type of experience you have provided depends entirely upon the conclusions drawn by those you intended to have the experience as they exercised selective interpretation. Did they walk away with the intended belief or not? Given the bias to hold on to old C^1 habits, perspectives, and beliefs, those interpretations will tend to defy all efforts to change them and will favor a C^1 view of the world. For example, a leadership team that others perceive as unreceptive to feedback or unwilling to collaborate cross-functionally might find it difficult to create experiences that cause people to see them in a new light; people may view attempts at newfound openness and inclusiveness as oddly out of character and nothing more than a fluke.

Overcoming this natural tendency toward belief bias takes some thoughtful effort, but you can overcome it when you approach the problem correctly. We remember early in our career working with "Telenetics," a manufacturing concern that had mushroomed into a $100 million company in just under five years. People loved working at Telenetics. Customers lined up to buy the company's product, and manufacturing could scarcely stay ahead of the forecast and keep product flowing out the door.

As we worked with the management team at Telenetics, we

administered a survey among line workers and their supervisors to assess the prevailing C^1 beliefs. One belief, widely held among line workers and their supervisors, greatly surprised the company's leaders: "Senior management is not committed to quality."

At first, the management team was tempted to filter out this feedback and ignore it altogether because of its glaring inaccuracy—after all, they knew they were committed to quality. However, knowing that their customers were complaining about quality problems, they acknowledged there might be something to the beliefs on the assembly line. We coached them to go to work to find out what experiences led to this widely held belief. When we facilitated candid discussions with their team leaders, we learned that line workers would frequently turn on the call light that signaled a line engineer to come and inspect an item that clearly fell below manufacturing's quality specifications. However, rather than scrapping these seemingly deficient products, the engineer would "always" give the green light to ship the item in question. With no interpretation of the decision, the message was clear: Delivery was more important than quality.

As the managers delved further into this disturbing revelation, they discovered that engineers often made the decision to ship a product that was out of spec because the deficiency in the product was only an issue of "goodness," usually involving minor issues, such as color mismatches, that did not affect the efficacy of the product itself. The issue may have even involved specs that were out of date and no longer applicable. However, because the line engineers allowed these products to go through, people working the assembly line stopped turning on the light to alert the quality control engineers that a problem existed, allowing truly deficient products to get shipped. The result: Telenetics was shipping bad products, and the customers did not like it.

Managers determined that to solve the quality issue and stop mismanufactured items, they would need to help line workers adopt a new belief: If an item was out of spec, it needed to be scrapped, period. While some good products would be sacrificed, the bad ones would be caught. They also determined that to avoid scrapping products with mere cosmetic defects, Telenetics would need to revise the out-of-date or incorrectly written specs.

We vividly recall the meeting when the managers met with the assemblers to announce their findings and their decision. In disbelief, one line supervisor stood up and challenged whether senior leadership really would support scrapping a cosmetically imperfect product, which the new policy would dictate until the revised specs were put in place. The answer: "Yes. If we need to rewrite a spec, we will do so. But until that happens, Telenetics will not ship a single product that fails to meet existing specs."

Over the next six months, people working on the assembly were provided a completely different experience from the past. Whenever they spotted a suspicious item, they routinely switched on the call light to alert the quality engineers, who, for their part, ordered the scrapping of any product that fell below spec. The interpretation remained constant: "We do not ship out-of-spec product." Whenever the company installed revised specs, engineers honored them to the letter, providing timely feedback whenever they thought a spec needed revision. Before long, Telenetics made measurable strides in terms of product quality and customer satisfaction: Quality increased fivefold and sales soared.

We administered the survey again six months later. The finding? To a person, people on the line now believed that senior leadership had changed and were completely committed to quality. It happened because leadership focused on the bottom of the pyramid and effectively accelerated a shift in people's beliefs by creating Type 2 experiences that changed their beliefs, their actions, and ultimately their results—a fivefold reduction in customer complaints over the next two years.

We once interviewed middle managers of another client about the Type 2 experiences they had observed within their organization. They told us how senior management had attempted to create greater personal ownership of company results by setting up a new program that would reward employees throughout the organization with stock options. As we probed further, we learned from the CEO that every member of the senior management team was involved in this initiative and felt proud of the fact that they had worked so hard to benefit employees throughout the company. They were confident that the stock would certainly rise in value with the significant growth in revenues they expected. What better way to provide a benefit that would enrich the lives of employees, improve their engagement, and let them participate in the company's growing earnings?

Everyone on the senior team enthusiastically participated in the launch of the new plan. You can imagine their shock when their announcement was greeted with a lukewarm response. The management team could not believe it. Why hadn't their people reacted to the announcement with enthusiastic applause?

Later, town hall–style meetings revealed that most employees did not understand how stock options worked and how they would benefit from them. They thought it obligated them to buy the company's stock, but they did not grasp the fact that if they chose to exercise the option at the current price per share, they could resell their shares at a higher price. It just looked to them as if management was coercing them to spend their hard-earned money without getting a return on their investment.

This episode was a classic Type 2 experience. Once senior leaders understood the need for interpreting this experience and began to explain the option program, people began to like the idea a lot. Sharing in the ownership of the company's performance, they started to think much more carefully about what they could do every day on the job to enhance their gains. They scanned the financial page to see daily fluctuations in the stock price, because they understood perfectly that if the company performed well, they would make more money. The moral of the story? When it comes to experiences that instill beliefs, never underestimate the power of conscious and deliberate interpretation.

During the initial stages of your own cultural transition, you will undoubtedly find that experiences need even more interpretation than usual, simply because the effort to change beliefs is challenged so persistently.

Belief bias is strong and selective interpretation is real. However, if you consistently implement the change methodologies in this book, you can overcome the tendency to see things through the C^1 lens, thereby helping people more quickly and readily interpret their new experiences in light of C^2. In short order, E^2 experiences will propel people in your organization to replace the culture's prevailing beliefs with preferred B^2 beliefs.

When it comes to Type 3 experiences, they do not alter prevailing beliefs, because, for good or ill, people dismiss them as events that fit into the normal pattern of things. Consider these examples:

Common Type 3 Experiences During Culture Change

1. Putting vision and values statements on the wall

2. Writing articles in the company newsletter

3. Posting notices and updates on the company Web site

4. Receiving a weekly paycheck

5. Making management team announcements

As a rule, people do not take such experiences to heart, and experiences they do not take to heart will not convince them to adopt new B^2 beliefs. While these experiences, in concert with other E^2 experiences, may play some role in promoting the change, you should keep a watchful eye out for needless investment of time and/or resources in Type 3 experiences. Instead, put these resources to work on Type 2 experiences, those that really will help you promote the shift from C^1 to C^2.

When it comes to Type 4 experiences, no matter how hard you try, people will never interpret them the way you intended. Type 4 experiences usually undermine the culture by reinforcing unwanted C^1 beliefs. You should make every effort to avoid providing such experiences, particularly during a culture change effort. One of our clients told us an interesting story about the perils of a Type 4 experience. For the first time in the history of this hundred-year-old company, "CGS" had undertaken significant budget cuts that led to workforce reduction at the senior executive level. Never before had

CGS's top executives laid off people they had known and worked with for many years.

In the midst of all this, the CEO called an executive management meeting with the top 120 people in the company, during which he announced his intention to buy another jet for the corporate fleet. He carefully laid out his reasoning. This purchase would, he insisted, speed up the process of closing the deals the organization needed to achieve its goals. The announcement came as a shock to everyone there. No matter how thoroughly and carefully this CEO might have detailed the reasoning behind the decision, it would fall on deaf ears. This classic Type 4 experience reinforced C^1 beliefs held throughout the organization that you could not trust leadership, that senior executives did not care about their people, and that the top brass only looked out for themselves. This was a Type 4 experience that never should have happened.

Sometimes you can avoid Type 4 experiences by seeking feedback from others before you create a planned experience. Seeking the perspectives of others will help you know how people might interpret that experience, enabling you to make necessary adjustments or scrap it altogether. Ask and listen before you act. However, if you see a Type 4 as your only choice, then you should move forward with your eyes wide open, anticipating the reaction, preparing for it, and taking the appropriate steps to minimize the negative effect of that experience on the B^2 beliefs you want to reinforce.

WHAT'S YOUR EXPERIENCE?

Experiences create beliefs that drive actions that, in turn, produce results. When people consistently interpret E^2 experiences in a way that fosters B^2 beliefs, R^2 results come more quickly. You can use the following exercise to stimulate your thinking about the experiences you need to provide in your own organization.

Consulting the chart below, identify a B^2 belief you need to create for your organization or team. Make sure the B^2 belief will play a major role in achieving R^2 results. Then identify either a Type 1 (if you can) or a Type 2 experience that you think will foster that B^2 belief. Consider, specifically, what you could do to create each type of experience.

Providing Experiences That Instill B² Beliefs	
Key B^2 belief you want to create:	
Experience Type	**Experiences that you could provide to instill the B² belief:**
Type 1 EXPERIENCE A meaningful event leading to immediate insight, needing no interpretation	
Type 2 EXPERIENCE An experience that needs to be interpreted in order to have the desired results	
	CHANGE_{THE}culture CHANGE_{THE}game

After you have given this some thought, you may well conclude that identifying the experiences you need to create will take some careful planning. That's generally true. But you can make it a whole lot easier on yourself when you take the right steps to ensure that the experiences you provide hit the mark.

THE FOUR STEPS TO PROVIDING E² EXPERIENCES

There are four important steps you can take to ensure that you provide experiences that will create B^2 beliefs. Skip a step, and you will likely find yourself, at some point, creating experiences that reinforce the old C^1 culture you want to change. These steps will help you create the right experience the first time and help you correct your approach whenever you discover that your effort is not influencing people's thinking the way you hoped it would.

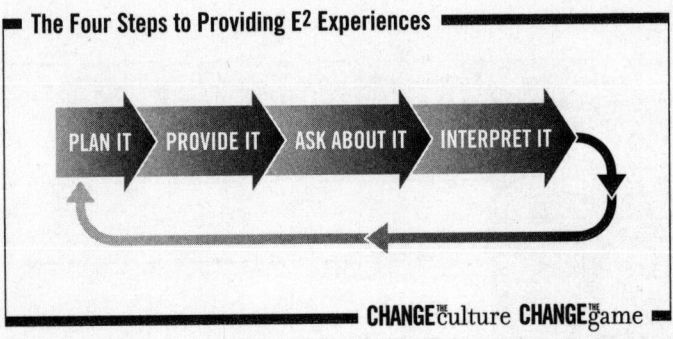

The Four Steps to Providing E^2 Experiences

PLAN IT ▸ PROVIDE IT ▸ ASK ABOUT IT ▸ INTERPRET IT

CHANGE the culture CHANGE the game

Note that these steps work in a cycle. As you strive to establish B^2 beliefs, you will find yourself planning the E^2 experience, providing it, asking for feedback on it, interpreting that experience, and then repeating the cycle over and over as you work to instill B^2 beliefs in the culture.

Step One:
Plan It

While you will find plenty of opportunities to create experiences spontaneously, you must also, and more importantly, learn to plan E^2 experiences in advance, both as a team and by yourself. When doing so, ask yourself a few essential questions.

Planning E^2 Experiences

1. What B^2 belief do I need to reinforce?

2. Who is my intended audience for the experience? Whom will they talk to about it?

3. What specific experience will I provide? Is it a Type 1 or Type 2?

4. How will I provide the experience so that it reinforces the B^2 belief?

5. When is the best time to do this?

6. Who can give me input on my plan?

You may want to add some questions to this list in order to tailor it to your own organization and culture change effort. Thoughtfully planning the experiences you provide will help you do what people need you to do to establish the foundation of E^2 experiences that are essential to creating the desired C^2 culture.

Step Two:
Provide It

Next, you follow your plan and provide the experience. That could involve a little practice, depending on the nature and scope of what you are trying to accomplish. Also, keep in mind that your experiences cannot be manipulative in any way. Your efforts must be sincere attempts to provide genuine experiences that signal real change. The people you are trying to influence for the good will smell an insincere effort a mile away, and when that happens, all bets are off.

It's not a bad idea to arrange for someone to observe how you go about providing the experience, perhaps a member of the team to which you are directing the new experience or anyone else whom you trust and whose presence would not be a distraction. Of course, that person would need to know the details of your plan and be looking for a few specific things. Here is a list of questions that you could have them use.

Observer Questions

1. Did I do what I planned?

2. What type of experience do you think I provided (1, 2, 3, or 4)? Why?

3. What feedback can you offer me on how I did?

4. How do you think people reacted?

5. Do you think the experience will have the intended effect on B^2 beliefs?

With questions like these, the observer can give you targeted input that will help you aim even more effectively at the B^2 beliefs essential to the culture change. If you are providing a one-on-one experience or a "virtual" one for people at remote locations, then invite them to participate in the process as much as possible. Their input could make a huge difference in terms of improving your ability to provide new E^2 experiences.

Step Three:
Ask About It

This is a critical step. If you don't check in, you will not know if you have hit the mark. Most of us naturally expect people to behave rationally, reasonably, and in line with how we see things. But you must remember their bias toward holding on to B^1 beliefs and seeing things through that lens. This bias always leads to selective interpretation, increasing the likelihood that people will interpret the experience differently than you might expect. Given this reality, feedback becomes critical to getting it right. Remember: *Don't believe everything you think!*

As you ask about the experience you have provided, it is quite possible that you could walk away from that feedback session pleased with the outcome, while those providing the feedback regret their candidness, thinking that whatever they said could come back to haunt them later. Even the experience of asking about the experience has an impact on people's beliefs. To find out how people are really interpreting the experiences you provide, you must ask them about the experience and the beliefs they are forming. Whenever you do ask, bear in mind a few do's and don'ts:

Do's and Don'ts of "Asking About It"

1. Don't get defensive.

2. Do be curious and listen to what people really think.

3. Don't cut people off by asking a thousand questions.

4. Do get as much input as you can from as many people as you can.

5. Don't ask leading questions that bias what people say.

One final don't: Don't forget that asking for feedback on the experiences you create becomes an experience in and of itself. If done well, it will surely foster desired beliefs. If, on the other hand, the feedback indicates that things are not on track, take step four in the cycle.

Step Four:
Interpret It

This final step in the process of providing E^2 experiences involves acting on the feedback that you received and taking the extra steps necessary to interpret the experience you provided in such a way that people form the desired B^2 beliefs. Interpreting experiences for people involves: 1. telling them the B^2 belief you want them to have; 2. explaining how the experience was intended to foster that belief; and 3. clarifying any confusion or answering questions people may raise. Tell; explain; clarify. Of course, you should always listen carefully to the feedback people will offer, as this will guide you toward understanding exactly what you need to do to interpret the experiences you are providing.

If you find yourself having a difficult time getting others to accept your interpretation, then you may have provided a Type 4 experience. If that is the case, either due to a misfire on your part or because you could not choose to do otherwise, then simply acknowledge that fact and move on with the cycle by providing new experiences that do move people in the right direction.

Remember, culture changes one person at a time, and the effort to change people's beliefs is worth it. When people participate in several belief-changing Type 1 or Type 2 experiences, they become game changers, driven to promote the new beliefs and the C^2 culture. They will share their observations and insights about these new experiences with others. After all, when you learn something new and positive, don't you want to tell someone about it? When you see something new and good in your environment, don't you want others to see it too?

Using the four steps to providing E^2 experiences will help to ensure that your efforts yield B^2 beliefs. While not every E^2 experience you provide will stem from deliberate planning—because you will, of course, seize many spontaneous opportunities to do the right thing—you will find that this approach does speed up your ability to move the culture toward C^2.

MANAGEMENT TEAMS MUST START WITH THEMSELVES

Almost invariably we find that when the team at the top decides to shift the organizational culture, it must also shift its own team culture. Tougher results, a changing business environment, or a new managerial focus can all generate a need for greater alignment, clarity, and accountability in the management team's own C^2. That means that any organization-wide change effort should begin by providing E^2 experiences for the management team.

One management team of a European company did just that. "Mécaniser," a small appliance manufacturer, had been struggling against more innovative competitors. Our assessment of senior management revealed a fragmented team focused solely on their individual roles and engaged in finger pointing to justify lackluster performance. The new president, "Claude Guillaume," had come into the organization to set matters straight. Immediately, Claude attempted to create a new E^2 experience for the team that would underscore the need for change. In management-team meetings, he openly confronted performance issues and decisively made strategic decisions.

His approach created new B^2 beliefs about how the team and the organization needed to change, and things began to change quickly.

In fact, Claude managed to shift Mécaniser's culture enough to generate considerable performance improvement in his first year on the team. However, progress plateaued as the company ran out of "low-hanging fruit" to harvest and found results harder and harder to achieve. Soon Claude recognized that he could not fundamentally shift the way the organization was operating without help.

That's when Claude asked us to assist the Mécaniser team in evaluating what they needed to do to change the culture and achieve next year's R^2 plan. The plan number posed a terrific challenge, signaled a moderate change in strategic direction, would require an important deployment of resources, and would necessitate the development of internal processes that did not currently exist. Although Claude and the team had made some progress, they knew that they would not be able to achieve plan without changing the culture, starting with the management team.

Claude also knew that, while he had intentionally and successfully created early experiences for the group that had won their attention, he now needed to bring the group together and forge a more effective team. They worked together to define Mécaniser's management culture and develop a Cultural Beliefs statement that captured the key B^2 beliefs the organization needed to adopt in order to achieve R^2. With this clarity of cultural direction, Claude set about creating the new E^2 experiences that would support the Cultural Beliefs for his whole management team. After obtaining feedback about how he could more completely demonstrate the new B^2 himself, Claude identified a Type 2 experience he could provide the management team: He would confront people less often and listen more attentively in order to establish a more consultative and collaborative decision-making process within the group.

As Claude shared this idea with his team, he was pleased to hear that everyone agreed that this Type 2 experience would forcefully drive the belief that "we are all in this together and we will succeed or fail as a group." While the team had always viewed him as a brilliant strategist, they had also felt that he gave them too little opportunity to participate in strategic decisions. He committed to create a stronger team approach to running the business by drawing out input during his routine meetings and sincerely seeking to understand other team members' perspectives. Claude's mere willingness to hear this feedback provided an E^2 experience that went a long way toward convincing the team that he was serious about creating the C^2 culture captured in the Cultural Beliefs.

The team also knew they needed to address the B^1 belief, widely held by others throughout Mécaniser, that management did not function well as a team. Could they create a Type 2 experience for the entire organization that would begin to shift this B^1 belief? How could they foster and promote the B^2 belief that the management team worked collaboratively for the success of the organization? They saw this as a crucial undertaking because, to date, other Mécaniser teams always followed their lead, thus explaining the current company-wide problem with dysfunctional teams and noncollaborative decision making.

Claude and his team determined to initiate the E^2 experiences they would provide by sharing lunch in the employee cafeteria. In the past, rarely did any one of them go there at all, let alone together as a management team. Imagine the entire senior management team entering the cafeteria as a group and sitting together at a table to eat. Their unified appearance at lunch attracted a great deal of attention and became the story of the day. More important, to anyone watching, they looked as if they actually liked one another and enjoyed one another's company. With a few well-placed comments to the right people, the team also offered clear interpretation: "We want to work better as a team, and we want everyone to know it."

The team also agreed that they needed some additional new E^2 experiences of their own. To begin, they would change the seating configuration in their staff meeting. In the past, Claude had taken the seat at the head of the table facing the team. This seating arrangement had seemed best suited to the small conference room they used for meetings, but why not move to a different room where they could sit around a table with no visible hierarchy and where they could look one another in the eye?

These E^2 experiences, along with others, began to instill new B^2 beliefs in both the management team and the organization. Consistently reinforced, the experiences Mécaniser's leaders created for one another led to the management-team culture described by their Cultural Beliefs and to progress toward achieving R^2 results.

BUILDING THE PYRAMID

To transform an organizational culture or to make tactical shifts to a more solid one, you must start creating new E^2 experiences consistent with desired B^2 beliefs. We often ask, "When it comes to living the Cultural Beliefs, who is the most important person who needs to change?" Of course, the right answer is "I am." Culture changes one person at a time. The most important E^2 experience that you can provide is the experience of you living the Cultural Beliefs, demonstrating their application in the way you do your work each and every day.

Taking accountability to live the Cultural Beliefs and creating the E^2 experiences needed to foster and promote them does more than anything else to accelerate culture change. When you model these key B^2 beliefs, you send the signal to everyone with whom you work that this is the way we need to do things around here. Doing so not only promotes the B^2 beliefs; but it also drives home your credibility as a leader of change.

With this chapter, we conclude our examination of how to use the four elements of organizational culture captured in the Results Pyramid—Results, Actions, Beliefs, and Experiences—and how to apply them to accelerate a change in culture. In Part Two, we will introduce some practical tools, tips, and techniques that will help you integrate the change and accelerate the shift in your culture from C^1 to C^2 so that, in the end, you achieve your R^2 results.

Integrate the C^2 Best Practices to Accelerate the Culture Change

Part Two of *Change the Culture, Change the Game* shows you how to apply the C^2 best practices at every level of the organization to accelerate the culture change and achieve R^2 results. Integrating the C^2 best practices into the existing systems, structure, and practices of the organization will reinforce the C^2 culture and speed you along the way to creating and sustaining a Culture of Accountability. We think you will find our client examples and best practice suggestions about integration extremely helpful in your own quest to achieve game-changing results.

CHAPTER 6

Aligning a Culture for Rapid Progress

WE BEGIN PART TWO of this book by presenting the key to successfully integrating the Results Pyramid and the Cultural Beliefs into your culture so that you consistently produce R^2 results. Lasting integration requires alignment at every stage of the process. First, the senior leadership team members must align themselves around the key R^2 results their organization needs to deliver, the fundamental shifts from C^1 to C^2 that need to take place in the way people think and act throughout the organization, and the B^2 Cultural Beliefs that describe the cultural shifts that are most critical to achieving the key R^2 results. Then, the team members must also align as to how they will use the key Culture Management Tools and how they will fully integrate those tools within the management practices of the organization.

Success in speeding up the culture change will only come when everyone's actions, beliefs, and experiences are aligned from person to person and across the various functions of the company. The more completely aligned the culture, the more everyone will concentrate on achieving R^2 results. Effective leaders of culture change manage in ways that get a culture aligned with results, and then they work to keep it aligned. They say and do things that provide the E^2 experiences that create or reinforce the beliefs that motivate the needed actions that produce R^2. They avoid saying and doing anything that puts the culture out of alignment, such as promoting someone who does not demonstrate the Cultural Beliefs in his or her daily work.

While this may seem obvious, promotions create a compelling experience that has a significant impact on the beliefs people adopt. Promoting people who do not live the Cultural Beliefs is like driving your organization over a huge pothole on the road to C^2. Those potholes can put you out of alignment; too many potholes will stop you dead in your tracks. That's why you must constantly create and maintain alignment at every level of the organization.

GETTING ALIGNED AROUND ALIGNMENT

The dictionary defines *alignment* as adjusting the parts of something in relation to one another so that they are properly positioned. As you work to accelerate the transformation from C^1 to C^2, you need to pay close attention to adjusting the parts of the culture so that they are positioned properly in relation to one another. Neither meaningful nor rapid culture change will occur unless the experiences, beliefs, and actions are aligned with and reinforce R^2 results.

When the different parts of the Results Pyramid fall out of alignment, people know it! People pursue their own agendas and protect their own turf, stress levels run high, decisions are second-guessed, and just about everything slows to a crawl, especially the culture change.

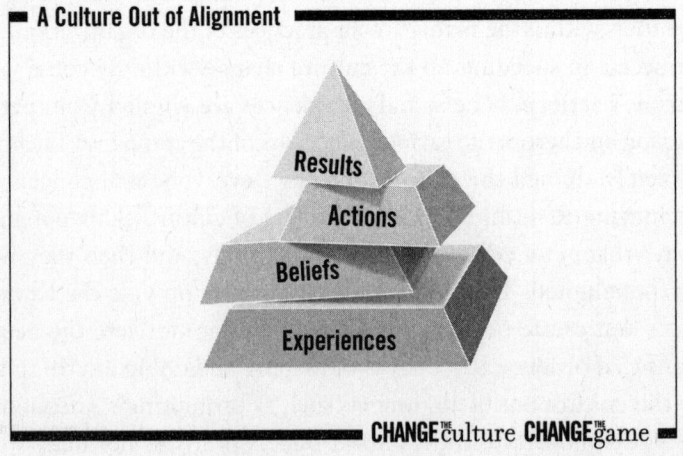

A Culture Out of Alignment

Results
Actions
Beliefs
Experiences

CHANGE the culture CHANGE the game

Using the Results Pyramid as a reference point, we have developed a definition of alignment that applies to every effort to change culture:

Alignment is common beliefs and concerted action in collective pursuit of a clear result.

This definition refers to lining up the parts of the Results Pyramid so that all of the parts are positioned in relation to the R^2 results you want to achieve. When all the parts are aligned and everyone is moving in the same direction, you get accelerated culture change; everyone stays on the same page, people feel less stressed, decision making occurs more efficiently, and almost everything speeds up.

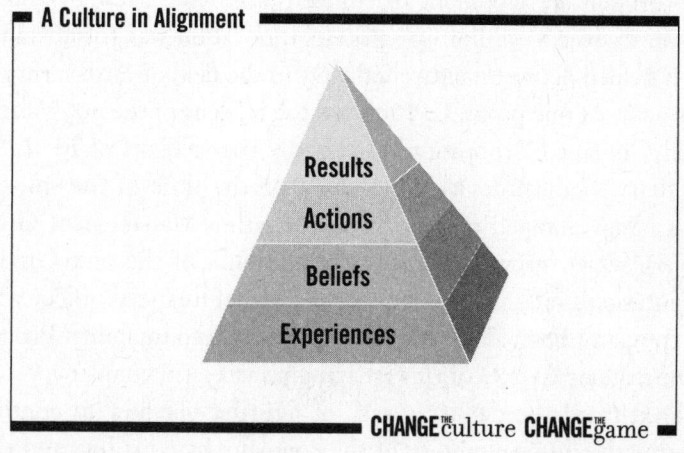

During the Culture of Accountability Process, the speed of the culture change will directly correspond to the level of alignment you create and maintain around R^2 and the Cultural Beliefs.

MAINTAINING ALIGNMENT OVER TIME

Like managing culture, maintaining alignment is a process, not an event. It never ends. You may gain complete alignment around R^2 and C^2, but at some point, R^2 will likely need to move to R^3 and C^2

to C^3. Learning how to manage culture to achieve R^X is an essential leadership competency that you must learn, and even master, as you work to shift your culture and produce R^X results.

A striking example of continuing to manage the culture for long-term success comes from part two of the Cardiac Pacemakers (CPI) story that we introduced in chapter 2. You will remember that at one point, CPI was described as a company traveling "ninety miles per hour on an icy road, headed toward a cliff." Unable to develop new products, people joked that it could not even "develop its way out of a paper bag." However, you will also remember that under the leadership of Jay Graf, and with the aid of the Culture of Accountability Process we describe in this book, it took just a few short years for CPI to change the game so dramatically that the organization became a "new product development machine" (its R^2) and grew from $250 million to over $1 billion in sales. Its innovation was so substantial that it helped define an entire industry in the field of cardiac rhythm treatment. At one point, CPI formed the nucleus of the newly established Guidant Corporation, created by the split-off of Eli Lilly's subsidiary medical device companies. At the time of the split-off, CPI's name changed to the Cardiac Rhythm Management Group (CRM), which grew to account for the bulk of the new Guidant Corporation's sales. Fred McCoy, CPI's chief financial officer when the company first adopted the Culture of Accountability Process, became the new CEO of this amazingly successful company.

Fred faced the daunting task of figuring out how to continue the growth and profitability of the company by equaling, and then exceeding, its past successes. The CRM Group continued to operate the best product development engine in the cardiac rhythm market-place. It produced products at a faster rate than its competitors. In fact, sales from products less than twelve months old accounted for more than 60 percent of CRM's total revenues.

However, while CRM's best-in-class product development and clinical development engines rapidly introduced new heart-related products to the marketplace, something had changed. CPI had become overly reliant on products and product features. In effect, its leaders had assumed that "if they built it, customers would come."

But despite the continuous flow of products, the company was not winning the market share it had assumed its technological edge would create. Customers wanted more than just new products; they wanted a company that was easy to do business with. Clearly, CRM needed to do more to win over customers and patients to the Guidant therapies.

To accomplish this, Fred knew that his leadership team needed to extend the sterling performance they had built in product development to all the other functions in the company. His first task aimed to get everyone in the company aligned with the shift from R^2 to R^3. Since the organization had done this before, he capitalized on the proficiency of the management team to get aligned around this new objective and then enlisted their help to get the company there. CRM's shift from R^1 to R^2 and now to R^3, along with the accompanying shifts in the culture, epitomizes the journey all organizations travel over time as they strive to stay competitive and at the top of their game.

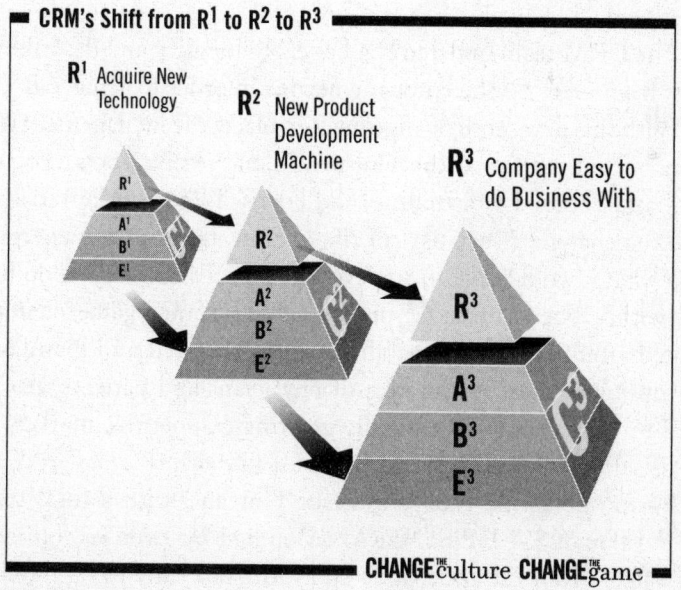

Culture is not something you can do once and then leave alone. It always needs to be managed relative to the results (R^x) you are working to achieve. Again, managing the culture is not an event, it is a process, and maintaining alignment among all the parts within the Results Pyramid requires constant and vigilant attention.

The CRM shift to C^3 reflected a tactical shift in culture, not an overall transformation. Since they had successfully done it before, they were confident that they could do it again. Their shift in Cultural Beliefs was simple: They needed to extend the winning culture they had built in product development to every other discipline in the company, so that every employee in the organization operated with the same heightened competitive edge as the product development group. Marketing, manufacturing, quality assurance, and every other function needed to provide a competitive advantage in their respective disciplines.

Fred worked with his management team to adjust the Cultural Beliefs that had served them so well in the past to reflect the change in the B^2 beliefs they needed to be successful. The chart on page 119 shows what the Cultural Beliefs looked like before and after that adjustment.

The CRM team updated the beliefs to identify and describe the shifts from C^2 to C^3 the company needed in order to achieve R^3.

With this new sense of alignment in place, the management team again put into practice the Culture Management Tools (Focused Feedback, Focused Storytelling, and Focused Recognition) to accelerate the change. Every part of the organization became energized to do what it would take to achieve R^3 and become "easy to do business with." The shift to C^3 proved to be another game-changing event. By building new capabilities, CRM created and maintained extraordinary value in the eyes of physicians and patients, participated fully in a tough and rapidly growing competitive market, and saw its sales revenue double again in just five years.

Boston Scientific then purchased Guidant, with a total transaction value of $27 billion. CRM accounted for over $20 billion of that value. From the time of its split-off from Lilly to its purchase ten years later by Boston Scientific, Guidant's stock price climbed

CRM Cultural Beliefs

R² CULTURAL BELIEFS

Customer Orientation
I am focused on the needs of our customers and do everything within my power to ensure that our customers are satisfied with our products and services.

Continuous Improvement
I work to improve my performance and my area of responsibility every day.

Risk Taking / Innovation
I take reasonable risks that will move the team forward toward its objectives, and I take an innovative approach to solving problems and dealing with obstacles.

Accountability
I am accountable for doing the things that I say I will do.

Development of People
I am committed to helping others develop through supportive, positive coaching and feedback.

Communication
I proactively report on my progress and that of my team, and I give and receive feedback on our progress toward our objectives.

Commitment and Consistency with Corporate Objectives
I commit myself to CPI's corporate objectives and act in a way that is consistent with what is necessary to achieve these objectives.

R³ CULTURAL BELIEFS

Thrill Customers
Patients and customers come first. I earn their trust through my every action.

Extend and Improve Life
I relentlessly pursue the delivery and adoption of our therapies.

Pioneer Solutions
I create distinctive solutions that cross the frontier of conventional thinking.

Take Accountability
I See It, Own It, Solve It, and Do It.

Unleash Potential
Turn it loose!

Celebrate Excellence
I see, applaud, and celebrate excellence.

Win
Winning is my habit. It earns me a place on our championship team.

CHANGETHE**culture CHANGE**THE**game**

from \$3.62 (adjusted for stock splits) to \$80.10 per share. Guidant and CRM turned in one of the top performances ever in the history of medical technology companies. The alumni of CRM have gone on to occupy high-level technical and executive positions in a variety of successful medical technology enterprises.

As the CPI/CRM story suggests, once you achieve alignment in the culture, you must work to maintain it over time. This requires clear and focused effort. You can never just "install" culture and then forget about it. Maintaining alignment in the culture is a critical leadership skill and capability that you must use every day to manage change in today's complex and competitive environment.

FORCES THAT CAN PUSH YOU OUT OF ALIGNMENT

A company's culture will not stay in alignment by itself. There are constant forces that will always threaten to push you, your team, your organization, and even yourself, out of alignment. These same forces are always exerting a strong gravitational attraction to pull people Below the Line and draw a company back toward the C^1 culture. You

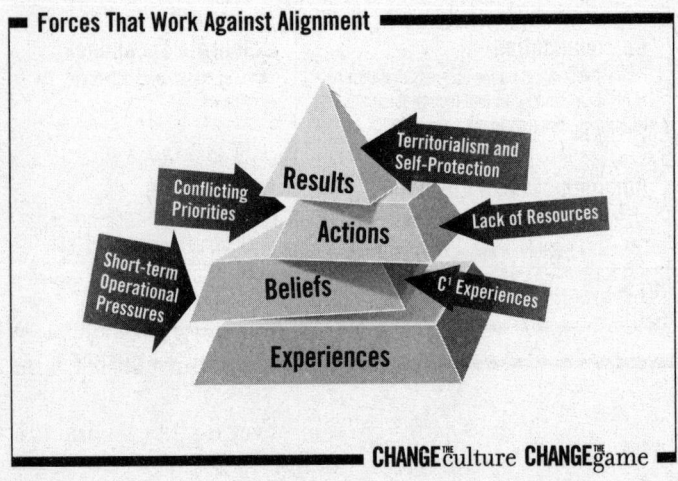

will surely recognize some of the key forces that leaders and their organizations must contend with almost every day.

To overcome the persistent C^1 experiences that reinforce the old B^1 beliefs and can push the organization in the wrong direction, you must keep an ever-watchful eye on these threats. It takes a lot of time and effort, because these forces never go away. You must learn to recognize when these forces have pushed your team or organization out of alignment or seem poised to do so. Consider this list of telltale signs of a lack of alignment.

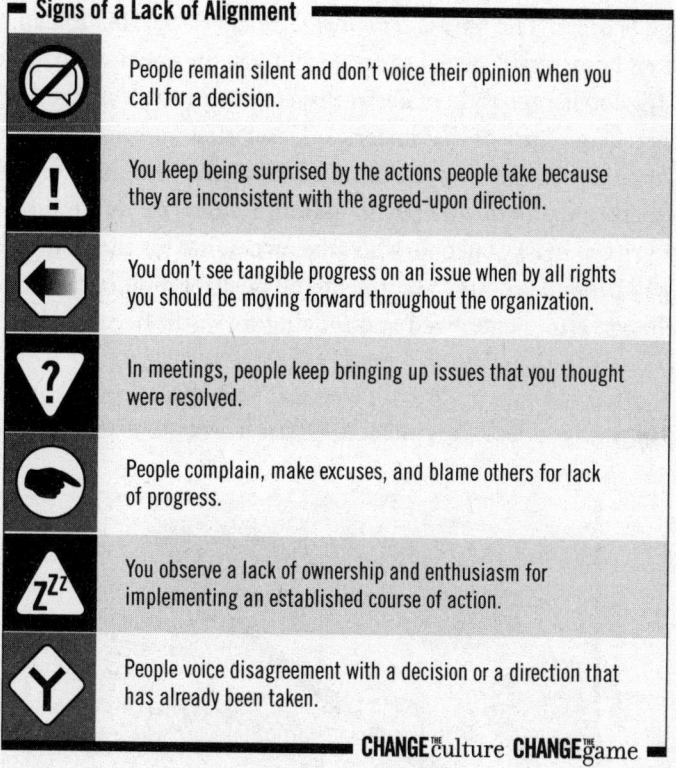

Signs of a Lack of Alignment

People remain silent and don't voice their opinion when you call for a decision.

You keep being surprised by the actions people take because they are inconsistent with the agreed-upon direction.

You don't see tangible progress on an issue when by all rights you should be moving forward throughout the organization.

In meetings, people keep bringing up issues that you thought were resolved.

People complain, make excuses, and blame others for lack of progress.

You observe a lack of ownership and enthusiasm for implementing an established course of action.

People voice disagreement with a decision or a direction that has already been taken.

CHANGE^{THE}culture CHANGE^{THE}game

While the threat of misalignment never disappears and is a fact of organizational life, you can do something about it. First of all, you must recognize when people and organizations are out of alignment and that this misalignment will slow down every attempt you make to create the new culture. With this reality in mind, you must remain vigilant, identifying any lack of alignment and striking quickly to correct the problem.

THE CASE FOR CHANGE

Gaining the needed "critical mass" that comes through alignment should preoccupy every management team engaged in the culture change process. The phrase *critical mass* refers to the smallest amount of the right material needed to create and sustain a nuclear chain reaction. It's not just the right material that sparks the nuclear reaction; it's the correct quantity of that material. To set off a "cultural chain reaction," you need to form a critical mass of people who take ownership for the change process and buy in to both R^2 and the Cultural Beliefs.

A critical mass of people who take ownership for the change process will produce enough alignment and positive momentum to keep the change effort energized and moving forward. Because the early

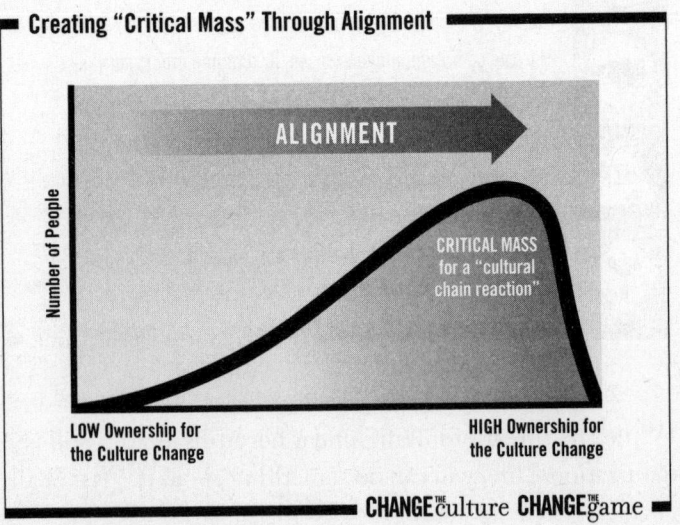

Creating "Critical Mass" Through Alignment

ALIGNMENT

Number of People

CRITICAL MASS for a "cultural chain reaction"

LOW Ownership for the Culture Change

HIGH Ownership for the Culture Change

CHANGE the culture CHANGE the game

adopters are important to the success of the overall effort, you should concentrate on cultivating and nurturing them. To achieve critical mass and true buy-in, you must get the key people in the organization on board. You know who they are. They're the people who will create the early E^2 experiences that will galvanize those who are "watching and waiting" to see what happens.

To initiate this cultural chain reaction, you must make a compelling Case for Change. Everyone wants to understand the basic rationale for R^2. The Case for Change addresses the why behind R^2, providing the context for *why* we need to change the culture and why we need to do it *now*. The more compelling the Case for Change, the more likely you will forge the ownership and buy-in you need. We've found that the most compelling Case for Change always incorporates the best practices.

The Case for Change Best Practices

1. Make it real.

2. Make it applicable to your audience.

3. Make it simple and repeatable.

4. Make it convincing.

5. Make it a dialogue.

Making it real means ensuring that the Case for Change captures the reality of the business environment, your competitive position, and the requirements of stakeholders. Couching the business case in terms of what matters to your audience may require some research and preparation, but that work will pay big dividends. When you keep it simple, those who hear it for the first time can easily repeat it to others. Repetition sustains the chain reaction. Of course, you should include any facts, figures, or essential points needed to make it convincing. The most convincing Case for Change paints a clear picture of R^2 and what achieving that will do for all involved.

When presenting the Case for Change, make it a dialogue, not a monologue. The more quickly you can begin the dialogue in the organization around the Case for Change, the easier you make it for the early adopters to get on board. That dialogue will also help you create the necessary critical mass. You can take it as a sure sign that the alignment process is working when you hear a lot of conversation about the Case for Change. If you are not hearing it pop up in the organizational dialogue, if you don't hear others spontaneously bring it up in meetings, and if people are not reminding one another about why the organization needs change, then you have probably not employed one or more of the best practices associated with formulating a strong Case for Change. If that happens, go back and try again. You simply must get it right. If you don't, the culture change process will not move forward as smoothly or as quickly as you'd like.

Quickly creating ownership will accelerate the cultural transition, fostering the experiences needed to shift beliefs, generating the appropriate actions, and achieving the desired results. Following the steps in the alignment process described below will help you create alignment and build critical mass early in the transition.

THE LEADERSHIP ALIGNMENT PROCESS

Over the years, we have developed a model we call the Leadership Alignment Process. We use this process early in the cultural transition effort to develop the Case for Change, define C^2, and draft the Cultural Beliefs statement. The model consists of six key elements that help ensure that real alignment is achieved.

You can apply these six steps of the Leadership Alignment Process, depicted below, to ensure alignment around key decisions with individuals, teams, or the entire organization.

Step One:
Participation—Get the Appropriate People Involved

To create alignment, you need to make sure you have the appropriate people involved in the decision-making process. When it comes

Leadership Alignment Process

1	Participation	Get the appropriate people involved.
2	Accountability	Identify who will make the decision.
3	Discussion	Ensure that people speak up and are heard.
4	Ownership	Promote the decision as your own.
5	Communication	Be consistent with the message.
6	Follow-Up	Check in and test for alignment.

CHANGE the culture CHANGE the game

to setting the direction for the culture change, the appropriate people will most likely include those at a senior level and, in many cases, members of the executive team. There are several key decisions that you will need to make early in the Cultural Transition Process when it comes to determining specifically who should participate in the process and when they should do it.

Early Key Decisions on Participation

1. Who should we involve in the initial assessment of the existing C^1 culture?

2. Who should help define R^2?

3. Who should help create the Case for Change?

4. Who should help write the Cultural Beliefs statement?

5. Who should design the way we will implement the Cultural Transition Process?

6. Who should communicate about the culture change with the entire organization and how should they do it?

7. Who should receive additional coaching as a leader of the change process?

As you select and involve the appropriate people, you should ask yourself, "Whom do we need to hear from in order to make the right decisions?" For example, the division president of a major grocery chain implemented the second track of our Three-Track process called the Culture of Accountability Process (the training and consulting process that we offer in conjunction with this book). This president identified eleven people he felt would provide the needed input, several of whom did not report directly to him, including a store manager whose store had scored at the top on internal "employee engagement" surveys. All of these people would participate in some of the early Cultural Transition Process decisions, particularly in crafting the Cultural Beliefs statement. As you determine who should get involved, you might also consider including some of the most important people who will take accountability for implementing these key decisions.

Step Two:
Accountability—Identify Who Will Make the Decision

In an effort to achieve alignment, those who participate in the decision-making process should understand who will make the decision and how they will do it. We have found that the Culture of Accountability Process works best with a leader-led, rather than a consensus-driven, decision-making model. You don't hold committees accountable for decisions; you hold leaders accountable. In our view, when it comes to cultural transition, a leader-led model is the most effective approach.

Identifying the accountable decision maker in advance will enhance and speed up the alignment process, especially when developing the Cultural Beliefs. Otherwise, the team can get lost in the process and stalled in their progress. While we help clients implement a collaborative approach that inspires intense participation of all team members in the development of the Cultural Beliefs, we have found that it is helpful for all participants to understand that the final word in terms of both the number of Cultural Beliefs and the final wording of the belief statements rests with the organizational leader. Attentive leaders will only resort to tiebreaking when absolutely necessary. Accelerating cultural transition is a leader-led endeavor in a team-participative environment.

Step Three:
Discussion—Ensure That People Speak Up and Are Heard

To create alignment in the Cultural Transition Process, you must encourage people to say what they think as they engage in an ongoing dialogue about the culture change. While teams do not make decisions, leaders do need help making the right decisions. They get that needed input when people say what they really think before a decision is made. To foster this kind of dialogue, everyone participating should work to make sure people feel that their voices are being heard as they talk frankly about changes in the business environment, the problems with the present culture, and the experiences that drive current beliefs.

Open discussion, free expression, and respectful debate enable people to talk honestly about the needed changes. To be most effective, you need to create an environment that welcomes positive confrontation so that real debate can take place in your conversations about the cultural transition. This is something you can do more easily if you follow the few simple ground rules presented in the chart on page 128.

Committing everyone to the ground rules and then encouraging ongoing, open dialogue will speed up the process of creating and maintaining alignment during the cultural transition.

Step Four:
Ownership—Promote the Decision as Your Own

Perhaps you've heard the expression, "When all is said and done, more is said than done." Once you have made a decision, once you have determined a course of action, then you must make sure

Ground Rules for Positive Confrontation

1 Focus on issues, not personalities, and avoid personal attacks.

2 Separate your own opinions from the facts as you know them.

3 Acknowledge your own "hidden agendas."

4 Make sure you can restate the views of others before you debate them.

5 Don't interrupt.

6 If you think someone is "hiding out," check in with the person and ask them what they think.

7 No "hallway" discussions; share your perspectives in the meeting.

8 Wear all of the hats you should be wearing during the discussion.

9 Remember, the goal is to move forward as a team—do not advertise the disagreement, but demonstrate full support of the decision.

CHANGE the culture CHANGE the game

everyone in the group owns the decision and promotes it as if they had chosen that path themselves. The bottom line is that promoting a decision means owning it as though it were your own, even if you don't entirely agree with it.

Leaders demonstrate their alignment and promote the cultural transition in one of four ways, as shown in the chart on page 129.

Someone in the Support category agrees with the logic of the decision to move to a C^2 culture but does not take real action to get involved. However, they do not resist the change effort. Those in the Advocate category talk about the need for the cultural shift and even share a sense of urgency that it needs to happen. They fully support the decision to move to C^2 but may be slower to step up and lead out in the process. Those in the Sponsor category allocate time and resources for the effort and play a leadership role by going first with bold strokes. Finally, Champions make a game-changing effort to promote the Culture of Accountability Process and keep it front and center on the agenda for the entire organization.

For the transition to succeed, an organization needs more than one or two Champions. In fact, any successful culture change will

Four Ways to Promote the Culture Change

Support	Agrees that the transition needs to occur and makes no effort to resist it.
Advocate	Vocally talks about the need to shift and shares a sense of urgency to make it happen now.
Sponsor	Someone who allocates time and/or resources to prioritize the transition high on the list of things to do.
Champion	Demonstrates accountability for the success of the transition by: • Ensuring that their daily actions visibly demonstrate the Cultural Beliefs. • Continually seeking and providing Focused Feedback while engaging in Focused Storytelling and Focused Recognition around the Cultural Beliefs. • Consciously creating new experiences for the people with whom they work.

CHANGE the culture CHANGE the game

come about because Champions throughout the organization, in every department and at every level, passionately promote the cause. They use the Culture Management Tools by reaching out to provide Focused Feedback, employing Focused Storytelling to exemplify the Cultural Beliefs, speaking constantly about the R^2 key results, and consistently using Focused Recognition. A Champion rallies the involvement needed to propel the cultural boulder forward.

Step Five:
Communication—Be Consistent with the Message

Effective leaders "talk the talk" and mean it! When members of the team walk out the door after drafting the Cultural Beliefs statement, each one must work hard to create a consistent experience in their own sphere of influence to reinforce the right beliefs, actions, and results. Too often, management teams do not spend enough time getting aligned around what they should communicate and when they should do it.

Effectively communicating the culture change to the organization may seem like an obvious step, but it takes conscious and deliberate effort to do it well. Your communication must overcome the common change-killing attitudes.

Change-Killing Attitudes

- It's another "program of the month."
- It's just the leader's "pet project."
- It's a "repeat"; it failed before.
- It's just to "punch their ticket."
- It's DOA ("dead on arrival").

Let's face it; people are usually a bit jaded when it comes to efforts to change the organization. They have witnessed too many previous failed attempts that resulted in Level One temporary changes that had no lasting impact. A communication plan that overcomes these past E^1 experiences and current beliefs about change efforts is critical to achieving alignment throughout the organization.

Each leader needs to do the homework and prepare to communicate the Case for Change, the R^2 results, the Cultural Beliefs, and the methodology for culture change in the organization in a compelling way that is aligned with the other members of the management team. Staying on message by conveying what everyone has agreed to communicate will help get the word out more quickly.

Step Six:
Follow-up—Check In and Test for Alignment

Culture change cannot succeed if managers don't follow through and take full accountability for doing what they said they would do. To ensure that this happens, you should continually check in and test for alignment. We have found that planning periodic checks with the management team is critical to the success of the cultural transition. As usual, these meetings require an open and candid dialogue about what is really going on and how people really feel about it. These Alignment Checkpoints are a good place to start when testing for alignment in these team meetings.

Alignment Checkpoints

- ✓ Are we aligned around the urgency to shift the way we think and act?

- ✓ Are we aligned around our Cultural Beliefs?

- ✓ Are we aligned around the actions we expect people to take?

- ✓ Are we aligned around the experiences we are creating as a team in leading the change?

- ✓ Are we aligned around the personal commitment each of us needs to make in creating new experiences for the organziation?

- ✓ Are we aligned around how we agreed to hold ourselves accountable for the change?

- ✓ Do we remain aligned around how we are communicating about the change in terms of what we are saying and how we are saying it?

CHANGE the culture CHANGE the game

For maximum effectiveness, we recommend that you develop your own specific checkpoints for use in a group setting. These checkpoints will help you continually monitor team alignment and direct your efforts to make corrections where they are most needed. The Leadership Alignment Process helps you do this effectively and quickly. Keep in mind this basic principle: The more effectively management teams align themselves and their entire organization around the cultural transition, the faster the organization will move toward a game-changing cultural transition.

Alignment is a process, not an event. It is something you must constantly work to achieve. During a cultural transition, nothing more powerfully affects a successful outcome than a management team fully aligned around R^2, the Case for Change, the Cultural Beliefs and the C^2 culture, and the methodology for changing culture. That alignment alone is one of the most important accelerators of the change process.

Either you will manage the culture, or it will manage you. When you decide to manage it, you must first create and then maintain the alignment necessary to move people in the direction you need them to go. Alignment is a leadership capability everyone must learn and master. Improving your own ability to sense when alignment does not exist and then to create and maintain it will pay dividends, not only during the Cultural Transition Process, but also in each and every aspect of your leadership as you focus on delivering results. In the next chapter, we will introduce the three Culture Management Tools that will help you accelerate your cultural transition and achieve your R^2 results.

CHAPTER 7

Applying the Three Culture
Management Tools

NOW THAT YOU UNDERSTAND how to create alignment for using the Results Pyramid to build a game-changing culture, you can start applying the three essential Culture Management Tools that will accelerate the change effort: Focused Feedback, Focused Storytelling, and Focused Recognition. These tools will help you integrate the Cultural Beliefs into your organization's culture and speed it toward C^2 and your desired R^2 results.

We have designed these tools to help you deal with a C^1 culture's strong resistance to change. One example of how they help our clients comes from Brinker International's successful efforts to change the culture of two of its well-known restaurant brands, Chili's and On The Border. After working for several months with the senior team, the time came to fully launch the project with a meeting of the top 1,500 leaders and managers from the two brands. The meeting was designed to help the field leadership and restaurant managers prepare to lead the culture change effort in each of their respective brands.

Using a metaphor we've found effective, Kelli Valade, COO of Chili's and On The Border, created a visual image of the concerted effort required to shift their culture by reenacting an unforgettable game-changing moment that had occurred on the PGA Tour.

Before the meeting began, Kelli arranged for a boulder weighing over 1,500 pounds to be lowered onto a reinforced stage. After managers from around the country had assembled for the opening dinner, the CEO, Doug Brooks, took the stage to paint the historical context for Brinker International's future vision and R^2 results. While he spoke, no one in the audience could keep from looking at the giant boulder. Who had put it there, and why?

The next day, as leaders began speaking about creating the culture change from C^1 to C^2 that would enable Brinker to achieve its key results, they drew attention to the boulder. They pointed out that the Brinker culture was much like the boulder on the stage: heavy and hard to move! Throughout the next two days, the boulder served as a consistent reminder of the weighty challenge facing the Brinker team.

On the last day of the meeting, Brinker's president came to the stage. We posed to him the single most important question that every leadership team that desires to change their culture and create accountability for results must answer: "Are you serious about this? Are you *serious* about moving the boulder, creating your C^2 culture, and achieving your key R^2 results?" The president turned to his team and exclaimed, "Totally!"

Reenacting what happened on the PGA Tour in Phoenix back in 1999, the president positioned himself behind the boulder, picked up his 5 iron and explained to the Brinker team that, while they could not see it, his golf ball had landed behind the boulder, which completely blocked the next shot to the green. If by some miracle he could continue play without the penalty of hitting the ball sideways or taking a drop away from the boulder, that move could provide a badly needed game-changing edge.

The president explained that most golfers assume that you can only move small and inconsequential impediments, such as stones, twigs, or leaves, but he quickly clarified that the rules of golf actually did allow players to move impediments, even ones as massive as the boulder, with the help of others and without penalty—a rule that ignited so much controversy after the Phoenix Open that the PGA changed it. With the Phoenix Open in mind, the president looked out over the audience and wondered out loud if there were any "Brinkerheads" who would join him on stage and help him push the boulder out of his way. Twelve members of his team, some with biceps like those you'd see on the front line of the NFL, jumped up on stage to join him behind the boulder. With looks of absolute determination, the team members surveyed the situation, strategically positioned themselves on the same side behind the boulder, and then put their shoulders to it. Counting together "One, two, three!" they began to push with all their might. The boulder began to move, and before long, they had moved it out of the way, allowing a clear shot to the imagined green. The president then stepped up and continued play by hitting a foam practice ball out over the heads of the audience. We'll never forget the scene as all in the audience shot to their feet as one and gave the president a rousing standing ovation.

MOVING THE BOULDER

We often use this boulder metaphor to illustrate the concerted effort required to create C^2, build a Culture of Accountability, and produce the desired R^2 results. Like a thousand-pound boulder, C^1 is hard to move. It's heavy, awkward, and hard to grasp, and it takes a lot of focused energy to get it moving. It never moves just because everyone agrees that it should. On the contrary, the C^1 culture, just like a boulder, moves only when everyone gets on the same side and pushes together toward C^2.

Defining which direction the boulder needs to roll provides the clarity everyone needs in order to join forces on the right side of the boulder. Imagine trying to move a gigantic boulder with people randomly dispersed all around it, unwittingly pushing against one another as they try to create movement. Sometimes a culture change effort looks just like that. Without a clear idea of where you want to go (R^2), even your most talented and passionately dedicated people will end up on different sides of the boulder. Good people, people who have signed up to make the change happen, may push with all their might, but if they are pushing against one another, they will eventually grow so weary and frustrated in their efforts that they'll abandon their commitment to move the cultural boulder and achieve R^2.

The direction of the desired movement is defined by the organization's key results (R^2), which in turn determine which way the cultural boulder should move. Your Cultural Beliefs statement identifies where everyone should place the energy and effort to start the change process and get things rolling; it determines which side of the boulder everyone should push against. Knowing where to start and what will give you the needed momentum to get things moving is critical to the success of the change process. The key R^2 results and the Cultural Beliefs do just that.

Despite the difficulty of "moving the boulder," an organization's culture can move and indeed will move when you integrate the right Culture Management Tools into the daily business practices of the individuals and teams in your organization. The three Culture Management Tools we have designed (Focused Feedback, Focused Storytelling, and Focused Recognition) create a daily, sustained, and tight focus around the Cultural Beliefs. Together these tools provide the needed leverage to get the cultural boulder moving and to keep it moving in the right direction over time.

To illustrate how to use the Culture Management Tools, we will detail the experience of Opthometrics, the client we introduced in chapter 2. This example thoroughly illustrates the application of the tools in a challenging retail environment that involves multiple sites (headquarters and retail stores throughout the United States), multiple levels (executive officers, middle managers, supervisors, and full-time and part-time store salespeople), and an economy unfriendly to retail—all the complexity one might need to suggest that culture change would present a sizable challenge.

The Opthometrics Cultural Beliefs are the central feature of their efforts to implement the Culture Management Tools. As you recall, Cultural Beliefs provide the essential framework for any successful cultural change, and they consist of both a title and a statement. For example, "Live the Brand: I apply the Opthometrics brand filter in everything I do." The Cultural Belief titles are extremely important. In essence, they provide the "handles" on the cultural boulder that everyone can grab as they personally take accountability to move the culture in the needed direction. These handles facilitate ease of movement. Leaders who are serious about changing the culture should learn the titles and the full Cultural Beliefs statement by heart. Those who fail to do this as an early demonstration of ownership of the Cultural Beliefs license their people to do likewise. Make sure you hold yourself accountable to know your Cultural Beliefs.

The full Cultural Beliefs statement serves to amplify and clarify the belief beyond its title. For example, when someone refers to "Live the Brand," the full statement tells everyone that they must personally, "lead, think, and act through the Opthometrics brand filter." The Cultural Beliefs statements remind people how they need to think and act in order to create C^2 and achieve the organization's key results.

We know leaders who have grown quite frustrated over their inability to change the cultures of their organizations. That frustration almost always stems from the fact that they lacked the tools essential to creating the desired change. Without the proper tools, leaders will struggle to accomplish meaningful change. With them, leaders speed up the change process and promote results in game-changing ways. Let's take a close look at each of them.

THE FOCUSED FEEDBACK TOOL

Feedback is rarely employed as the tool for change that it can and ought to be. However, when it is used effectively throughout all levels of the organization, it can greatly accelerate the shift to C^2. To achieve this, feedback must be focused around the C^2 Cultural Beliefs. We call this Focused Feedback, and it should be both appreciative and constructive. Appreciative Focused Feedback lets people know you value their demonstration of the Cultural Beliefs. It reinforces the thinking and behavior needed to move the cultural boulder forward. Providing appreciative Focused Feedback in a timely way not only clarifies desired C^2 behavior; it also supplies the repetition needed to reinforce the desired A^2 actions.

Constructive Focused Feedback offers positive and candid suggestions and guidance on what else people can do to demonstrate the B^2 beliefs more fully. This type of feedback is critical to helping people succeed in the new C^2 culture because it helps them know what they can improve in a timely way. People who don't receive it get left behind, mired in C^1. A lack of constructive Focused Feedback will cause every culture-change effort to stall and eventually die out.

"Bill Jones," a division director at Opthometrics, learned this lesson early in the company's cultural transition. Although Bill's co-workers viewed him as someone who wholeheartedly embraced the culture change on a personal level, he was not performing in the job and delivering the desired results. His inconsistent use of the Focused Feedback tool hampered the pace of improvement and did not reflect his deep personal commitment to the dramatic shift in the Opthometrics culture. The problem could have gotten a lot worse if his own boss had not provided Bill with Focused Feedback. His boss told us, "Bill was always using 'pillows' when delivering constructive feedback. In listening to one conversation he had with a store manager, I heard Bill soften the feedback he gave him at least five different times, and as a result, the feedback didn't connect. After making this observation, I gave Bill the feedback, cited various examples, and showed him how it was affecting his results."

Bill's Category 2 belief (introduced in chapter 4) about constructive feedback needed to change. Constructive Focused Feedback should be candid, clear, and complete. It is not criticism, which simply expresses disapproval of someone's shortcomings and mistakes. Rather, constructive feedback points out what people might be doing wrong and provides suggestions as to how they might change for the better by demonstrating the Cultural Belief even more effectively. It builds rather than undermines people, with the goal of helping them succeed in becoming C^2.

After receiving appreciative and constructive Focused Feedback around the Cultural Beliefs from his boss, Bill began to change and his performance began to improve. His boss continued, "Bill accepted the feedback I gave him without hesitation and started copying me on messages and stories where he had taken the 'pillows' off. That was ten weeks ago, and Bill has made plan eight of those ten weeks, has a fifteen-week trend over a hundred percent, and has made plan for December and January." Bill's turnaround illustrates how Focused Feedback around the Cultural Beliefs can positively affect A^2 actions and R^2 results.

THE LANGUAGE OF FOCUSED FEEDBACK

What does Focused Feedback sound like? If you had eavesdropped on a Focused Feedback session around the Cultural Beliefs between "Jen" and "Robert," two Opthometrics field leaders involved in the company's cultural transition, you might have heard something like this:

> "Robert, here's where I feel you demonstrate 'Stay Focused' [an Opthometrics Cultural Belief]. You do a tremendous job on your developmental visits. You get to the root cause of nondelivery on key results and quickly uncover the competency gaps among the division directors who are leading territories that are not delivering. And you correctly allocate your time to develop the right people.
>
> "Here's where I feel you could demonstrate 'Stay Focused' even more. There are two impending division director openings on the horizon. I think you need to weigh the time you are spending developing people you are working with right now against the time needed to hire two top-tier division directors in the next two weeks. I know it would be a heroic effort to get them hired and get them to the conference in Dallas, but that's what the business really needs."

This actual Focused Feedback session prompted Robert to hire the two new division directors within two weeks, an action that almost immediately increased sales within the respective territories. It also set a new standard for quickly filling key positions throughout the company.

Jen also received some Focused Feedback around the Cultural Beliefs from one of her direct reports, who also offered feedback on the same subject:

"Jen, here's where you demonstrate 'Reject Average' [another Opthometrics Cultural Belief]. You have been very focused, ensuring that your team knows and understands with clarity what is expected at the regional general manager (RGM) level. This clarity of expectation has created an opening within the RGM team.

"Here's where I feel you can demonstrate 'Reject Average' even more. As you work through the numerous candidates, do not settle for someone who can just do the job; rather, bring someone into the company who can raise the excellence of the current RGM team, someone who will turn heads."

Jen told us that she acted on this Focused Feedback and did, in fact, hire a new RGM, who, beginning with her very first month on the job, has consistently delivered excellent results. Focused Feedback around the Cultural Beliefs will speed up needed change and help deliver R^2 results.

While the content of Focused Feedback will differ from person to person and from session to session, it should always center on the Cultural Beliefs. We have found that accelerated culture change occurs only when you focus the feedback on the Cultural Beliefs. For example, when you want to reinforce a B^2 belief, such as "Live the Brand," you should say something like, "Here's where I feel you demonstrate 'Live the Brand…'" When suggesting ways in which that same person might more fully demonstrate that belief, you should offer something like, "Here's where I feel you could demonstrate 'Live the Brand' even more…"

The words *I feel* convey that you are sharing a subjective opinion that the feedback recipient may find helpful, not an objective or absolute truth that could make the person feel harshly judged. Feedback rarely represents "the truth" about an individual. Instead, it offers a perspective that may help someone improve their situation. The word *I* conveys a feeling of personal ownership of the perceptions you are sharing. Also keep in mind that people tend to respond more favorably to feedback when you give it in a direct and straightforward manner from your own personal perspective. Feedback loses power when you replace *I* with *we*, because the plural robs the feedback of the personal ownership that all effective feedback requires. When it becomes too anonymous, it can begin to seem manipulative. We also recommend using the phrase *even more* when giving constructive feedback, because it suggests that, to some extent, the recipient of the feedback has already demonstrated the desired belief in some way.

When seeking Focused Feedback around the Cultural Beliefs for yourself, we recommend that you simply ask, "What feedback do you have for me?" This question is a much better one than, "Do you have any feedback for me?" The former assumes that the person actually has feedback to give you. They probably do! The latter prompts the answer yes or no, and because many people find it difficult to give feedback, they usually answer "no." Remember, if you really want Focused Feedback, the question is, "What feedback do you have for me?"

Nobody's perspective is 100 percent correct, or even useful, 100 percent of the time. You probably know the supposedly true tale about the Yale University management professor who graded Federal Express founder Fred Smith's paper on the possibility of a reliable overnight delivery service. The professor reportedly wrote, "The concept is interesting and well informed, but in order to earn better than a C, the idea must be feasible." Fred Smith listened to the feedback, evaluated what he heard, ignored it, and went on to found his delivery service empire. While sometimes you will not act on the feedback you receive, you will always benefit from hearing what people think. Remember that what they think (their beliefs) guides what they do (their actions). Accurate or not, people operate based upon their beliefs. Understanding those beliefs will go a long way toward helping you speed up the culture change effort.

To guarantee that people will continue to give you feedback over and over again, try responding with a simple thank you. When you say, "Thanks for the feedback," you send the message that you appreciate their demonstrating their accountability to provide the feedback. That simple response avoids the impression that you are evaluating whether the feedback was useful to you and instead emphasizes that you want them to keep it coming.

FEEDBACK FILTERS

What you do with the feedback is your choice, but it's a choice you ought to weigh carefully. Often, people defensively try to explain away the feedback they receive. Years ago we worked with an executive, an engineer by training, who acted only on what he considered "useful" feedback. At the time we met him, he was the vice president of manufacturing for a large medical device company. He told us that when he received feedback, he would sequentially apply a series of four questions to filter and evaluate it. First, he asked himself, "Is it accurate?" If so, he would then ask, "Is there a basis for this feedback?" If it passed through this second filter, he would then ask, "Is it relevant or irrelevant?" Finally, he would ask "Is it right or wrong?" With pride in his voice and a sly smile on his face, he assured us that he acted on all feedback that made it through his filters.

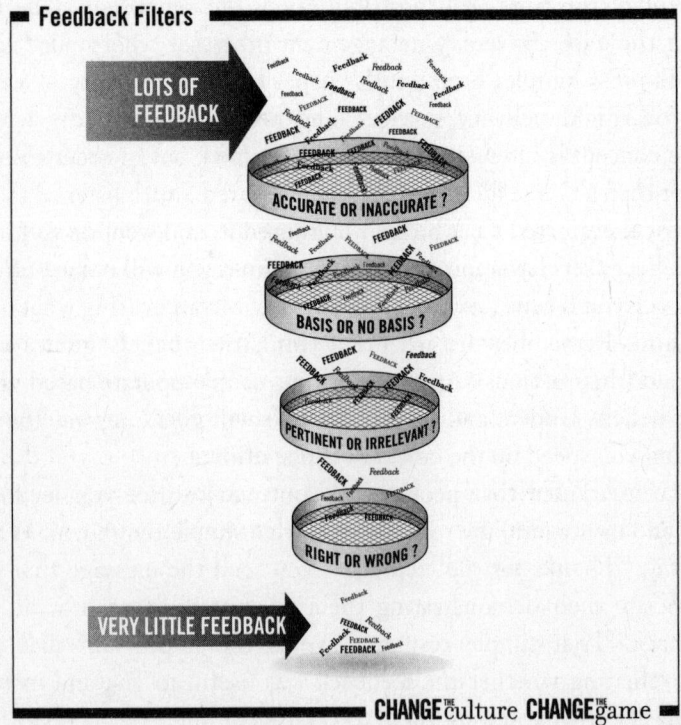

Feedback Filters

LOTS OF FEEDBACK

ACCURATE OR INACCURATE ?

BASIS OR NO BASIS ?

PERTINENT OR IRRELEVANT ?

RIGHT OR WRONG ?

VERY LITTLE FEEDBACK

CHANGE the **culture** **CHANGE** the **game**

When we asked this manufacturing VP just how much feedback actually survived the filtering process, he replied, "That's just the problem. I don't get any good feedback!" In truth, by the time he finished running the feedback through his filters, precious little feedback survived. Of course, while this VP was filtering the feedback he received, others were forming a belief about him. When we interviewed a number of the members of his team, asking them to tell us about the feedback they had given their boss, every one of them said pretty much the same thing: "Oh, we stopped giving him feedback years ago. He doesn't want it!" Think of the price paid when a VP of manufacturing in a medical device company receives no feedback from the people who report to him. People tend to filter the feedback they receive more than they should. That's why we offer one consistent recommendation to everyone who receives feedback. Rather than getting defensive, simply ask yourself two questions: "Is that a belief I want them to hold?" And if not, "What do I need to do to change it?"

Rather than defensively filtering out feedback, ignoring it, discounting the source, or invalidating what you have heard, take the feedback at face value. View it as information or a point of view and consider this key point: "Since the belief exists and will serve as a basis from which others will act, does that belief work for me? Will that belief help create C^2?" If not, work at the foundation of the Results Pyramid and the basis of people's beliefs by asking, "What experience will I need to create to change that belief?"

We have worked with enough leaders to know that it never makes sense to dismiss feedback out of hand or to become defensive when receiving it. Thank those who give feedback, reflect on it, and consider whether you may benefit from responding to it. If you decide that it doesn't merit action, you may want to close the loop with the individual who offered the feedback and let them know why you have chosen not to act on it.

THE FOCUSED STORYTELLING TOOL

While Focused Feedback accelerates change, organizations can pick up the pace of the transition even more when they add Focused Storytelling to the mix of Culture Management Tools. People tell stories every day throughout the organization. These stories simply describe people's experiences and convey their beliefs about what is important and how work should be done in the organization. Some stories even become legendary and bridge generations. For good or ill, these stories transmit culture in a powerful way and have a significant impact on people at every level of the organization. As a result, stories are among the strongest influencers on the bottom half of the Results Pyramid.

Do you know what stories people in your organization tell each other? What beliefs do those stories drive? Do those stories promote the C^2 culture, or do they entrench B^1 beliefs and the C^1 culture? What stories do *you* tell to others? Are you conscious of the stories you tell? When it comes to the impact of stories, there is no neutral ground. To someone hearing it for the first time, a compelling story can seem as real as it did to the person who first experienced it. One person's story is often another person's experience.

These stories move the organization either toward C^2 or back to C^1. If you want to speed up the journey to a C^2 culture, then you must identify and tell C^2 stories.

STORYTELLING LANGUAGE

Like feedback, Focused Storytelling centers on the Cultural Beliefs. Specific stories that describe people living these Cultural Beliefs reinforce their importance and show people how to put the beliefs into practice. Every story you tell using Focused Storytelling includes three parts: a beginning, middle, and end. You begin by referencing the Cultural Belief title that corresponds to the story, using specific words to frame the context of the story: "Here's what 'Live the Brand' looks like to me." This approach identifies a specific B^2 belief and alerts the listeners that they will hear a story that depicts what the Cultural Belief, in this case "Live the Brand," looks like to the person telling the story. The "Live the Brand" story transforms an idea into an experience, one that will reinforce desired Cultural Beliefs.

The middle is the story itself. A well-crafted story takes approximately forty-five seconds to tell. Of course, you want your stories to make people think, but more important, you want them to show people what A^2 actions and B^2 beliefs look like. The right stories help people see the culture change right before their eyes. As people hear C^2 stories, they *see* the changes they personally need to make, motivating them to adjust their own actions accordingly.

The story ends by addressing the impact on the key R^2 results. We have heard enough Focused Storytelling to know that if you fail to describe the impact on key results, the story will, without exception, have little or no impact on beliefs. We recommend you conclude your story by using the same simple language with which you began: "That's what 'Live the Brand' looks like to me." This concluding statement is important because it anchors the focused intent with which the story began: "Here's what 'Live the Brand' looks like to me." Bookending the story with these statements reminds everyone listening to the story why you chose to tell it. The reference to the Cultural Beliefs reminds the listeners of what they should both look for in others and personally demonstrate themselves. In this case, "Live the Brand" means "Live the Brand: I apply the Opthometrics brand filter in everything I do."

Focused Storytelling caught fire at Opthometrics. In fact, scores of stories flooded in via e-mail and were distributed in weekly communications to the entire field. Here are some examples of C^2 stories told at Opthometrics using the Focused Storytelling pattern. This first one reinforces the Cultural Belief "Live the Brand: I apply the Opthometrics brand filter in everything I do."

> "This is what 'Live the Brand' looks like to me. A customer came into our store very concerned. She had just gone to her doctor, who diagnosed her with diabetes and

recommended she have a diabetic eye exam. This patient was very reluctant and stated over and over that she just did not have the money to do it now, but that she would be back. One of our associates tried to convince her that we could fit anyone's budget but that we needed to help her take care of this today. The customer still left, saying she would be back. Well, that wasn't good enough for store staff. They went out to the food court, found the customer, and told her they would make sure she could afford the visit. 'The doctor really wants to see you today!' they told her. Long story short, the exam was completed, only to discover this patient was hemorrhaging behind both eyes. The doctor helped the patient reach her own physician, who requested that she go to the emergency room right then and there. Needless to say, the patient was very emotional and thankful, and she shared with our entire team how moved she was that we would not let her walk away without that exam! The words she used were 'overwhelmed at the generosity and passion Opthometrics has for its customers.' The entire store staff and our customer were moved to tears. The doctor gave the customer his home number to make sure she made the follow-up call. Not only did our team use the Cultural Belief 'Live the Brand,' they also added a customer for life. The store not only delivered this experience to the patient, but they delivered it to each other, as everyone on the team understood that this is why we do what we do. By the way, the team hit plan that day and are ahead of plan year-to-date. That's what 'Live the Brand' looks like to me."

The next story reinforces the Cultural Belief "Stay Focused: I align all that I do to the Opthometrics priorities."

"This is what 'Stay Focused' looks like to me. At the start of the day yesterday, we had a light schedule of exams on the books with unpleasant weather threatening our traffic.

Instead of going Below the Line and settling into a 'wait and see' mentality, we didn't blame the weather and instead focused on 'What else we could do' to be successful. In our huddles, we focused on the Cultural Beliefs, engaging and delighting every potential customer who came into the store and working to convert walk-ins to patients. We were able to convert four walk-ins for exams the same day. Out of the total of twelve exams yesterday, half were contact lens patients who received comprehensive exams with the doctor. Even though we had many contact lens patients, we still converted three fourths of patients for both eyeglasses and contacts. The team members kept their focus all day and also converted walk-ins with outside prescriptions, as well. By staying focused on delighting customers and uncovering their individual needs, we finished above plan for the day. That's what 'Stay Focused' looks like to me."

These are but two of the numerous C^2 stories that people have recorded at Opthometrics. To have the desired impact, the sheer number of C^2 stories crafted and told during a time of culture change should almost overwhelm the current C^1 culture. These stories create experiences that depict with great clarity what it looks like to demonstrate the Cultural Beliefs for everyone hearing them. This clarity becomes compelling as the stories accumulate over time. Leaders at every level of the organization must take accountability to tell stories that reflect and demonstrate the Cultural Beliefs. As Focused Storytelling reinforces the C^2 culture, and as leaders take accountability for the daily story line of their organizations, individuals at every level move with greater determination to take accountability to think and act in the manner necessary to achieve results.

THE FOCUSED RECOGNITION TOOL

Focused Recognition builds on Focused Storytelling to increase the momentum of the change effort throughout the organization. We often ask people in our training workshops if they feel that they get too much recognition. They always answer, "No!" When it comes to recognition, most people feel underappreciated and overlooked. We have observed over the years that people rarely perceive their leaders as "getting recognition right," mostly because their leaders fail to recognize "me!"

To understand the impact of appreciation and recognition on performance, consider what parents choose to focus on when teaching their young children to walk. When a child takes that first step, what does every parent do? Cheer! But what does every child do after taking that first step? Fall! How many times have you heard parents begin booing when a child falls? Never. Instead, they pick the child up and, with appreciation for the first step forward, they encourage the toddler to try again. Parents instinctively ignore the fall and focus instead on the step. Because of this focus on the steps rather than the falls, children learn to walk in a matter of days and begin to run within weeks.

There is much to be gained if you apply this same approach to the first steps people take to create the C^2 culture. We all know that people will sometimes "fall down" while learning to live the Cultural Beliefs. Acknowledging the step forward with recognition, in spite of the fall, will speed up the culture change effort. Focused Recognition, like storytelling and feedback, must center on the Cultural Beliefs. Focused Recognition allows anyone in the organization to observe and then to recognize other employees for what they do to demonstrate the C^2 Cultural Beliefs.

When we asked one of the Opthometrics operations directors where he saw Focused Recognition happening, he answered, "Everywhere!" He went on to say, "When someone receives Focused Recognition, they deeply appreciate it. I have been amazed at the impact it has on recipients. I gave Focused Recognition to someone in Operations, uncertain whether it would mean anything to her. I learned a lesson from her about just how much it means. She was tearful as she told me that my appreciation could not have come at a better time." Focused Recognition is a 360-degree positive-reinforcement tool unhampered by more formal top-down processes. Everyone can get in on the act, regardless of job title, position in the company, or organizational affiliation. The positive reinforcement boosts morale and gets people looking for what's working when it comes to making the cultural shift happen.

We suggest you use some kind of recognition card that anyone can fill out and hand to the recipient either electronically or in person. Our clients have found that the cards help to facilitate the recognition and provide physical evidence that progress is occurring. In fact, when the culture change gets rolling, you'll see a lot of cards on people's desks and in their cubicles. As with Focused Feedback and Storytelling, the recognition begins by identifying the Cultural Belief the individual has demonstrated, continues with a brief description of the A^2 actions that reflect the Cultural Belief, and ends by identifying which of the key R^2 results the demonstration of this Cultural Belief supported.

Take a look at this example from Opthometrics.

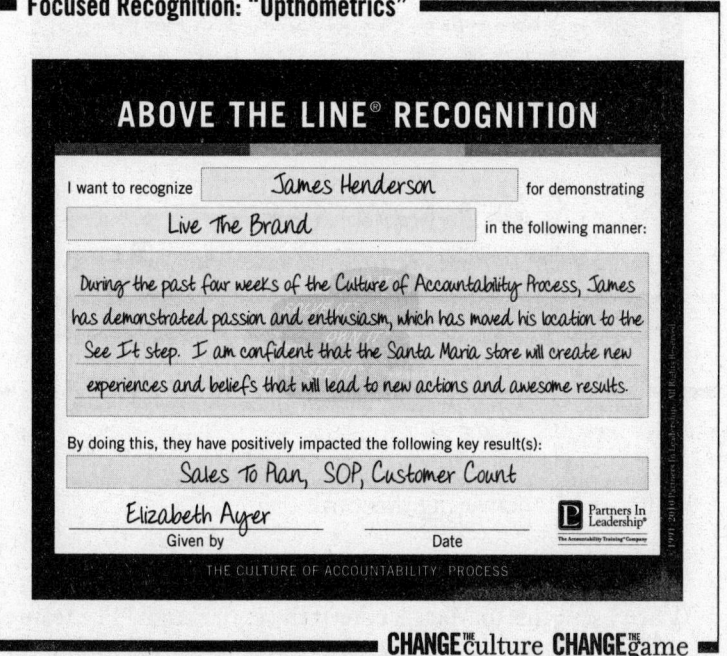

Focused Recognition: "Opthometrics"

ABOVE THE LINE® RECOGNITION

I want to recognize **James Henderson** for demonstrating

Live The Brand in the following manner:

During the past four weeks of the Culture of Accountability Process, James has demonstrated passion and enthusiasm, which has moved his location to the See It step. I am confident that the Santa Maria store will create new experiences and beliefs that will lead to new actions and awesome results.

By doing this, they have positively impacted the following key result(s):

Sales To Plan, SOP, Customer Count

Elizabeth Ayer
Given by   Date

Partners In Leadership®
The Accountability Training™ Company

THE CULTURE OF ACCOUNTABILITY PROCESS

CHANGE the culture CHANGE the game

Focused Recognition powerfully motivates individuals to think and act in the manner necessary to achieve the key results. It helps people line up on the same side of the boulder and provides appreciation when they do so. It clarifies the linkage between the A^2 actions and the key R^2 results they produce.

One final recognition card example comes from a member of the senior executive team, "Walter Gonzales," who led Opthometrics field operations across the United States. He gave the card to "Mary Wilson," the Midwest Division director.

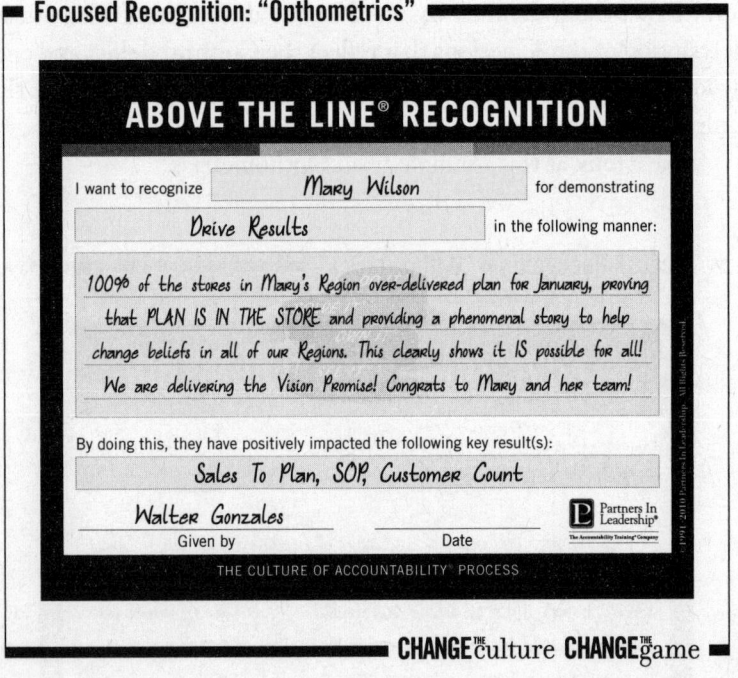

Focused Recognition: "Opthometrics"

ABOVE THE LINE® RECOGNITION

I want to recognize *Mary Wilson* for demonstrating *Drive Results* in the following manner:

100% of the stores in Mary's Region over-delivered plan for January, proving that PLAN IS IN THE STORE and providing a phenomenal story to help change beliefs in all of our Regions. This clearly shows it IS possible for all! We are delivering the Vision Promise! Congrats to Mary and her team!

By doing this, they have positively impacted the following key result(s):

Sales To Plan, SOP, Customer Count

Walter Gonzales _____
Given by   Date

Partners In Leadership®
The Accountability Training® Company

THE CULTURE OF ACCOUNTABILITY® PROCESS

CHANGE the culture CHANGE the game

Walter recalls delivering this card:

"This was the first recognition card I gave in Division 5. When I sent this to Mary, I copied the entire team. The team then copied their stores as well. The Midwest Division was just coming off a year when they delivered sales plan only four weeks out of fifty-two. However, now every single store in Division 5 was overdelivering on sales plan. This changed a *huge* belief, not only for the entire team, but for all of her stores as well. They were able to clearly show that *plan* is in every single store: You just have to go out and get it. When a hundred percent of the stores in this market were able to achieve this, no one could any longer blame sales on traffic. What a great way to start off the New Year—nothing had changed in this market except our beliefs and actions. This was the first real experience that sent our cultural momentum into action in the Midwest Division. It blew the minds of all the other division directors. They realized that anything is possible when we embrace the changes needed in ourselves as leaders!

"The Midwest Division was able to prove that results are possible in every single location when we 'own' it. In January, the Midwest Division ended up at number one in the company for sales to plan. This had not happened in a very, very long time. When I asked the team what had changed—their answer was 'We have!'"

In our experience, everyone who uses Focused Recognition, Focused Storytelling, and Focused Feedback to manage culture change finds these tools both powerful and simple to use. The tools provide clear direction to all individuals in the organization about what C^2 looks like and what they must do, and keep doing, to create the new culture. Properly implemented, these tools provide momentum for moving the cultural boulder to achieve the key R^2 results. However, you must integrate them into the daily, weekly, and monthly business practices of the organization to sustain movement over time.

We like what Winston Churchill once said: "First we shape our dwellings, and afterwards our dwellings shape us." Of course, he was recognizing the cause-and-effect relationship that exists in any society of people, where we first form our traditions and then those traditions work to shape us. We are, after all, creatures of habit. And that is exactly how culture works. Once you create the C^2 culture you need, it takes over and perpetuates itself, reinforcing at every turn what is important and the way things should be done, reaffirming the beliefs, practices, and traditions that are fundamental to your particular organizational culture.

That's the good news. Culture can and will work for you as you craft and shape it to produce R^2. In the next chapter, we will examine the three culture change leadership skills essential to making the transition effort successful.

CHAPTER 8

Mastering the
Three Culture Change Leadership Skills

THE PHILOSOPHER GEORGIY IVANOVICH GURDJIEFF suggested that most people live their lives with insufficient conscious thought. He called this "sleepwalking." When it comes to creating culture, many leaders do the same, investing far too little conscious thought in the process of shifting the beliefs people hold to create the C^2 culture and realize R^2 results. However, in addition to sleepwalking, they also do a lot of "sleep-talking," paying too little attention to the experiences they are creating for their people that bring about those shifts in beliefs. When leaders move unconsciously through the organization, they fail to provide the experiences that will create the desired culture. That's why we suggest every culture change effort include the clarion call, "Leaders, awake!"

Leadership of the Culture of Accountability Process does not require an oversize personality, arcane manipulation of others, inspirational speeches, or wild lunges at greatness. Instead, it calls for honest motives, conscious thought, and a focused effort to provide a good example of C^2 in action. Our model of leadership puts this kind of influence within the reach of every manager and employee, and it begins with modeling the new culture for everyone in the organization.

Every leader is empowered, by virtue of his or her position, with the visibility and authority either to spearhead or to undermine the transition to the new culture. Just one or two managers who fail to adopt the C^2 culture can throw the whole organization out of alignment by continuing to think and act in a C^1 manner. Their actions send a confusing and counterproductive message to employees: "It's acceptable to get on the wrong side of the boulder, to push against the change effort, and to continue to think and act according to the tenets of C^1." The experiences created by leaders who don't buy in and who are not invested in achieving the cultural transition often provide the most visible experiences, ones that strongly and negatively affect those who are struggling to make the change.

In sharp contrast, leaders who consistently use their visibility and influence to promote the new culture have a powerful impact on accelerating the culture change. As a result of their consistency, these leaders quickly get their people believing that they are serious about the importance of the change effort. That belief, in turn, encourages people to ignore any experiences that betray the cause as the organization moves toward C^2.

Every leader will, from time to time, manifest beliefs and actions that are inconsistent with the desired C^2 culture. Like everyone else in the organization, they have been living in C^1. As a result, all leaders must take a first and vital step toward accelerating culture change by acknowledging that they, too, will need to change in order to exemplify C^2. This acknowledgment, in and of itself, accelerates change and signals to people throughout the organization that the change effort is authentic. After all, their leaders have acknowledged that they were and are part of the C^1 culture and did a lot themselves to create it. This acknowledgment gives everyone else in the organization permission to do the same.

Culture change always requires leaders to become proficient in the skills needed to lead the transition effort. Without a concerted effort at the top of the organization to develop greater proficiency with the skills needed to lead the culture change, leaders frequently slow down the process and make the change effort less efficient and less successful. Developing these skills will accelerate the cultural transition while enhancing leadership capability in every other endeavor. The three culture change leadership skills every leader will need if they want to move the culture from C^1 to C^2 are: 1. the skill to Lead the Change, 2. the skill to Respond to Feedback, and 3. the skill to Be Facilitative. These three leadership skills are essential to ensuring that the culture change effort stays on track and achieves R^2.

THE SKILL TO LEAD THE CHANGE

Culture change must be led. You cannot delegate the initiative to Human Resources, Organizational Development, or anyone else. While these and other organizational functions play important roles, the senior leadership team simply must maintain ownership of the process and lead the culture change at every level of the organization, ensuring that the change effort is prioritized correctly at the top of every management team agenda.

To bring about the C^2 culture and R^2 results, leaders must take personal ownership of the implementation of each of the cultural transition best practices, shown on the chart on page 156, throughout the organization.

Many leaders will be doing some of these things for the first time in their careers. While skill building is always necessary for leaders to be most effective in the cultural transition, the speed at which culture change needs to occur does not usually allow for the luxury of building capability before leaders begin the process. Consequently, building skills to increase leadership proficiency in applying all of the best practices must occur in real time, simultaneously with the implementation of the cultural transition.

The coaching of leaders must commence in parallel with the change effort, and it must be implemented in the proper sequence so that they are developing, practicing, and applying the three leadership skills as they move forward with the Culture of Accountability Process. As shown in our C^2 Leadership Proficiency Model (on page 157), training, planning, and coaching help leaders perfect their ability to implement the C^2 best practices.

Leaders at every level need training in how to implement the C^2

■ C² Best Practices Leaders Must Own ■

Establishing Above the Line Accountability as a foundation of the change effort	**Chapter 1**
Defining and communicating R² results	**Chapter 2**
Engaging the assessment dialogue about shifts from A^1/B^1 to A^2/B^2	**Chapters 3 & 4**
Developing and implementing the Cultural Beliefs statement	**Chapters 4 & 10**
Providing new E^2 experiences	**Chapter 5**
Developing the Case for Change	**Chapter 6**
Using the Leadership Alignment Process to create and maintain Alignment	**Chapter 6**
Applying Focused Feedback	**Chapter 7**
Applying Focused Storytelling	**Chapter 7**
Applying Focused Recognition	**Chapter 7**
Reinforcing the three culture change leadership skills	**Chapter 8**

CHANGE the culture CHANGE the game

best practices. That training should incorporate practice and role-play to ensure the necessary skill proficiency. Preparing is vital to a leader's effectiveness in implementing the C^2 best practices and involves the necessary preplanning every step of the way. While shooting from the hip can work sometimes with the best practices, it will seldom produce the long-term impact you need.

The coaching required to increase proficiency must come from both outside and within the team. Outside couching affords the team added perspective and expert advice to ensure that they successfully implement C^2 best practices. Inside coaching encourages peer-to-peer support on the senior team, where advice aims to calibrate and

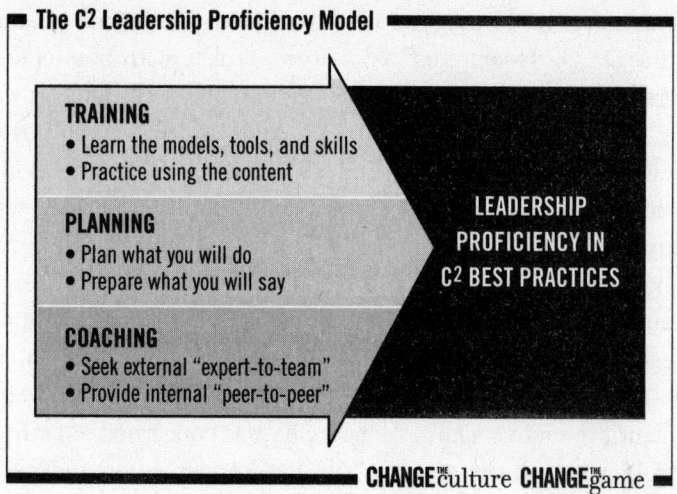

target everyone's efforts for maximum impact. Leaders do all of this in parallel with the implementation of the cultural transition.

A good example of a leader demonstrating the skill to lead the change comes from one our clients, "Universal," a large packaging manufacturer whose leaders decided they needed to "go big or go home" with one of their key units, the Flexible Materials Division (FMD), a North America–based business. At one point, FMD accounted for over 30 percent of total company revenues and won praise as Universal's flagship division. With the implementation of a global strategy for organization-wide growth, however, FMD's revenue contribution to the parent company had dropped to less than 10 percent, motivating the Universal board to question whether FMD should remain in the portfolio. The board threatened that if the FMD business could not get itself above the cost of capital and realize a reasonable return on that capital, then the parent company would find more promising opportunities for investing its money in the global markets.

In a final attempt to turn things around, the board decided to bring in someone from the outside to run FMD and recruited "Ken Jones" to serve as the division's CEO. With prior experience in the steel industry, Ken brought a fresh perspective to his job. He knew that FMD's "boss-centered" C^1 culture, replete with boss-centered leaders, did not make sense for his division and its unionized workforce. He had learned that in such an environment, employees who were closest to the problems and who often had good ideas about how to solve them would not speak up and talk about what wasn't working, that they would not easily tolerate risk, and that they would fear punishment for any and all failures. After quickly assessing the current culture, Ken determined that to save the business and drive success, the division would need to create an "employee-centered" C^2 culture in which everyone at every level was engaged in making the plant productive again. As far as he was concerned, creating C^2 meant blowing up the current "silo-like" organization and putting the business back together flatter, with more responsive pieces.

At this point, Ken brought us in to help implement the Culture of Accountability Process and change the culture of the organization. He needed game-changing results and knew that a focus on culture could make that happen. As the central theme of the new C^2 culture, Ken encouraged what he called a new-business owner mentality. His Case for Change argued that the company's survival as a viable entity depended on its ability to reduce costs rapidly while at the same time making the business more competitive. Ken believed, and communicated to every member of his team, that because Universal would probably end up selling them anyway, they might as well operate as though they had just bought FMD and take the risk to make the changes they thought the business needed. He convinced his management team to step up and act as if they were the new owners of the FMD business.

In order to enroll his top team in the cause, he took them off-site for two days to a seaside retreat, where they engaged in a major Level Three transformation effort. Ken told them, "We're going to challenge everything, and we're going to involve the entire organization in running the business. We're going to share it with the shop floor. We're going to tell Universal to leave us alone and let us manage our business." The team signed up and got aligned. For them, the motivation was simple: They had nothing to lose and everything to gain. They found the Case for Change personally compelling. They knew they had the ability to save the plant, grow the business, and advance their own careers.

Immediately, Ken and his team set about creating early experiences meant to communicate that they were serious about owning the business. They moved their corporate office from a showy glass building, with its leather furniture and ivory tower status in North Carolina, to the rugged and smoky production plant in Kentucky, a bold Type 1 experience no one could misunderstand. As we discussed in chapter 5, a Type 1 experience is a meaningful event that leads to immediate insight and needs no interpretation. For the first time in the over hundred-year existence of the plant, the firm's top executives would reside permanently on-site. For another first-time experience, Ken required executives to begin reporting how much time they spent on the plant floor interacting with workers on the line. This Type 1 experience needed no explanation: Executives were expected to make their presence known on the floor throughout the plant and engage with those who ran the daily operations of the "new business."

Ken knew that in order to become competitive and save the business, his team needed to boost return on capital (ROC) from 2 percent to over 10 percent. This became FMD's R^2: 10 percent–plus on ROC. To do that, he knew that one of the plant's key production lines needed to produce 10 million more pounds than it currently churned out and that it needed to do it with the same number of people. With R^2 in mind, he challenged his team to figure out how they could make that happen.

Ken and his team created a Cultural Beliefs statement that captured the essence of the change they needed to make in order to achieve R^2. At every opportunity, they reinforced those beliefs, which included major cultural shifts like Think FMD, Step Up!, Speak Up!, and Proudly Invest.

To reinforce the importance of creating an environment in which people would eagerly offer their input and ideas to improve plant operations, Ken's team attended safety meetings, team meetings, and other gatherings. The senior leaders took the initiative to create mechanisms for people to share more information, offer more feedback, and challenge every practice and policy that did not make sense to them. Ken made sure everyone knew that there would be no sacred cows.

Ken and his management team routinely participated in formal training meetings that helped them understand how to apply the best practice key activities. In fact, after the initial training, they came together every sixty to ninety days to ensure that they continued to manage the transition and stay on course. During these meetings, they also planned upcoming events and facilitated feedback and coaching between team members and our firm as outside advisors. All this effort focused on increasing their leadership proficiency so that each experience they created reinforced the new C^2 culture. The ongoing commitment of the senior team members to their own development was instrumental in helping them provide the necessary leadership throughout the cultural transition.

The end result? A 12 percent return on capital! Ken and his team changed the game for both FMD and Universal. They not only staved off the threat of closing the plant; they returned to their profitable status as a revenue producer in Universal's portfolio. The culture changed so completely that it survived the turnover of almost every key player involved in establishing the new cultural direction, including Ken, who tragically died shortly after the transformation. The new leader, "Bill Weston," found, to his surprise, that the culture did not depend on Ken's personality, but on the B^2 beliefs that had been instilled at every level of the organization. On his first day, someone handed him a card containing the Cultural Beliefs, suggesting that he should start asking people about what they had done to change the way they work to reflect the Cultural Beliefs. He was also told that he should seek Focused Feedback from a wide mix of people throughout the plant. Bill quickly learned that the way a leader responds to that feedback can make all the difference in continuing to move the culture change forward.

THE SKILL TO RESPOND TO FEEDBACK

It's natural for a leader to slip up occasionally and manifest old A^1 actions, particularly when the cultural transition first gets under way. After all, leaders are only human and are also making the transition. During the change effort, people watch leaders even more closely, and rightfully so. Of course people will see all the good experiences, but they also look for any signs of slippage or backsliding. They intuitively understand the power of belief bias and know that everyone finds old habits hard to break. Because people selectively interpret and find what they are looking for, those looking for leaders who are providing experiences that are not consistent with the Cultural Beliefs and the desired C^2 culture will spot them in a flash.

As you implement Focused Feedback early in the process and tap into the perceptions of others, you will undoubtedly learn what you need to do in order to improve your ability to create more compelling E^2 experiences that reinforce the desired Cultural Beliefs. Every leader with whom we have ever worked during cultural transition has faced this challenge and asked, "How do I change the beliefs people hold about my willingness and desire to live each of the Cultural Beliefs?"

To answer this question and to help you respond effectively to all the constructive Focused Feedback you will surely receive, we developed the Methodology for Changing Beliefs, which is presented in the chart on page 162. This methodology, used by countless leaders over the years, helps you acquire another simple but powerful skill that you can use to overcome B^1 beliefs about yourself and speed up the transition process for the organization. With this proven approach, you can efficiently and effectively change people's beliefs about your leadership and what it says about your willingness and desire to model the Cultural Beliefs. It also helps you create needed E^2 experiences that make a lasting and memorable impact on the beliefs people hold. Of course, this methodology will only work in the long term if the new experiences you create represent real and sincere change.

When you receive feedback that you have created an experience that is inconsistent with the Cultural Beliefs, you can use the

Methodology for Changing Beliefs

STEP	DESCRIPTION	WHAT YOU SAY
1	Identify the belief you need to change.	*"That's not the belief I want you to hold."*
2	Tell them the belief you want them to hold.	*" The belief I want you to hold is..."*
3	Describe the experience you are going to create for them.	*"Here's what I'm going to do..."*
4	Ask them for feedback on the planned experience.	*"Will that be enough; is there something else I need to do?"*
5	Enroll them in giving you feedback on your progress.	*"Will you give me feedback along the way?"*

CHANGEthe**culture CHANGE**the**game**

Methodology for Changing Beliefs to get people looking for evidence of your true alignment and your deep desire to embody the new culture. Both individuals and teams can employ this methodology to stimulate productive dialogue as they work to target specific beliefs. Lets walk through each of the methodology's five steps.

Step One:
Identify the Belief You Need to Change

First, you need to identify the B^1 belief you need to change. It will undoubtedly emerge as you solicit Focused Feedback and ask people what they really think. As you hear people's comments and observations, you should test the belief you think these people have formed by restating what you have heard. Sometimes these beliefs will surprise you. You may even wonder how on earth people could draw that conclusion, make that judgment, or form that impression. Surprised or not, you should try hard to understand the beliefs people hold because, accurate or not, they will guide how people act, and how they act will, obviously, affect results.

Once you have clarified the beliefs people hold, you simply need to ask yourself, "Is that a belief I want them to hold?" If the belief will not move the organization toward C^2, then you will want to change it. If that's your conclusion, you should simply state to the person or team, "That's not the belief I want you to hold." Take care not to invalidate their belief, make them feel stupid for feeling that way, or try to convince them that they are seeing it the wrong way. Once you disengage your feedback filters, then you can work to change the beliefs people hold by changing the experiences they are having.

Step Two:
Tell Them the Belief You Want Them to Hold

In the next step, you identify the belief you want them to hold. Make sure you put this belief in the context of the B^2 Cultural Beliefs. By making this connection, you reinforce the importance of the B^2 beliefs and communicate your commitment to those beliefs. Don't shy away from talking about beliefs. Leaders who successfully instill beliefs talk explicitly about them. Here, you say to the person or team, "The belief I want you to hold is . . ." By identifying the belief you want them to hold, you predispose them to look for evidence of it. You are simply reframing the situation so that they will give you the benefit of the doubt and interpret experiences in the way you intend them to be interpreted. It sounds simple, but it powerfully influences what people end up seeing and believing.

Step Three:
Describe the Experience You're Going to Create for Them

After stating the belief you want people to hold, you should describe the experience you are going to create to reinforce that belief. This is when you convince people that you mean what you say and that you will do what you promise. Be as specific as you can when you describe the experience(s) you want them to have. Explain, "Here's what I am going to do."

Resist any temptation to jump directly to step four by asking

others what they think you should do. People want to know that you
are sincere and serious about creating new experiences. Communicating what you plan to do lets them know that you have given this
some thought and are taking accountability for changing their belief.
At this point, everyone will be watching to see if you go Below the
Line to justify the experiences you have provided in the past or if you
will rise Above the Line and shoulder the responsibility for taking
the steps to See It, Own It, Solve It, and Do It.

Step Four:
Ask Them for Feedback on the Planned Experience

Seeking feedback on the planned experience will help you calibrate what else you may need to do to meet the needs of your intended
audience. Because you probably will not have thought of everything,
the very act of asking for input from others about what beliefs they
really need to change builds credibility. Ask, "Will this be enough?"
and "Can you think of something else I will need to do?" At this
point, we should stress that you are not looking for everything you
could do but for what would most likely "ring their bell" and cause
them to adopt the new belief. You cannot skip this critical step. If you
do, you may not learn what you need to know in order to prompt the
desired change. Be sure to consider the practicalities of what people are telling you. If you hear a good, usable idea and you're willing
to do it, then say so. Likewise, you should also let them know if it's
something you do not think you can do.

Step Five:
Enroll Them in Giving you Feedback on Your Progress

Finally, you enroll others in giving you feedback on your progress.
You measure progress in terms of the degree to which your intended
audience is adopting the new beliefs you want them to hold. To determine this, ask for both reinforcing and constructive feedback. The
former pinpoints those times when you have created experiences
that reinforce the desired belief; the latter spotlights those times you

failed to do so. Even after people agree to give you feedback, you may still need to work to convince them that you really want it.

When people know that you will be asking for feedback on your progress, they will begin looking for that progress, a major step in shifting beliefs. Enrolling others in providing you feedback now places the focus on exactly the right behaviors: working collaboratively to establish the C^2 culture and achieve R^2 results. Leaders and their teams help each other co-create the new culture. Establishing internal peer-to-peer (or boss-to-team) coaching, in addition to the expert-to-team coaching, will help you calibrate the experiences you create on a day-to-day basis to demonstrate the Cultural Beliefs. To be successful in leading the transition, leaders must fully involve their teams in helping them demonstrate the B^2 beliefs.

While this methodology helps leaders effectively respond to Focused Feedback and demonstrate the Cultural Beliefs, it also produces an interesting side effect by automatically and subtly focusing the audience's attention on their own beliefs and behaviors. When leaders faithfully execute each of the five steps of the Methodology for Changing Beliefs, they ignite the same thought process in those who are watching. When people see leaders reinforcing B^2 beliefs, everyone gets the message that "I ought to be doing that too." As a result, others will look for that behavior, think about that behavior, and seek that behavior both in their fellow workers and, most important, in themselves.

HOW THE METHODOLOGY FOR CHANGING BELIEFS WORKS

Let's look at a real example of this methodology in action. Suppose that an organization's leaders have committed themselves to creating a culture in which people believe they can express themselves freely and that the leadership team has captured this idea in the Cultural Belief "Speak Up." Leaders on the management team want to provide experiences consistent with this B^2 belief, experiences that will get everyone in the company to take accountability to say what they think.

At a management meeting, suppose further that one of the

attendees, Karen, experiences C^1 behavior from one of the leaders, Jim. The following dialogue between the two traces the steps of the Methodology for Changing Beliefs and exemplifies what should happen when you get Focused Feedback that your behavior is out of alignment with the Cultural Beliefs.

Step One:
Identify the Belief You Need to Change

Jim: Karen, what feedback do you have for me about our meeting this morning?

Karen: Jim, I'm actually glad you asked. I've been a bit hesitant to bring this up, but, as you know, we've made a commitment to "Speak Up" and be open to the perspectives of others as a part of the culture change effort. But during the meeting, I felt you were very defensive. Based on the experiences I have had with you recently, I don't really feel that you're demonstrating our belief about being open to the perspectives of others.

Jim: OK, Karen, I'm a little surprised by this feedback. Help me understand why you believe I'm not being open to the views of others and that I'm defensive when I hear things I don't like.

Karen: Well, you're not always defensive, and you're open to some perspectives, but when any of us from Marketing say something about the new product requirements, I feel you close up and get defensive.

Jim: Yes, I probably do feel that. Sometimes I'm afraid you're going to throw a wrench into the current plan and slow down our ability to get the product out the door. So, I can see that I probably do come across a bit defensive and closed. Good point.

Karen: A lot of people in Marketing are beginning to believe that you're not very interested in their views, so, just like me, they are hesitant to "Speak Up."

Jim: Well, Karen, thanks for that feedback. That's not the belief I want you to hold. And I can see how some experiences I'm providing are causing people to feel I am not committed to that Cultural Belief.

Karen: Yes, and not only not committed to it, but not committed to helping us do it either.

Step Two:
Tell Them the Belief You Want Them to Hold

Jim: I get it, Karen. Again, that's not the belief I want you to hold. The belief I want you to hold is that I am open to the perspectives of others and want to support you in living the belief "Speak Up." Honestly, I really do feel that I need to know Marketing's true views. Of course, I also need to manage my concerns about the production timeline. I know I need to change the experience I'm creating for you and the Marketing Department.

Step Three:
Describe the Experience You Are Going to Create for Them

Jim: So, here's what I am going to do. At every meeting with Marketing, I'll be the one to ask, "What does Marketing think about that?" Then I will listen carefully to everyone's opinions.

Karen: That would be great.

Step Four:
Ask Them for Feedback on the Planned Experience

Jim: Karen, will that be enough? Or is there something else I'll need to do?

Karen: I think you could also talk with people prior to the meeting about any big concerns you anticipate coming up, so that you're not surprised by their reactions. That will open the lines of communication with Marketing even more.

Jim: That's a good idea. It would probably help the conversation in the meeting be even more productive. Is there anything else?

Karen: I don't think so. I honestly think those actions would make a big difference in how you are perceived.

Step Five:
Enroll Them in Giving You Feedback on Your Progress

Jim: Karen, will you give me feedback along the way?

Karen: Of course.

Jim: Karen, I want you to let me know when you think I'm not supporting "Speak Up," and when you think I am. Would you be willing to give me feedback on how that's going immediately after our weekly meetings?

Karen: Sure. I would love to do that.

Jim could also approach the entire marketing team and apply the methodology with them. He might also want to think about Karen's input before acting on the Focused Feedback he received from her, perhaps asking others for their perspectives to check his assumptions and make sure he has not missed some other important perspective. In any case, this example demonstrates how leaders can use the Methodology for Changing Beliefs to respond to Focused Feedback when the experiences they are providing are out of alignment with the C^2 culture. The methodology works by helping you live the B^2 beliefs more fully and consistently, providing the experiences people need to reinforce the commitment that the Cultural Beliefs should become a way of life for the organization. Once you clearly identify what else you can do to move the change effort forward, then you can turn your attention to helping others do it more effectively as well.

THE SKILL TO BE FACILITATIVE

It usually takes some effort to become thoroughly facilitative in your communication style—an important culture change leadership skill. Getting everyone to engage in a meaningful dialogue about what needs to change and making sure that conversation occurs at every level of the organization is essential to accelerating culture change.

In our view, lasting culture change always requires collaboration, teamwork, and dialogue. Your ability as an organizational leader to ask questions, seek input, create dialogue, and get people talking about the right topics will speed up the adoption of C^2 beliefs. Take, for example, our experience with Sony's VAIO Service organization, a client that had set an ambitious goal to improve its repair-related customer satisfaction scores by 15 percent over its previous year's results. VAIO Service Vice President Steven Nickel recalls the exact moment this R^2 result was presented to his team: "I still remember the silence in the room when everyone fully realized how challenging this result would be. Although we had communicated it numerous times in meetings and assemblies, it wasn't until we sat down as a team and dissected every aspect and implication of this goal—what we needed to do more of, what we needed to eliminate, and what new ideas we would have to come up with—that the true nature of the challenge became apparent. Let me tell you, the room got real quiet."

Steven and his team energized the organization around R^2 by opening the door to an ongoing dialogue about what it would really take. Once fully engaged in the conversation, they found it much easier to make significant daily progress on this initiative. The team's weekly Key Performance Indicator meetings buzzed with life as members from all areas, many of whom had never spoken up in these meetings before, enthusiastically shared numerous improvement ideas and quickly took ownership to implement them.

The engagement facilitated by the senior leaders helped the organization achieve and ultimately exceed its ambitious goal. The parent company recognized the members of VAIO Service with an award from Sony Electronics. Steven Nickel said, "I learned the equivalent of several volumes of business books from this experience. . . . Getting people to talk about the right things, like the goals of the organization, and then getting them to buy in . . . doesn't come from slide shows or speeches. It comes from engaging everyone on the team to help define what success looks like and how we need to change to achieve this success."

Facilitating the right conversations requires a passion for wanting to know what people really think and an ability to ask the right questions to get, and keep, that dialogue going. To do that, you should ask three questions a lot.

Three Questions You Should Ask, a Lot

1. What do you think?

2. Why do you think that?

3. What would you do?

Of course, when you ask these questions, you need to listen carefully to the answers you hear. Improving your active listening skills will help you stimulate the dialogue. Never forget that people can tell if you are listening or not. The degree to which you pay attention will speak volumes about whether or not you sincerely want to know what they think.

Rest assured that you can learn a great deal from the dialogues you facilitate about what else you can do to move the change forward. One of our clients tells what people in the organization call "the watermelon story," which nicely illustrates the value of facilitating input from others. In the words of the manager involved:

"One of the guys asked me to come walk the floors with him one day and said, 'It's interesting, you know, how we used to have these daily inspections.' He went on, 'Let me show you how I inspect the valves. Come with me for a minute.' So we walked together while he checked the valves. We came to the first valve, and he said, 'Look at this.' I looked at the valve and found the glass was broken and covered with black grime. You could not even see the number. Worse, he told me that the valve doesn't even move anymore. He then pointed to the book he was carrying and said, 'See here in my little workbook; it says, "Check valve." I'm checking the valve. But that's not really what they want. What they want is to know if there is coolant in here, because it's the coolant that determines whether or not this 1950s machinery is going to work.' I was stunned. We were doing everything we could to improve productivity on the line, but this had never come up.

"The line worker said, 'How can I tell if there is coolant? I pound on it. I know the sound that it should make, based on what level of coolant is inside of it. And that's how we run the plant. I knock, and depending on that sound, I know whether or not we need more or less coolant. It has nothing to do with the valve. But management feels good because they have a checklist that says check the valve. But every day I've been asked to check the same broken valve. And I report every day that the valve is broken.'

"Here is a guy who knows the ins and outs of the plant well enough that he can knock on a piece of machinery, like you would a watermelon, and tell by the tone how much coolant is inside that piece of machinery that literally determines if that plant is going to run! He had raised the issue before, but no one seemed to listen."

From this experience, this manager understood that getting people to tell you what they think, and what they know, garners the kind of valuable information that can move a change effort forward at a more rapid pace.

Learning how to be facilitative in your communication style and get people to talk frankly with you will not only help engage people in the change effort, but it will also help you identify and share best practices across the organization. During culture change, everyone is learning what works best, and as they do, they discover best practices that can be leveraged across the entire organization. Sharing best practices optimizes the effort. Herb Henkel, CEO of Ingersoll Rand, promotes the notion of "dual citizenship" as a key value of the organization. At Ingersoll Rand, being a dual citizen means that you are not only a member of your own team or function, but you are just as much a member of the larger organization. When good citizens share best practices, not only with their teammates, but also across internal organizational boundaries, they not only avoid reinventing the wheel, but leverage everyone's efforts as well. Many good ideas about how to promote the culture change will come from the ground up, as people engage and take ownership for making the change happen.

Becoming more facilitative also means structuring your town halls and other communication meetings in a way that allows for Q&A. Small group meetings can also provide the needed forum to facilitate conversation. "Breakfast with Bob" was a popular and helpful forum in one culture change effort. The CEO met once a week in a breakfast meeting with different groups in the organization. Employees loved this meeting's open forum agenda.

Whatever approach you use, always remember to ask the three questions a lot: What do you think? Why do you think that? What would you do? Then listen carefully to what people say. Your ability to master a facilitative communication style will not only engage people more completely, it will speed up the change in culture.

The role leaders play during the transition is key to accelerating change. Their effectiveness in leading the change is greatly improved when they work to develop their leadership proficiency in applying the C^2 best practices. Leaders face the unique challenge of leading the change while simultaneously changing themselves. Every effective cultural transition that we have ever witnessed has included the leadership development of key leaders throughout the organization targeted around the C^2 best practices.

Leadership of a cultural transition requires leaders to do more than just expect everyone to change; leaders must help people make the change. Successfully changing the culture is one of the most personally rewarding leadership endeavors anyone can participate in. It not only brings the satisfaction of improving the organization in a lasting way; it also escalates individual performance and the personal benefits that come from game-changing business success.

In the next chapter, we will share with you what we have learned over the last two decades about how to integrate the cultural transition effort into the practices, processes, and procedures of the organization so that the culture change is sustained over time.

CHAPTER 9

Integrating the Culture Change

ONCE THE CULTURAL TRANSITION gets under way, most leaders ask, "What is the key to making sure people use the C^2 best practices to move the change forward?" Our long, successful experience with a vast variety of clients has helped us formulate the answer to this question: You must not only implement the C^2 best practices, but you must also completely and fully integrate them into the existing meetings and systems of the organization. Otherwise, you are not likely to create and maintain the discipline and focus needed to sustain the cultural change over time. Doing it well saves you money, time, energy, and effort; doing it poorly will most likely result in frustration and limited progress. It's that fundamental!

Change is hard for people, but sustaining change can pose an even greater challenge. One of the authors will never forget the time when five of his children, each under the age of eight, had been leaving their bicycles strewn all over the driveway and blocking the front door to the house. Every morning when the author left the house, he navigated the same death-defying walk through the pile of bicycles in order to reach his car and drive to work.

The first attempt to get the children to change came in the form of a fatherly request: The bikes needed to be parked in an orderly fashion because that's the right thing to do. As you can imagine, the father's request did not alter the children's behavior and prompted a myriad of excuses: "I forgot," "The car was in the way," "Mom called us to dinner. . . ."

In the father's second attempt to get the children to change, he called upon his business acumen and offered a small payment in the form of their favorite candy bar, provided the children cooperated with the requested change. The father thought bribery might do the trick. The result: immediate compliance! However, to his dismay, the change lasted for only one day. Then the children got back to business as usual, piling up the bikes and offering the same old excuses.

The third attempt to get them to change was the result of a brainstorm. Why not establish a process that would essentially *require* them to do what they were being asked to do? As the centerpiece of this strategy, the father ordered a sturdy bike rack that would accommodate all five bikes, hold them upright, and keep them stationary in the designated spot. Because the children loved dessert after dinner, he reinforced the new process with the understanding that there would be no dessert for any child who did not use the rack.

He anxiously awaited the arrival of the perfect rack he had ordered over the Internet. When it arrived, he quickly assembled it and placed it in a strategic position, away from the front door but near enough to make it easy to park the bikes. During a special training meeting with the family, everyone gathered around and listened to the carefully crafted instructions about how to use the bike rack. Then everyone practiced the procedure. After the last bike stood upright in the rack, all the children applauded and agreed that it looked marvelous. The bikes were neatly organized, the walkway was clear, and order had been restored to the driveway. The children seemed committed, enthusiastic, determined, and motivated to follow the new process. (True, the "no dessert" clause sealed the deal.)

It was a sight to behold as the father strolled to the car the next morning and saw all those bikes lined up in the rack. With a triumphant whoop, he went off to work. On the drive home that night, his anticipation mounted as he imagined that row of neatly parked bikes. But anticipation immediately plunged to disappointment as he pulled up the driveway. Oh, the bike rack still stood there in all its glory, but the five bikes lay all around it on the ground, neatly surrounding the rack. It almost looked as if the children had gone out of their way to make the point that the rack would not be tolerated. The author consoled himself with the fact that at least some progress had been made. The bikes no longer blocked the front door!

This experience illustrates the difficulty that often accompanies a leader's efforts to integrate change throughout the organization. The same ineffective pattern—tell 'em, bribe 'em, force 'em—is often employed with the same results: temporary and partial compliance. No matter how good or important an idea may be, people often struggle to adopt the change, and they struggle even more to make those changes permanent. We have learned from our own experience that without an effective mechanism for integrating the changes you wish to make into the daily routines of the people who need to make them, you will likely fail. All the inducements to change, including asking people to do it because it is the right thing to do (tell 'em), providing incentives (bribe 'em), or structuring it into the process and systems of the organization (force 'em), can fail to bring about the intended effect. Change requires a combined and consistent effort at both the top and bottom of the Results Pyramid. Knowing how to integrate the change will help you accomplish the lasting culture change that produces R^2 results.

Warning! We relentlessly emphasize integration because we know that without it, the implementation of the Cultural Beliefs and the C^2 best practices will, at best, be hit-or-miss. People simply will not find the time or muster the necessary motivation to employ the C^2 best practices if the change requires extra effort or time. That's why learning how to incorporate all of the best practices seamlessly into the current management practices of the organization is such an essential step at this point in the journey.

INTEGRATION MEANS INTEGRATE

Leaders who are managing the culture change effort must ensure that people throughout the organization receive consistent and frequent reminders that the leaders are serious about changing the culture and moving the cultural boulder forward. You build these reminders into the organizational process as you integrate the C^2 best practices into the daily routines of the organization and encourage their use on a regular basis.

As we have outlined in this book, changing culture involves both implementing the best practices (Part One of the book) and integrating them (Part Two of the book). These two activities form a continuous loop, as the diagram below depicts.

Leading culture change means working ceaselessly to implement and integrate. Each activity enhances and then mutually reinforces the other. Implementation sets up integration and integration sustains implementation. They go hand in hand.

Integration is not about convening additional meetings, creating a longer list of things to do, or lengthening the workday. On the contrary, when you integrate the Culture Management Tools into the organization, you insert them into carefully selected, already existing meetings and activities, where they provide leverage to move the cultural boulder forward to C^2. It bears repeating: Integration means integrating the tools into the current organizational processes, procedures, and systems. When done correctly, integration weaves the Cultural Transition Process seamlessly into the way things are done in the organization. If you do it poorly, people end up feeling that you have just added another burdensome program to the many they already need to implement.

One of the authors' daughters took a job at a local bookstore, Deseret Book, while attending college. At the end of her first week, she called to tell her father how much she enjoyed her new job. She said that on her first day at work, her manager handed her a name badge with a set of Cultural Beliefs printed on the back. She learned that when she or any other employee saw another associate in the store doing a good job, they could give that person a DB Dollar (Deseret Book Dollar), which they could use to acquire free products from the store. When the author confided to his daughter that the bookstore chain was a client and that she was experiencing the Culture of Accountability Process and the integration of the Cultural Beliefs we talk about so much, she laughed. It was exciting to experience a rather random sampling of a client's integration efforts, witness the process working, and hear the enthusiasm this daughter felt about what could otherwise have been a rather ordinary job.

The C^2 best practices are high-leverage activities that help move the boulder forward and build the desired culture. Using them early in the process will help you create momentum and get everyone moving in the right direction. Unfortunately, many organizations fail to formalize and integrate these types of activities early enough in the change process.

The most common mistake leaders make in the Cultural Transition Process is failing to integrate *as soon as* they begin to implement. Remember, implementation and integration progress on parallel paths and mutually reinforce and depend on one another.

THE THREE STEPS TO EFFECTIVE INTEGRATION

Successful integration of the C^2 best practices into the culture change process depends on effectively applying each of the three distinct steps.

First, you identify opportunities for integration into meetings.

Second, you identify opportunities for integration into the organizational systems. Third, you make your Integration Plan. Taking these steps sequentially will allow you to spot the best opportunities for making integration happen in a way that optimizes your effort and minimizes distractions.

Step One:
Identify the Opportunities for Integration into Meetings

Integration is most effectively accomplished within intact teams. While the opportunities for integration will differ from team to team, your initial list of opportunities should include all of the different meetings the team currently holds, including one-on-ones.

Here are some meetings we've seen clients use to seize the opportunity for integration:

- Developmental store visits by district managers
- Staff meetings
- Safety meetings on the plant floor
- Shift huddles (short employee meetings)
- One-on-ones between boss and subordinates
- Departmental meetings
- Management meetings
- Board meetings
- Predictable yet spontaneous ad hoc meetings
- Project updates
- Standing "corridor" updates with employees
- Sales meetings
- All-hands company meetings
- Town hall–style meetings

These kinds of activities occur in every organization with varying degrees of regularity: daily, weekly, monthly, quarterly, or annually. You will want to make your own list of meetings, which, at the very least, should include already scheduled one-on-one meetings and long-standing team meetings. Once you have listed every meeting that could serve as an integration opportunity, you can then select the very best opportunities for integration by filtering the opportunities according to the following criteria:

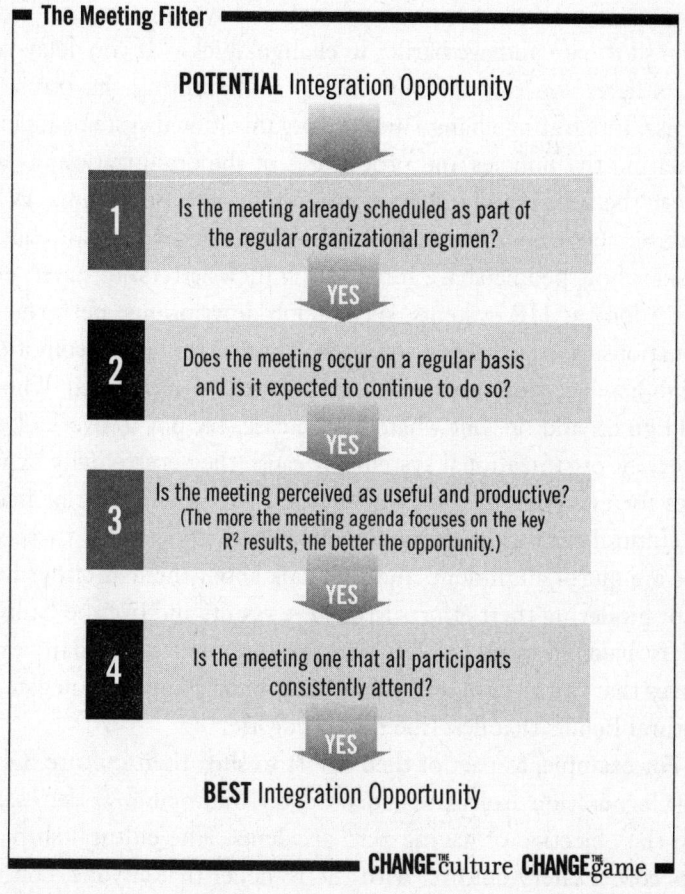

The Meeting Filter

POTENTIAL Integration Opportunity

1. Is the meeting already scheduled as part of the regular organizational regimen?

YES

2. Does the meeting occur on a regular basis and is it expected to continue to do so?

YES

3. Is the meeting perceived as useful and productive? (The more the meeting agenda focuses on the key R^2 results, the better the opportunity.)

YES

4. Is the meeting one that all participants consistently attend?

YES

BEST Integration Opportunity

CHANGE THE culture CHANGE THE game

With these criteria in mind, you should be able to build a strong list of opportunities quite quickly. Selecting the best opportunities may be a judgment call, but identifying those with the greatest leverage for helping you move the cultural boulder will allow you to focus your efforts where they will bring the biggest return.

Step Two:
Identify Opportunities for Integration into Systems

In addition to building the C^2 best practices into meetings, you also need to examine the organization's formal systems for integration opportunities. In most cases, organizational systems are less flexible in the short run and are harder to change quickly. If you delay your efforts here, you can actually end up undermining the transition process. Integrating change into the organizational systems includes evaluating the policies and procedures of the organization, as well as both the formal and informal application of those systems. When thinking about your organizational systems and what can change, consider how people share information (newsletters, intranet, etc.). Take a look at HR systems, such as job descriptions, performance evaluations, job postings, rewards, incentives, and promotions. Weigh how decisions are made and how work is authorized. The list could go on and on, but whatever the case, try not to overlook any important organizational systems, because they create daily experiences for everyone in the company that either reinforce or betray the cultural transition effort. People usually know when these systems are out of alignment, and they talk about them as either helping or hindering their efforts to achieve results and live the Cultural Beliefs. Keep in mind the fact that these systems create daily experiences that can sustain, call into question, or completely negate the Cultural Beliefs that describe the C^2 culture.

For example, as part of their effort to shift their culture, Chevron Corporation executives focused on improving worker safety with the objective of having zero accidents. The cultural shift had at its core a safety culture, with the B^2 belief that anyone, contractors and employees alike, who saw a behavior they would consider unsafe, could issue a stop-work order. Previously, in Chevron's C^1 safety culture, only those in positions of authority could stop the work. The company consciously changed its organizational systems to reinforce the new belief that everyone must take accountability for safety. As a result, Chevron enjoyed its safest year in history and boasted one of the best safety records in the industry. It happened because Chevron integrated this core belief into the practices associated with its organizational systems. This success underscores the point that integration into the policies and procedures that lie at the heart of organizational systems brings a big payoff in terms of achieving R^2 results.

Making needed changes to organizational systems can be complicated and become even more difficult when the cultural transition effort is occurring within a department or division of a larger organization and is subject to policies and procedures determined by that parent organization. However, even in these situations, there may be subtle changes that can be made to send the right messages and motivate the desired C^2 behavior. At the very least, when needed adjustments to systems that are misaligned with the Cultural Beliefs cannot occur quickly, you must effectively interpret such Type 2 experiences. Failure to do so can create Type 4 experiences out of those that would have otherwise been Type 2.

Step Three:
Make Your Integration Plan

Successful integration of the C^2 best practices into your culture-change effort hinges on forming a C^2 Integration Plan based on the first two steps you have taken. This plan should specifically capture what you are going to do to integrate the best practices into the activities you have selected.

A good example of how to do this comes from our earlier client story about "Eastside HealthPlans." After the Eastside management team evaluated steps one and two in the integration process, they arrived at the plan on page 182.

The team took early steps to align the organizational systems as well. As a result, they unleashed organizational thinking and began to make changes on a variety of fronts. Lean process teams were

■ **Integration Plan: "Eastside HealthPlans"** ■

1 Director's Pre-Briefings
- Deliver at least one recognition card for a Cultural Belief.
- Tell at least one Cultural Belief story at every meeting.
- Create new experiences for people to help them change beliefs.
- Provide time on the agenda for cross-divisional sharing.

2 Divisional Staff Meetings
- Deliver at least one recognition card for a Cultural Belief.
- Tell at least one Cultural Belief story at every meeting.
- Create new experiences for people to help them change beliefs.
- Provide time on the agenda for cross-divisional sharing.

3 First Mondays
- Deliver some recognition for Cultural Beliefs.
- Tell at least one Cultural Belief story in every video.
- Discuss progress toward business results.
- Continue to keep the Case for Change message in communications.

4 Eastside News
- Alternate with VPs telling stories, giving recognition, educating employees on their results and/or key initiatives.

5 Town Halls
- Schedule and conduct Cultural Belief activities at every Leader Town Hall meeting.
- Share C^2 stories.

■ CHANGE^{THE}culture CHANGE^{THE}game ■

formed to address the waste, inefficiencies, and administrative costs within the organization. For the first time in twenty-five years, leaders began to create significant experiences that suggested the company would not tolerate waste. These teams ultimately achieved line-item cost savings of over $200 million.

Cross-functional work teams were given the task to create forums for better collaboration between functions within the organization. The Cultural Beliefs were posted at the employee entrance and on the back of every employee badge. Stories of people living the beliefs were regularly published in all employee communications.

Taking it one step further, the company added a weekly pop-up to the sign-in screen on its intranet home page. This pop-up posed a question to test employees' understanding of the desired R^2 results. A good answer to the question-of-the-month won a raffle prize. A new Web site contained links that sent people to an update on all the key results. Teams also began conducting quarterly thirty-minute tele-conferences on business results. All employees gained access to electronic versions of a recognition card linked to the Cultural Beliefs, and posters, surveys, and other reminders constantly reinforced the use of the Culture Management Tools.

These efforts led to the results we described in chapter 4: a game-changing shift in culture that resulted in the top-ranking health care provider among all the providers in the Eastside system for the first time in the history of the company.

Another example of effectively integrating the C^2 best practices comes from Opthometrics, whose story we have outlined throughout this book. Without a doubt, this company's efforts to integrate the three Culture Management Tools and change its culture paid huge dividends in terms of improved performance. The Opthometrics field leadership team put together an In-Field/In-Store Integration Plan that included a number of integration activities, such as twice daily "shift huddles," weekly store manager meetings, and regular developmental store visits by field leaders.

In the shift huddles, managers briefly met with associates and doctors to review performance and discuss needed adjustments to a store's efforts to deliver planned performance. The shift huddles met all of the Meeting Filter criteria: They were already scheduled to occur every morning and every afternoon in every store, they were a recognized part of the ongoing store regimen, they were seen as useful and productive with high impact on key R^2 results, and they were consistently attended by each of the associates working in every Opthometrics store.

The company integrated many of the C^2 best practices within the shift huddles, specifically the Culture Management Tools. "Raymond Ramirez," an Opthometrics store manager, said of his experience with daily shift huddles, "We prepare for each huddle by using what we call the shift huddle notepad. The notepad is set up as a guide to help us plan how to use the Culture Management Tools and Models. As we meet in a shift huddle, we begin with a brief story about someone who has demonstrated a Cultural Belief." The story quickly reminds everyone of the need to live the Opthometrics Cultural Beliefs as they work to achieve plan. With this in mind, the people involved in the huddle move into a targeted discussion of how everyone in the store can take more accountability for store performance. They go over the numbers: yesterday's results, where they stand for the week, and where they need to improve in order to deliver their plan.

Typically, the accountability discussion reveals any beliefs people hold that may be getting in the way of performance. For example, Ramirez commented, "Yesterday in our huddle, we talked about prescriptions for sunglasses and acknowledged that we were under plan for the week. I asked everyone in the huddle to consider what beliefs we had, if any, that were keeping us from providing our customers with sunglasses. One belief surfaced quickly: A pair of sunglasses is believed to be a second pair of glasses. We talked about changing that belief to one in which we consider the customer's sunglasses as the first pair of sunglasses, not the second pair of glasses. Everyone agreed that this was a more empowering belief that would guide A^2 actions and engage associates with customers in a better way."

Ramirez continued, "We quickly made the decision to change the belief. So here's what happened in terms of results: That very day we had two people sell well over their prescription sunglasses goals, and we finished the week achieving our plan." It is worth noting that the team did not achieve the prescription sunglasses results by concentrating on those results but by concentrating on changing the beliefs that impeded their ability to deliver those results. That's what it looks like to work with the bottom two levels of the Results Pyramid and integrate the model into the huddle.

Each shift huddle concludes with an exchange of Focused Feedback. Normally, the store manager leads this process and begins by asking, "What feedback do you have for me?" As people offer Focused Feedback around the Cultural Beliefs, the store manager writes it all down and then seeks additional feedback on how well the team has implemented what they have already agreed to do, how well they feel the week is going, and what else they think they may need to do to achieve plan and/or deliver the brand promise.

According to "William Lake," a division director, the integration efforts throughout the Opthometrics stores have been consistent, and Focused Storytelling is becoming a part of the culture. He told us, "Stories no longer simply begin shift huddles, they bubble up from within the stores throughout the day. We've got associates, lab employees, doctors, and everybody else telling stories, and they're doing it without being prompted. It's not 'Hey, tell me a story' or 'We want to hear a story'; it's happening spontaneously with an underlying understanding that great C^2 experiences ought to be shared!"

Regarding the strength and consistency of the integration of Focused Recognition, Lake observed, "When we first started integrating the tools and models into our huddles, it was very new to us. The managers led the meeting and recognized the people. Now, when you walk into a store and get involved in a shift huddle, you'll hear associates recognizing lab employees, lab employees recognizing doctors, and so on. Everybody is involved in recognizing people for demonstrating the Cultural Beliefs and achieving results."

Concerning the overall success of the integration effort, Lake commented, "The integration in these huddles has been so complete that leadership for the huddles has moved from the store managers to other key players on the team. Lab managers, retail managers, and sometimes even strong associates are leading the huddles; they're doing the storytelling; they're asking the questions. And they're taking accountability for changing the culture!"

The second key opportunity of the In-Field/In-Store Integration Plan was the weekly managers' meeting. This meeting included the store manager, lab manager, retail manager, and eye-care specialist, and it began with a review of the store's current results. When performance fell below expectations, the managers used the Steps to Accountability (introduced in chapter 1) to identify what else they could do to deliver plan. For example, a discussion of a store scheduling problem resulted in the discovery of a customer-count trend that consistently moved up on Tuesdays by one percentage point. To address that newly revealed issue, the managers scheduled an additional doctor for a half day on Tuesdays, a move that measurably improved performance.

The managers rely on the meeting not only to discuss issues related to running the day-to-day business, but also to work together to manage the store's culture and make tangible movement toward achieving R^2 results. They discuss the use of Focused Storytelling in the store, specifically evaluating the impact of the stories told the previous week and identifying new stories they should tell to their associates in the coming week. During their meeting, the managers seek and provide Focused Feedback and identify people they should recognize for demonstrating the Cultural Beliefs and achieving needed results.

The final opportunity seized by the Opthometrics In-Field/In-Store Integration Plan was the regular field leaders' developmental store visits. The field leaders use the Results Pyramid model to guide their developmental visits. Working from the top down on the pyramid, they begin the visit by checking results. Then they consider the prevailing beliefs and experiences in the stores and how those beliefs and experiences are affecting their results. They do all of this within the context of the seven Opthometrics Cultural Beliefs.

Integration is the very heart and soul of the developmental visit. As Lake put it, "Everything we talk about ties back to a Cultural Belief. It's rolled up in everything we do. In some cases, we have fun with it and quiz people on the seven Cultural Beliefs; we tell them we want the names and the definitions." No one says that you do not need to focus on numbers during the visit. On the contrary, they will tell you that by internalizing the Cultural Beliefs and integrating the C^2 best practices, they draft "the blueprint for achieving the numbers." Ramirez not only agrees, but he's proving it's true: His store hit plan halfway through the year!

Lake concluded, "Every other business I've been associated with has always gone on store visits and focused on actions and results, the top two levels of the Results Pyramid. We would go and dictate what we wanted people to do and expect results to change and then be sustained over time. They weren't! Now, we focus on the core beliefs, which influence the actions needed to deliver our desired results. We've seen a significant rise in joint accountability—everybody's doing whatever is needed to achieve the key results! This new culture has helped us redefine each of our job descriptions as well as our top three objectives. We don't have just one person standing in front of the customer saying, 'This is my job, and I have to do it.' Instead, whoever is available will step in to meet the need; everyone in the store thinks, 'If it affects our key results, it's my responsibility!'"

The three steps to effective integration—(1) Identify opportunities for integration into meetings, (2) Identify opportunities for integration into systems, and (3) Make your Integration Plan—will help you integrate the C^2 best practices into the day-to-day operations of your own business.

In one of our training workshops, a nuclear power plant superintendent, who had experienced the Culture of Accountability Process five years earlier at a different nuclear power plant where he had worked for twenty years, told the group about the impact of integration: "To this very day," he said, "the most common phrase you hear at meetings is 'Thanks for the feedback.'" He went on, "The one reason feedback has stayed alive after five years is simply because we successfully integrated this feedback process into our meeting structure. I hope we can do the same here, because it works." Indeed, it *does* work! Integration will sustain the C^2 culture and the R^2 results over time.

We remember a time in the early days of our consulting practice when we were meeting with Jay Graf, then the organizational leader of Cardiac Pacemakers Inc. (whose story we introduced in chapter 2). Jay asked us to tell him what we considered the most important element of the culture change process for his organization. "If I integrated only one part of the process and did that part exceptionally well, which part would you recommend I focus on for greatest impact?" Based on the needs of his organization, we knew exactly which tool he most needed to apply: Focused Feedback! We told him that his number-one priority should be quickly opening the channels of feedback throughout his management team and getting the members of his team to feel comfortable telling each other the truth about how they demonstrated the desired culture and how they needed to demonstrate it even more completely as they moved forward.

Jay took the cue and went to work on integrating Focused Feedback into his next staff meeting. He began the meeting by asking a pointed question: "What feedback have you received this week that you found valuable, and what are you doing to act on it?" While few could answer Jay's question that day, everyone was prepared to do so at the very next staff meeting. Not surprisingly, this crucial question remained an integral and regular part of the senior staff meeting agenda from that point forward.

Jay had created a truly significant experience for his team. His VPs began to believe that he was serious about the exchange of Focused Feedback and that he was going to ensure that they held themselves individually accountable to seek and receive it and then to act upon it. He clearly expected each and every VP to go out and get feedback, and not just any old feedback, but feedback around the Cultural Beliefs. Everyone soon understood that no one would get away with a comment like "I received feedback but did not hear anything that I found useful." Jay consistently created the experience for his direct reports that they were each accountable to get feedback they valued, to act on it as part of their work, and then to report to him and to their peers that they had done so.

As a result, the functional staff meetings held by these VPs ended up mirroring those held by the CEO. As a result, everyone at the company began exchanging feedback focused around the Cardiac Pacemakers Cultural Beliefs on a consistent basis, a development that quickly contributed to creating the culture the company needed to produce R^2 results.

INTEGRATION MAY MEAN ADDITIONAL IMPLEMENTATION

When making your Integration Plan, you may find that you need to begin a practice that you have not previously implemented. For instance, Universal, a client we mentioned in chapter 8, faced the challenge of installing a new culture in a unionized environment where management and the workforce had developed an adversarial relationship. Union supervisors resisted any effort by Universal's management to get them to do "extra" work, even during defined working hours. This us-versus-them mentality, shared by both sides, had erected a real barrier to shifting the culture and making the needed changes.

When Universal's leadership applied our Meeting Filter criteria during the development of their Integration Plan, they identified monthly crew meetings as a perfect forum. But when it came time to implement that idea, management discovered that the expected crew meetings were not happening anywhere in the plant. Thus, before they could proceed, Universal's management needed to correct this problem and ensure that monthly crew meetings really did occur as scheduled. This involved training crew leaders in designing agendas for the meetings and in adopting the C^2 best practices so that the crew chiefs, in turn, could train their crews. While implementing new practices should not top your own list of Integration Plan considerations, you may find that you cannot proceed without doing so.

In Universal's case, crew leaders provided the training one piece at a time in the crew meetings. The culture-change effort remained unnamed because leadership wanted to ensure that plant workers did not perceive the change effort as a new program or extra work. Crew chiefs incorporated the models and tools into their existing hour-and-a-half monthly crew meetings, introducing the best practices to the plant workforce in a way they accepted and readily embraced. In the end, this highly integrated implementation plan made a huge difference at Universal. As you may recall, the company's return on capital shot from 2 percent to 12 percent!

Another example comes from Alaris Medical Systems, the company that we introduced in chapter 1 and that enjoyed such amazing game-changing results (a 7,000 percent return on equity investment). Leaders called their culture change effort the Alaris Cultural Transition, or ACT. Early on, the Alaris manufacturing group realized that they needed to start using Focused Recognition with people on the assembly line to reinforce the C^2 culture.

One team came up with an approach they called "Caught in the ACT." The idea involved purchasing a couple of Polaroid cameras and placing them on a table near the assembly line. Anyone could take a picture of someone on the line who was visibly demonstrating the Cultural Beliefs. All of the pictures would be pinned on a bulletin board with a tag beneath each photo identifying the Cultural Belief people were demonstrating. Within a few short months, workers had plastered the wall with Polaroid pictures of their associates. To top it all off, regular staff meetings provided the opportunity to tell the stories behind the pictures and celebrate progress.

Marianne Gill, formerly on the management team of Alaris, summed up the value of integration of the C^2 best practices with a memorable story she recalled from her experience with ACT. "One of the things that I vividly remember is that we had some ongoing cross-functional sessions using Focused Feedback to build the team. We talked about being able to work together and talk to each other in a nonthreatening way, one of the tenets of the C^2 culture we were working to create. I was in Sales Support and having a really difficult experience with the Marketing Department. I felt we were in silos and were not working well together. I remember getting a Focused Recognition card from the Marketing Department, thanking me for being a good team player and for communicating well and for helping the Marketing and Sales and Customer Service teams work better together. It was the first time that Alaris ever got these siloed work teams together, and it was the first time that we were honestly able to appreciate each other. We would never have done that without some sort of training and without the application of some tools prior to that; we just didn't know how to do it."

Marianne went on to talk about her interaction with the director who had given her the recognition card. "I remember he was in Marketing and I was in Sales Support, and we struggled with getting aligned. We struggled with turf issues; we struggled with roles and responsibilities, who was going to do what, who didn't do what. His acknowledging that my leading our department in taking down barriers really assisted in forming a better functioning team." The recognition not only pleased Marianne, but it also opened the floodgates to better communication between the sales and marketing functions. The more they provided Focused Feedback to each other, and the more they talked frankly about issues, the stronger their teams became. As she put it, "It is one of the more memorable experiences of my professional career. I have to tell you, and I'm not exaggerating, the relationships between Marketing and Sales got stronger, and the culture transformed and changed."

One of the authors has experienced the value of integrating Focused Recognition in a very personal way. When each of his sons graduated from high school and looked forward to going to college, each took a job at Partners In Leadership in the shipping department. Whenever anyone received a Focused Recognition card, that person would post it on one of the walls in the department where all those in shipping could see it. These cards virtually became wallpaper. Everyone in Shipping took pride in receiving recognition for helping the business achieve its key results. The author did not know just how much the recognition meant to his sons until one of them left to pursue his education. A few weeks later, the author happened upon a drawer in which his son had safeguarded some his most favored possessions. Smack on top of the pile lay the Focused Recognition cards the young man had received while working in the shipping department. That little pile drove home the power of recognizing people for demonstrating the Cultural Beliefs that constitute the heart of the C^2 culture.

That's what integration is all about: helping people throughout the organization adopt the Cultural Beliefs and live C^2. When that happens, they demonstrate A^2 actions and achieve R^2 results. Full integration sustains the cultural change over time and should receive the undivided attention of every management team once the cultural transition gets underway.

The next and final chapter will show you how to enroll the entire organization in the effort to achieve accelerated culture change.

CHAPTER 10

Enrolling the Entire
Organization in the Change

UP TO THIS POINT in the journey through our methodology for accelerating culture change, we have shared with you the best practices associated with creating the C^2 culture, including B^2 beliefs, R^2 results, and a whole array of culture management models, tools, and skills. Now we will review the strategy we recommend for enrolling the entire organization in accelerating the culture change. We have learned that, when it comes to culture change, as with most things in life, experience truly is the best teacher, and our hard-won experience over the past twenty years has taught us a lot about what works and what does not when it comes to getting the entire organization enrolled in the process.

Recall the C^2 Best Practices Map we presented in the introduction to this book and which we present again below. The map provides an overview and summary of the best practices we have discussed and that you will need to accelerate the culture change and sustain it over time. By now it should come as no surprise that the enrollment process focuses on the R^2, which sits at the very top of the pyramid. Culture change always aims to create an environment in which people take accountability to think and act in the manner necessary to achieve desired organizational results. The bottom line is that culture produces results, and a C^2 culture produces R^2 results.

We have purposely designed the C^2 Best Practices Map in the shape of a pyramid because it reflects the fact that your R^2 results,

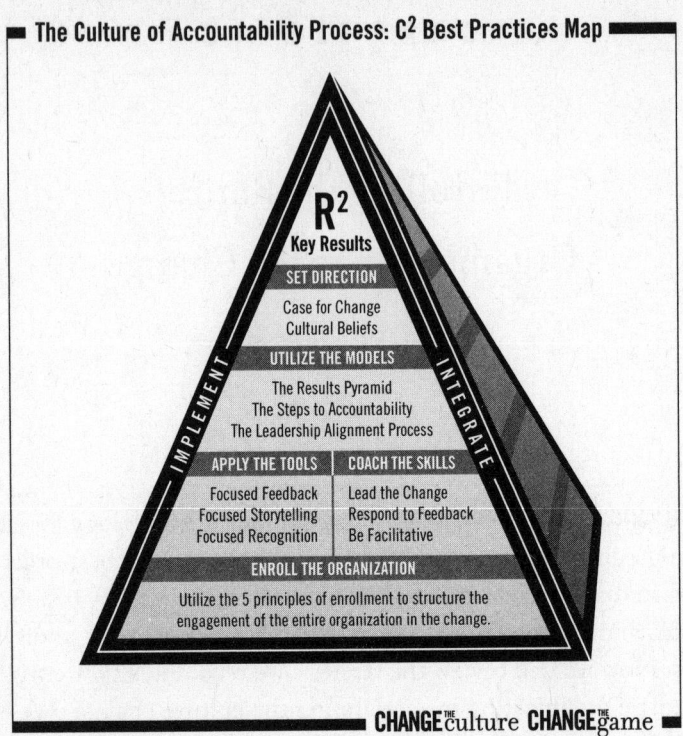

The Culture of Accountability Process: C² Best Practices Map

along with the processes, models, tools, and skills you use to manage your culture, all work together in the context of the Results Pyramid.

A McKinsey & Company Global Survey of successful transformations studied the variables of successful culture change that were identified by leaders participating in organizational transformations. We find this survey particularly interesting because it offers strong third-party validation of our approach to culture change. The McKinsey survey asked executives who had previously participated in large-scale, enterprise-wide organizational changes to identify the approaches to organizational change that they considered most successful in transforming their own organizations. We found it quite validating to note the strong correlation between what the executives said helped their transformation succeed and the C² best practices we have presented in *Change the Culture, Change the Game*. In the chart below, we have taken the comments from executives who

Executive Survey Responses about what made the transformation most successful	Corresponding C² Best Practice that ensures a successful Level 3 Transformation
"Setting aspirational clear targets."	Identifying R² key results.
"Assessing a company's present situation rigorously, identifying the current state of corporate capabilities as well as problems."	Defining the C¹ to C² shifts needed in order to achieve R².
"Explicitly identify the mind-sets that must change for the transformation to succeed… the more companies also focus on their employees' mind-sets and behavior, the more successful they will be."	Developing the Cultural Beliefs statement.
"Employee engagement as early as the planning process emerges as a key success factor," and "staff members are entirely or very able to participate in shaping the change initiatives."	Enrolling the entire organization in the change using the five principles of full enrollment to achieve employee engagement.
"Frontline staff members feel a sense of ownership to take the initiative to drive change" mostly through "leadership initiatives."	The Leadership Alignment Process and the Steps to Accountability.
"Communications… that focused solely on reasons for change" and "the organization was engaged and energized through ongoing communications and involvement."	The Case for Change and integration of the C² best practices into meetings and systems.
"Exercising strong leadership" and "Transforming leadership capacity."	The three culture change leadership skills (Lead the Change, Respond to Feedback, and "Be Facilitative) and C² Leadership Proficiency Model.
"Communications…celebrate success."	Applying Focused Feedback and Focused Recognition.
"Collaboration and co-creation" with employees.	The Culture of Accountability Process and the five principles of full enrollment and alignment.
"Our best talent was used to carry out the most critical parts of the transformation."	Creating alignment by nurturing "early adopters" and developing C² Leadership Proficiency.
"Leaders role-modeled the desired changes."	The four steps to providing E² experiences.
"The right information was available at the right time for managers to monitor the transformations progress and to troubleshoot where required."	Integration Plans with C² best practices process controls to maintain alignment.
"Define targets, role, and structure of the transformation clearly."	The C² Best Practices Map.

participated in the survey and listed them on the left side, with the corresponding C^2 best practice on the right.

Notice that when the executives responding to the McKinsey survey described what mattered most in their experience with successful organizational transformation, they identified the C^2 best practices to a tee. No surprise there. Anyone interested in accelerating culture change can rest assured that doing the right things, the things we identify as the C^2 best practices, will yield real Level Three transformational change.

In order to achieve this transformational change, you will need to adopt the right process for enrolling everyone in the organization in the change effort. Five principles should guide you as you engineer and build full employee engagement in the change:

The Five Principles of Full Enrollment

1. Start with *accountability*.

2. Get people ready for the change.

3. Begin with the relative top and intact teams.

4. Establish a process control and keep it honest.

5. Design for maximum involvement and creativity.

Relying on these five principles to guide the enrollment process will give you the structure you need to engage everyone in the organization and help speed your journey to C^2. Over the past two decades, we have experienced the strategic power of each of these principles as we have worked to help clients achieve game-changing results by enrolling their entire organizations in the process of creating and sustaining needed changes in their cultures.

Principle No. 1:
Start with Accountability

The first of the five principles is plain and simple: Start with accountability. You will recall from chapter 2 our strong belief, based on substantial experience, that accountability for R^2 should always begin with clearly defined results. Always! Kimberly-Clark Health Care (KCHC), one of our clients, provides us with another clear example of just how fundamental this concept is to both successful culture change and the achievement of R^2.

Several years ago KCHC was a budding star in the overall Kimberly-Clark business portfolio. Projected high sales and profit-growth rates, a function of organic business growth in the North American and international markets, coupled with plans for selected acquisitions in related businesses, painted a bright picture. However, the performance of the past year had not lived up to the advanced billing. With two months remaining in the year, the organization would not meet budgeted targets for net sales and operating profit for the second straight year. To make matters worse, the forecast for the coming year looked even more discouraging, with a relatively flat sales projection and continued erosion in profit, all caused by rising input costs and an increasingly competitive marketplace.

With this picture as the backdrop, we began assisting Joanne Bauer, the KCHC president, with the culture change process. At the very beginning of the culture change effort, we asked Joanne to define the top three R^2 results KCHC was accountable to deliver. After some very productive dialogue, her team narrowed their focus from seventeen different results to just three, which they called "the Big Three." These results targeted net sales, operating profit, and gross margin. Defining the Big Three was the first crucial step toward creating accountability to deliver their desired R^2 results.

According to Jeff Schneider, director of Strategic Business and Resource Planning, talk around the Big Three spread through the entire organization like wildfire, and people discussed them in every meeting they attended. In fact, the same sort of talk began showing up everywhere, as people realized just how serious the senior leaders were about achieving the Big Three, which people saw printed on binders and notebooks and posted on walls throughout the organization. The Big Three even appeared on labels affixed to packages in intracompany mail.

With this clear focus, people at every level of KCHC asked themselves, "What else can I do?" to achieve the R^2 results. The impact was nothing short of astounding. Net sales exceeded prior year sales by 12 percent and budget by 10 percent. Operating profit surpassed the prior year by 65 percent and budget by 19 percent. On top of all of this, KCHC announced the acquisition of two sought-after technologies for their portfolio of medical device offerings.

In chapter 1 we introduced you to the Steps to Accountability model and showed you what it means to operate Above the Line, to See It, Own It, Solve It, and Do It.

Just as it did at KCHC, building on the foundation of greater personal accountability always speeds up culture change and, for that matter, any other organizational endeavor. With it, people internalize the change, asking what else they can do to demonstrate the Cultural Beliefs and implement the C^2 best practices. Without it, people externalize the change and fall Below the Line, excusing and justifying their lack of participation in the change process. Below the Line, people ignore the change effort or flat-out deny that it involves them. They avoid any additional work because it's not their job. They blame others for a lack of progress towards R^2 results. In an attempt to get off the hook, they express confusion about how to implement the culture or about what the Cultural Beliefs really mean. Confusion is the great defender of the status quo; how can you possibly expect anything from the "confused"? Even worse, confusion leads to a "then just tell me what to do" attitude, in which all of the accountability shifts from the person who is actually responsible to the person who falls into the trap of doing the telling.

Below the Line, people spend time covering their tails, just in case the culture change effort gets derailed and they need to explain away their involvement and try to justify a lack of progress. Still,

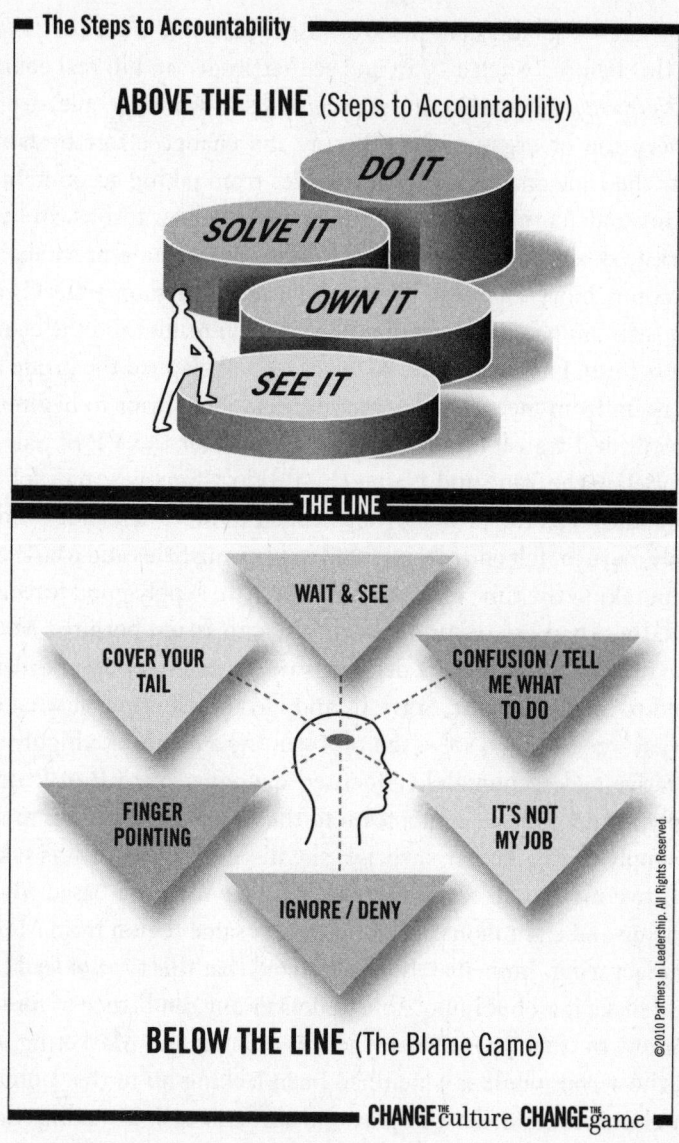

The Steps to Accountability

ABOVE THE LINE (Steps to Accountability)

DO IT

SOLVE IT

OWN IT

SEE IT

THE LINE

WAIT & SEE

COVER YOUR TAIL

CONFUSION / TELL ME WHAT TO DO

FINGER POINTING

IT'S NOT MY JOB

IGNORE / DENY

BELOW THE LINE (The Blame Game)

CHANGE the culture CHANGE the game

in our estimation, the greatest Below the Line threat to the progress of any culture change is a "wait and see" attitude. In this state of mind, people simply wait and see if anything at all is going to happen, pretending they are enrolled in the change process, when all along they do nothing meaningful to move it forward. They say things like "This too shall pass" or "Let's just wait it out" or "We've seen this before." Such a "wait and see" attitude can kill real change.

We have witnessed countless scenarios in which people, even at the very top of organizations, betray the change effort by falling Below the Line and excusing themselves from taking accountability to think and act in the manner necessary to deliver results. In sharp contrast, two senior executives at KCHC overcame a previous lack of accountability and rose Above the Line to demonstrate C^2 and the positive impact that accountability has on results and the change process itself. For some time, back orders had plagued the group and kept them from meeting customer expectations. Prior to beginning their cultural transition, it was quite natural for the VP of Sales to drop Below the Line and blame the Product Supply group for not giving sales reps the product they needed to meet demand. Product Supply, in turn, felt entirely justified in blaming Sales and Marketing for not taking the time to make it a priority to supply good forecasts.

Rather than let this problem continue to fester, both the Manufacturing and Sales leaders demonstrated accountability and determined to See It, Own It, Solve It, and Do It by looking at what else they each could do to solve the problem. As a result of a highly collaborative and accountability-focused dialogue, the VP of Product Supply, Gail Ciccione, sent a team to the Asia Pacific Region to map the supply chain. To her surprise, she discovered that it was taking up to five months to service Asia Pacific from China-based Manufacturing and eight months to service that same region from Mexico Manufacturing. Immediately, she realized that this type of lead time would make it all but impossible to deliver any semblance of forecast accuracy. In turn, John Amat, the VP of Sales and Marketing, created the accountability, which had been lacking up to that point, to gain clarity around the complex and difficult task of nailing down the demand forecast. In this instance, they modeled an important C^2 behavior by taking accountability and providing an example of what it looks like to internalize and personalize the needed change.

At the next global leadership meeting with the top fifty KCHC leaders, these VPs created an accountability experience for the entire team. Gail reinforced her commitment to customer satisfaction and improving the supply chain, and John reinforced his commitment to accurate forecasting as a key driver in customer satisfaction. Sales and Manufacturing emphasized the Cultural Beliefs by showing total solidarity in their joint accountability to get Above the Line and take on and solve a problem that crossed organizational boundaries.

The VPs for both Sales and Manufacturing committed to take accountability to work together to simplify the supply chain and improve demand forecast accuracy. They created an experience that suggested to others that leaders were serious about change at KCHC. This experience became a story that has been retold by others to reinforce the cultural direction and the need to get on board. The moral of the story? Start with accountability. Without it you will not move the organization forward and enroll people in providing the effort needed to change your culture.

Principle No. 2:
Get People Ready for the Change

The second principle of enrollment is getting people ready to change. Changing culture has never been, nor will it ever be, a spectator sport. Your culture will not change unless you get everyone in the organization enrolled in making the change happen. But most of us can acknowledge, based on life's experiences, that people do not readily sign on to change anything until they are ready to change.

This fact was brought home to one of the authors in a striking way. Some years ago, his two eldest teenage daughters shared the downstairs bedroom. Whenever he returned home, he would typically enter through the front door, look to the left at their bedroom, wince at what looked like the aftermath of a tornado, then immediately shut their door. How could his girls live with such a mess? He and his wife talked a lot about how to motivate a change in their behavior. They discussed the problem with their daughters, trying to impress upon them the importance of a tidy room. To get them to comply with the desired change, they came up with any number of creative incentives, all to no avail.

They even cleaned the room themselves one Friday night while the girls were away from home, piling everything that had been strewn on the floor into large trash bags they stashed in the attic. They vacuumed and dusted. They polished the mirror. When they finished, several hours later, they turned on soft lights and music, then waited for the girls to return. Later that night, the girls came home to find their parents resting on their perfectly made beds. Wow! They loved the sight of their neat, clean room and thanked their parents profusely. But it took little time for the tornado to strike again.

One evening, as the family arrived home after an activity, they found a police car parked in their driveway. Both doors of the police car stood open, as did the front door to their home. Climbing out of their van, the family saw a policeman striding down the walk to meet them. Astonished, they immediately asked, "What's going on?" The officer responded, "Your house alarm went off while you were gone. When we arrived, the alarm was still sounding, so we searched your house. I'm sorry to inform you that your house has been burglarized, and that this job was done by a professional!"

The father immediately asked the officer what made him believe that. "Oh," replied the officer, "They must have known what they were looking for. Everything in the house is fine except the downstairs bedroom. That's been torn apart. Everything in the drawers was dumped on the floor. The room is a disaster." Can you imagine the look on the faces of the father's two eldest daughters standing beside him in the driveway? He couldn't resist turning around and asking them if they wanted to offer some other explanation for why their room was such a mess. They sheepishly explained to the officer that, in reality, *they* were the "professionals" who had done the job.

Clearly, before that night, the author's daughters were not ready to make the change their parents desired. They did not Own It; the parents did! That's how it always goes when people are not ready to change: Their efforts to make the change fall far short of expectations and usually only serve to disappoint all concerned.

Whether it be at home or at work, in order to get someone ready to own the change, you must first help them see why the change is needed, so that they develop some level of agreement with the change. Second, you must get them involved in making the change happen. By gaining both their agreement and their involvement in the culture change, you can secure people's personal ownership for making that change happen.

We have captured this idea in what we call the Levels of Ownership model, which shows the four different levels at which people can own the culture change process.

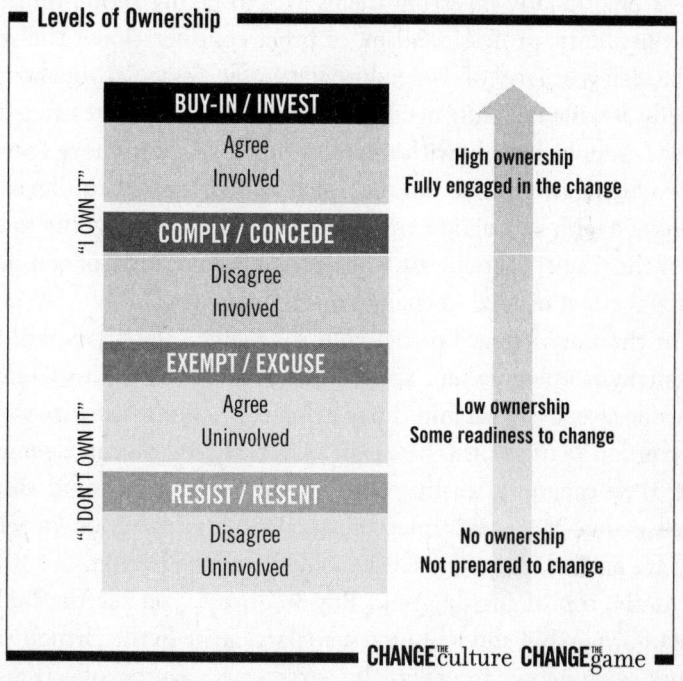

At the lowest level, where people disagree with and are uninvolved in the change effort, you find no ownership at all. People at this level resist the change effort and resent the fact that they are being asked to do it. They have committed neither their minds nor their hearts to the endeavor. Entrenched in the old C^1 culture, they do not recognize any need to change.

At the next level up, Exempt/Excuse, people are essentially saying, "I don't Own It." They agree intellectually but remain uninvolved emotionally. Either they will hold themselves exempt because they're "too busy," or they'll make excuses because they "can't get to it." People at this level of ownership will not move forward even though they may find changing the culture a good idea. At this level, they believe the culture change may apply to everyone else, but not to them. They will offer any number of excuses for why they are, in their own minds, exempt from the undertaking.

Moving up to the next level, Comply/Concede, you see people intellectually disagreeing with some aspect of the change but nevertheless emotionally investing themselves in taking action on it due to loyalty, duty, professionalism, or other considerations. You've no doubt seen that level of ownership. It's not necessarily bad, and realistically, it's all you really need in certain situations. Quite often people who simply comply with requests and concede to move forward do produce solid results. On the other hand, people at this level can be aligned with a direction and still lack what it's really going to take to get the result, particularly when it requires the kind of consistent personal effort needed to change the culture.

In the initial stages of the culture change effort, you will find that many people, perhaps the majority, will reside at this Comply/Concede level of ownership. They exhibit A^2 actions, but with wavering commitment. At the first sign of backsliding on management's part, they can quite easily revert to the C^1 way of doing things. Because they feel some uncertainty about the direction in which they are headed, they may fairly easily disengage from it.

At the top of the diagram, Buy-In/Invest, you see the highest level of ownership and willingness to participate in the change. This occurs when people intellectually agree with a course of action and emotionally commit themselves to it. Both their minds and hearts are engaged, and they are thoroughly invested and vigorously involved. These people are probably already demonstrating C^2 behavior. They find it easy to "sign up" and readily see the advantages that the company will gain by shifting the culture.

Getting people to Buy-In/Invest personally in the culture change process is one of management's key tasks and greatest challenges. You should expend every effort to get people ready for the change by persuading and convincing them of the merits of the change and by getting them involved in the process. Each step of the enrollment process should be designed to facilitate these two criteria: agreement and involvement. When you do it this way, you simultaneously prepare people for the change and enroll them in the process of the change itself.

Principle No. 3:
Begin with the Relative Top and Intact Teams

Successful culture change must always start at the top or "relative top" of the organization. By *relative top*, we mean that, regardless of where you initiate the culture change process, in a team, a division, a function, a subsidiary, a country affiliate, or the entire organization, you must begin the process at the top of that organization to be most effective. Because culture change is leader-led, the leader of the organization must get immersed in leading the change and work hard to enroll the maximum number of people and implement the change in a lasting way.

Initiating culture change without involving the relative top can be disastrous. When the leader at the relative top does not support and promote the new culture, that leader will continually create E^1 experiences that hinder the adoption of C^2. As we have already discussed, every leader possesses the position and power to create memorable experiences that signal to everyone else in the organization whether or not they should take the change process seriously. By not creating E^2 experiences, a leader actually creates resistance to change. Attempting culture change in any group without the buy-in of the leader at the relative top throws that group out of alignment and, essentially, dooms the effort.

Quite frequently, we assist clients who wish to initiate a culture change effort that is not an enterprise-wide undertaking. Such a culture change may take place at a division, department, or functional level. Almost always, the process migrates upward in time to involve the entire organization. Regardless of where the process starts, the leader of that organization must lead the change.

As you work with the relative top, you also need to include intact teams. Culture change begins in the context of intact teams. Establishing peer-to-peer accountability within these teams is essential to building the right foundation for the culture change effort. We always recommend that you work with teams that already exist within the organization, rather than with teams put together expressly for the purpose of culture change. While the latter may make sense at some point in the process, such groupings work best after intact teams have spent time working together on the culture.

An intact team is any group of people who work together regularly and share peer-to-peer accountability to accomplish some objective. Culture change occurs most surely and quickly when you work with such teams, because each team already has a culture that it carries into any endeavor it tackles. Culture change is a team sport. The fastest and most effective method for changing the way an organization thinks and acts is to focus on getting intact teams to help each other live C^2. When they do that, they use their everyday work experience as a vehicle for culture change.

While cross-functional work sessions on the culture are an important part of a cultural transition, such efforts must occur at the right time. When intact teams have practiced using the Culture Management Tools and skills, they can then apply those methods to help make the culture change happen between themselves and other organizations. This essential step does need to occur, but you should probably not attempt it until intact teams have embraced the change fully.

Principle No. 4:
Establish a Process Control and Keep It Honest

Every process needs a process control, or it will succumb to the forces of entropy and tend toward chaos over time. This particularly holds true with culture change, because the change depends so much on people's choosing to change their behavior, determining to form new habits, and adopting new mind-sets. Culture changes one person at a time, both when you are trying to get people to adopt the new culture and when you are helping them abandon the natural tendency to sustain the old culture. To be most effective, you should adopt agreed-upon process controls at both the individual and team level.

Important process controls are formed as you enroll others in the culture change process and as they take personal accountability to live the Cultural Beliefs. When this happens, you create a self-governing process control throughout the organization. You know this is working when you frequently hear people saying, "Thanks for the feedback," "That's not a belief I want you to hold," "We need to move Above the Line," "What else can I do?" "Here's what 'Speak Up' (one of your Cultural Beliefs) looks like to me," and "the key results." As you integrate the Culture Management Tools and C^2 best practices, people will use the language of Focused Feedback, Focused Storytelling, and Focused Recognition to help the process stay on track. When the language of the models and tools becomes a part of the way people do things, it acts as a real-time, self-governing process control, probably the most powerful monitor of implementation you can create.

Another important process control involves tracking the progress of the organization toward achieving R^2. While you may find it fairly easy to track progress toward desired R^2 results, you should make certain that you are communicating that progress widely throughout the organization. Although a more anecdotal measure, you should also track whether people are thinking and acting differently as you work to create C^2. To do this, some of our clients like to use online organizational assessments to measure progress. Establishing a baseline at the beginning of the process and then using checkpoints to measure progress along the way can give you a good qualitative key indicator of what people are seeing with respect to desired changes. You should particularly monitor progress toward living the Cultural Beliefs. When culture really does change, everyone knows it and can readily identify that it is occurring.

However, as you plan how you will involve everyone in the organization, you should identify milestones that will reflect progress in both implementing and integrating the change. These milestones should include deadlines by which certain activities should take place, including follow-up on specific Integration Plans developed by the team.

Some of the more common process controls include:

- Embedding the language of the tools and models.

- Tracking progress toward R^2 results.

- Using online assessment tools to capture perceptions of progress toward adopting the Cultural Beliefs.

- Establishing milestones for process implementation and integration.

- Ensuring follow-up and reporting on Integration Plans.

A word of caution: You do not want to make the mistake of over-structuring the process of enrolling the organization in the change effort. Some well-intentioned senior leaders try to plan every inch of the journey to C^2, relying too much on process, rather than people, to make the necessary changes. This overly strong focus on actions and process can take their eyes off the lower levels of the Results Pyramid, Experiences and Beliefs. As we have mentioned before, leaders often prefer working with the more concrete top of the pyramid, with Actions and Results. We've seen far too many cases in which leaders have unintentionally processed all of the life out of their culture change efforts, to the point that their overly prescriptive and structured approach to the undertaking deteriorates into little more than a "check the box" activity. Without knowing it, they end up choking off individual initiative, creativity, and leadership.

The Results Pyramid model, the basis for our culture change process, suggests a principle-centered, rather than a process-centered, approach. Note the difference:

Process: A continuous action or operation, taking place in a definitive manner and requiring the response or participation of others.

Principle: A personal or specific basis of conduct; a fundamental truth from which action is derived.

A principle-based approach allows correct principles, or B^2 beliefs, to guide people to self-select the A^2 actions they need to take, rather than waiting to be told exactly what to do. While you always want to strike the right balance between process and principle, when it comes to culture change, you will usually find that *a principle-driven and process-supported approach* works best.

When it comes to implementing and integrating the change

effort, one thing the enrollment process must be designed to do is help everyone avoid the trap of just "going through the motions." It should keep everyone honest in the way they apply the Culture Management Tools and C^2 best practices. If people begin to mistake activity for results, or motion for action, then the change process will become stalled, even though it may appear that everything is right on track.

For example, the Northeast management team at "HGS" challenged the quality of their storytelling early on. The organization was deeply committed to the cultural transition, but many people felt that the stories making the rounds of the organization celebrated ordinary things that had always occurred, rather than new behavior that really illustrated the Cultural Beliefs. Some team members challenged this perspective, insisting that they ought to celebrate the very act of telling stories, because that was a new activity for all of them. Others worried that if they required that stories meet too high a standard, they would actually end up lengthening the ramp-up time and overcomplicating the process.

The HGS management team debated how they could keep themselves honest in the process and ensure that the right sort of Focused Storytelling was driving the desired C^2 beliefs. They agreed not only to tell the stories, but also to give feedback on every story in order to determine whether or not the story described how someone had changed a C^1 belief and manifested a C^2 belief. The feedback would reinforce the use of the story, suggest that the story stop being told, or prompt that it be reframed in a way that better reinforced the new culture. As a result of people keeping one another honest in their efforts to tell stories that reflected and reinforced the move toward C^2, Focused Storytelling took on a whole new life in HGS's culture change process.

Principle No. 5:
Design for Maximum Involvement and Creativity

Culture change is a highly collaborative effort and requires the engagement of everyone at every level as co-creators of the culture.

You must design the enrollment to achieve this maximum involvement and creativity from everyone in the organization. You can't just "roll out" a cultural transition to all employees. Rather, you must enroll and engage everyone in the change effort. We have seen a lot of companies try to roll out new programs, but we have yet to see such a rollout fully engage people in the process. The stated objectives of a rollout often target little more than getting everyone trained by a certain date. That focus on the activity does not generate ownership. Incapable of instilling personal investment throughout the organization, such rollouts get rolled back when it becomes clear that they are not working. At other times, they are simply replaced by a new "flavor of the month" rollout.

To enroll everyone in the culture change requires structuring specific experiences that produce engagement. First, use the Leadership Alignment model to ensure participation in the implementation of the C^2 best practices. That will help you get the right people involved at the right time in each aspect of planning the engagement process. Also, the formation of the Cultural Beliefs statement can facilitate collaboration beyond the executive team. When dealing with large divisions, country affiliates, or far-flung geographical sites, you might find good reasons for them to formulate a Cultural Beliefs statement unique to each.

We also recommend utilizing people from throughout the organization to help facilitate the training meetings used to introduce the Cultural Beliefs. While you always employ a leader-led approach, people at all levels of the organization can cofacilitate the enrollment process as it cascades to include everyone. Remember, you want to make every step of the engagement as facilitative as possible. For example, when you introduce the Cultural Beliefs statement, you should do it in a highly engaging and participative way that mimics the same experience created for the senior team, using a scaled-down version that stimulates everyone in the organization to arrive at the same general conclusions in a very participative way.

You can take it as one sure sign that you have enrolled the entire organization and that people are engaged when you start hearing a lot of ideas about how to change the culture. For instance, team members in one Finance Department started an Oz Hour (named after *The Oz Principle*, our first book on accountability, which introduced the Steps to Accountability). The Oz Hour concentrated on Focused Recognition, Focused Storytelling, and Focused Feedback. By shining a bright light on their Cultural Beliefs, the department leaders ignited a lot of new ideas about promoting the culture change.

Another team started Breaking-News Huddles; anyone in the organization could call an ad hoc meeting at any time. The huddles allowed people to share important and relevant news the minute it popped up. That way people could stay current regarding both progress made and progress needed around their key R^2 results. Yet another company started using the Cultural Beliefs in the application and interview process for new hires. A letter to the prospective employee explained their Cultural Beliefs around accountability:

> "If you can commit to and live with these principles, then you're the type of person who will be successful and help our company thrive. If you feel that this level of accountability is not right for you, that you're not willing or able to offer feedback, not willing to take the necessary steps to do what you will say you will do and be accountable for your actions, then we are not the employer for you. We understand that not every person is ready for this level of commitment, and we appreciate the honesty of those who decide this is not the place for them."

This letter represented one of the first E^2 cultural experiences the company wanted to create and sustain. Ideas like these come from the creative force of fully engaged employees who own the culture change and are working hard to make it happen.

To put a fine point on the idea of designing for maximum involvement and creativity, we'd like to share the story of TransEnterix, a client that integrated the Cultural Beliefs and C^2 best practices into its recruiting strategy. TransEnterix, a start-up medical device company specializing in innovative, minimally invasive surgical devices, put together a great management team, received regulatory approval in record time in the worst economy in eighty years, and raised $76 million before it sold its first product, raising the bar for pre-revenue capital raised. TransEnterix reached all of their other milestones, including the first product launch, on time or ahead of schedule. In less than two and a half years, they launched twelve products into the $10 billion general surgery market. When commenting on their early success, Todd M. Pope, president and CEO, said, "A lot of what we have achieved can be attributed to what we have done with our Cultural Beliefs." While true for any business, the need for talent escalates exponentially in a small, young company. Success depends primarily on recruiting the right talent and putting that talent in the right positions at the right time. Todd told us how important it has been, while recruiting for TransEnterix, to emphasize the corporate culture when talking to prospects. While you can easily communicate facts and details about the TransEnterix business, none of that expresses what truly differentiates the company from other organizations: its culture! The leaders actually walk the prospective hire through the Cultural Beliefs, which they can recite from memory. They let the recruit know exactly why they chose that statement and then take time to provide some real-world examples of how people exemplify that statement at TransEnterix, day in and day out.

What they do next takes confidence. They encourage all potential recruits to ask anyone they meet about the TransEnterix Cultural Beliefs, what they are, the impact they have, and how employees are living them. They encourage the prospects to talk to people about the recognition cards posted on the walls. They confidently ask the potential new recruit to observe the culture at work and note what they see.

When asked about this approach, Todd stated, "It has made a huge impact. I think it's a differentiator for us." He continued, "When recruits feel the kind of culture that we are building, as it is communicated by the stories our people tell them, they want to be a part of that. Most recruits tell us that the culture we are building at TransEnterix was 'the single biggest determinant for them to come and join our company.' Just recently we had a family picnic for the company, and I can't tell you how many people told me that the reason their spouses were most excited about joining this company was what they had heard about the culture!"

Creating maximum involvement by thoughtfully planning to enroll everyone in the organization in the change effort will foster creativity throughout the organization around implementing and integrating the cultural transition. That creativity will accelerate the adoption of the B^2 beliefs and the overall culture change.

FINAL THOUGHTS

As we have shown throughout this book, culture change can provide the differentiator that brings competitive advantage and game changing results to any business. In today's competitive environment and challenging economy, performance improvements grow ever harder to achieve, and game changers become more important every day. Real game changers take more than a superb business strategy, a huge capital investment, or a better mousetrap. They can be hard to find.

"It advanced the technology, but it's not a game changer."

Certainly the development of the club made a difference back in the day. However, it was an incremental improvement, a Level Two transitional change. True game changers don't come easily. No matter how much time you spend optimizing performance with incremental improvements, they will take you only so far.

When the business model demands R^2 results, the game is no longer just about optimizing current performance; it's about transforming organizational results. Game changing, transformational results can and do come from well-executed culture changing initiatives. When you change the culture, you change the game, and with that new game comes the desired results that shape and define success for your organization. We have confidence in this process. It works!

When you approach culture in the manner we describe throughout this book, culture change raises the spirit of the entire organization and energizes everyone involved to make the change successful. With the combination of accountability and the application of the C^2 best practices, you will accelerate the change in your culture and achieve the results you seek.

We began our exploration of culture by proposing "Either you will manage your culture, or it will manage you." By now, this statement should have taken on a whole new meaning for you. We know that as you take accountability for your culture and manage it well, you will produce amazing results that will greatly benefit yourself, the people you work with, your entire organization, and, most important, your customers. Change the culture, and you will change the game!

A World of FREE Resources

join THE PARTNERS IN LEADERSHIP ACCOUNTABILITY community®

To access the following resources,
visit www.ChangeTheCultureChangeTheGame.com/resources

Live Author Webinars - Participate in the FREE online discussions with the *New York Times* bestselling authors on workplace accountability.

Accountability Assessments - Take complimentary online individual self-assessments or team assessments to find out how well you or your organization practices the principles of results-focused accountability.

Success Stories - Read and watch the people who have experienced Accountability Training talk about the ROI impact it brings to the bottom line in three areas: increasing revenues and profitability, reducing costs, and implementing key initiatives.

White Papers - Watch video segments of Partners In Leadership Executive Facilitators in action as they present the Accountability Training.

Executive Book Summaries - Read Soundview's distillation of the three *New York Times* bestsellers—handy also as a quick reference tool for those who have already read the books.

Author Articles And Interviews - Receive unlimited access to a collection of articles written by *New York Times* bestselling authors Roger Connors and Tom Smith, the worldwide experts on workplace accountability.

Workshop Videos - Curious what the training is like? We have provided a few samples of some of our training sessions to give you an idea of what we have to offer. They're good online, they're life changing in person.

Executive Video References - One of the best ways to understand the value of Accountability Training is to hear from the people and companies that have experienced its impact.

Author Audio Interviews - Listen to the *New York Times* bestselling authors speak about the powerful groundbreaking principles of accountability discussed in their Oz Series books.

The Oz Principle Blog - Continue the accountability conversation by reading the *New York Times* bestselling author's weekly commentary about applying accountability in the workplace.

www.ChangeTheCultureChangeTheGame.com or www.3CGbook.com

Partners In Leadership®
THE ACCOUNTABILITY TRAINING
& CONSULTING COMPANY

27555 Ynez Road, Suite 300 • Temecula, CA 92591
(800) 504-6070

Index

Above the Line actions, 20–23, 149–50, 156, 164, 198–201, 207

accountablity, 61–62

creation of, 5, 15, 39, 46, 50, 56, 65, 197, 200

effectiveness of, 16, 28

importance of, 2, 20, 28, 44, 49–53, 201

joint, 40–42, 187, 201

lack of, 18, 40, 80, 83, 200

and organizational enrollment, 196–201

peer-to-peer, 205–6

and results, 11, 43–44, 46, 147, 193, 214

steps to, 20–23, 185–87, 195, 198–200, 211

See also Culture of Accountability Process

accountability, individual, 1–3, 18, 20–21, 23, 28, 46, 51, 66, 83–84, 119, 147, 184–85, 198

accountability, organizational, 1–3, 11, 20–23, 37, 44, 46, 51–53, 165, 187, 196–201

actions, current, 24, 27, 51–52, 54–55, 58–62, 65–66, 77, 161

actions, desired

and Culture Management Tools, 137, 139, 145, 149–50

demonstration of, 191, 204

guided by beliefs, 77–78, 81–84, 86–87, 184, 208

and Results Pyramid, 24–28, 42

shifting to, 51–52, 58–63, 65–66

successful execution of, 56–57, 67

that produce results, 18, 41–42, 49–52, 87, 124

airline industry, 94

Alaris Medical Systems, 7–15, 28, 189–91

alignment, 48, 106

achievement of, 41–42, 81, 117, 120, 130–33, 156

and the Case for Change, 122–24, 130, 132, 158–59

definition of, 114–15

forces threatening it, 120–22, 154

importance of, 113–14, 132

lack of, 41, 80, 114, 121–22, 166, 180, 205

and leadership skills, 162, 168, 195, 205

maintaining of, 115–16, 118, 120, 131–32

model developed for, 124–32

Amat, John, 200–201

Amy's Ice Creams, 89–91

Apple, 67–68

automobile industry, 17–18, 180–81

Bauer, Joanne, 197

behavior, rewarding of, 55–56

belief bias, 72, 95, 98, 104, 161

beliefs, current, 24, 75, 81
  and experiences, 91–93
  identification of, 76, 162–63
  negative aspects of, 76–79, 121
  remaining stuck in, 71–72, 93,
    104, 144
  shifting away from, 67–68, 70, 78–79,
    108, 130, 161
beliefs, desired, 76, 168, 180, 213
  and actions, 56, 62, 66–67, 71, 77–78,
    81, 184, 208
  creation of, 66, 91, 93–94, 106–7
  and Cultural Beliefs statement,
    82–84, 109
  and experiences, 91–95, 100–109
  and Focused Feedback, 137, 140–41
  and Focused Storytelling, 144–45
  fostering of, 28, 88–89, 100–101,
    105, 108
  and leadership skills, 160, 163–68
  need for, 3, 18, 72
  and Results Pyramid, 24, 26–27, 62,
    67, 69, 109
  shifting to, 68, 70, 72, 79, 86–88, 99,
    124
  that produces results, 25, 27, 41–42,
    66, 76, 78, 81, 118
Below the Line actions, 20–21, 31, 52,
  62, 147, 164, 198–200
blame game, 20–21, 23, 106, 198–99
Boston Scientific, 47, 118
Brinker International, 133–35
Brooks, Doug, 134
business environment changes, 24,
  35–36, 49–50, 86, 106

Cardiac Pacemakers Inc. (CPI), 44–47,
  116, 120, 187–88
Cardiac Rhythm Management Group
  (CRM), 116–20
Cardinal Health, 8, 15
Case for Change, 122–24, 130, 132,
  156, 158–59, 182, 195
Case, John, 90
Chamberlain, Joshua Lawrence, 33–34
Chevron Corporation, 180–81
Churchill, Winston, 58, 151
Ciccione, Gail, 200–201

client examples / stories, 2–3, 11, 15,
  111. See also specific companies;
  specific industries
collaborative effort, 65, 107–8, 135,
  165, 169, 190, 209–10
communication / dialogue, 24, 160, 207
  and accountability, 2, 22, 46, 200
  and alignment, 48, 125, 127–28,
    130–31
  and the Case for Change, 123–24
  and Cultural Beliefs statements, 84
  facilitative, 169–72
  and Methodology for Changing
    Beliefs, 162, 164, 166–68
  and results, 32, 34, 48, 119, 156, 197
  See also meetings
competitive advantage, 4, 7, 12, 16, 18,
  20, 28, 34, 48, 68, 117–18, 213
Cultural Beliefs, 75–84, 160–61, 168,
  206–8
  and alignment, 113–15, 122, 132
  and Culture Management Tools,
    136–41, 144–49
  demonstration of, 165, 184–85,
    190–91, 198, 209
  essential for culture change, 136, 144
  and Focused Feedback, 138–41, 188
  implementation of, 175, 180
  integration of, 113, 133
  shifts in, 118–19
Cultural Beliefs statement, 76, 81–84,
  87, 107–9, 125–27, 129–30, 136–
  37, 156, 159–60, 177, 182, 186–87,
  195, 210–12
Cultural Beliefs titles, 136–37, 144
Cultural Transition Process, 157, 189,
  206
  and alignment, 127–28, 131–32
  commitment to, 209
  early stages of, 125–26
  integration of, 176–77, 181, 191
  and leadership skills, 153–55, 160–61,
    165, 172–73
Culture Best Practices, 171–72
  chart for, 155–56
  identification of, 196
  implementation of, 173–77, 198,
    209–10, 214

integration of, 173–91, 195, 207
map for, 3–4, 193–95
culture, 116, 118
culture change
    central aspects of, 15–16, 104
    four ways to promote it, 129
    implementation of, 10, 35, 39, 41,
        45–46, 48, 76–77, 173, 205, 207–9,
        213
    importance of, 17, 28
    ownership of, 203–5
    three levels of, 53–54, 62–63
culture, current, 78, 91, 166
    boss-centered, 158, 180–81
    deconstruction of, 27, 76–77, 96, 125
    employee centered, 181
    reinforcement of, 99–100, 102
    remaining stuck in, 39–40, 63, 72,
        95, 133, 135, 138, 144, 154,
        203–4, 206
    returning to, 120–21
    shifting away from, 37, 41, 62, 89,
        99, 109, 113–14, 134–35, 147, 155,
        195, 209
    strengths of, 27, 61
    weaknesses of, 27, 64
    won't produce results, 24–25,
        34, 81
culture, desired, 41, 132, 181, 193
    accelerating achievement of, 72, 106
    and actions, 62, 65
    creation of, 3, 27, 42, 44, 52, 56, 61,
        103, 134–35, 137–38, 143–44, 148,
        152, 190, 207
    crucial elements of, 78, 83, 191
    and Cultural Beliefs statement, 81,
        83–84, 87
    and Culture Management Tools, 133,
        144–47
    defining of, 124, 137
    demonstration of, 200, 204
    employee centered, 158, 169
    and experiences, 99, 103, 108–9
    and leadership skills, 153–56,
        165, 168
    reinforcement of, 160, 189
    shifting to, 27, 37, 66, 75–76, 89,
        113–14, 128, 154–55,

195–96, 209. See also Culture
    Best Practices
culture management, 3, 11, 16–18,
    27–28, 42, 48, 62, 76, 90, 106, 113,
    116, 118, 151, 186, 194
Culture Management Tools, 113,
    118, 129, 153, 176, 183–85, 189,
    206–7. See also Focused Feedback;
    Focused Recognition; Focused
    Storytelling
Culture of Accountability, 87,
    89, 92–93, 111, 135. See also
    accountability
Culture of Accountability Process,
    81, 115–16, 126, 128, 153, 155,
    158, 177, 187, 195. See also
    accountability
customer satisfaction, 79–82, 85–87,
    90, 95–97, 119, 146–47, 169, 184,
    200–201

Deseret Book shop, 177

employees, 7, 13, 56, 109, 153
    and beliefs, 85–86
    commitment of, 28, 32
    and creating culture, desired,
        151, 158–59
    and culture change, 49, 50, 106
    and decision making, 124
    "go-to," 9–10, 12, 15, 18
    and Methodology for Changing
        Beliefs, 162
    and performance, 15, 30
    and shifts in action, 66
    and shifts in thinking, 54
engagement, 48, 50–52, 65–66,
    98, 159, 169–72, 195–96, 203–4,
    209–11
experiences, 92, 130, 154, 205
    creation of, 18, 28, 123, 153, 156,
        161, 163–64, 188, 211
    four steps to, 101–6, 195
    interpretation of, 92–95, 98–99, 102,
        104–5
    and leadership skills, 161, 163–65,
        167–68, 188, 205
    and management teams, 106–9

experiences (*cont.*)
  and Results Pyramid, 24–28, 42, 56
  types of, 93–101, 103, 105–8, 159, 181
  used to create beliefs, 28, 42, 89–92,
    113, 124

Federal Express, 141
feedback, 27, 95–96, 100, 102, 104–5,
    107–8. *See also* Focused Feedback
financial
  failure, 8–9, 13, 17–18, 29, 45, 197
  focus, 10, 85–86
  improvement, 18, 31–34, 39–40, 47,
    64–66, 97–98
  success, 8, 13–15, 44, 68, 116, 118,
    139, 146, 151, 160, 198, 212
Flexible Materials Division (FMD),
    157–60
focus, 68, 106
  on actions, 56, 62–63, 65, 69–70,
    120, 208
  on beliefs, 72, 105
  on experiences, 89–90
  lack of, 41, 80
  on results, 2, 28, 41–42, 49, 65, 132, 193
  See also Focused Feedback; Focused
    Recognition; Focused Storytelling
Focused Feedback, 133, 136–43, 151,
    156, 160–68, 182, 184–88, 190–91,
    195, 207, 209, 211
Focused Recognition, 133, 136, 147–
    51, 156, 182–83, 185–86, 189–91,
    195, 207, 211–12
Focused Storytelling, 133, 136, 144–47,
    151, 156, 182, 185–86, 190, 207,
    209, 211–12
food industry, 58–59
Fortune 500 companies, 39, 63
Fortune magazine, 85, 87

General Motors, 17–18
Gill, Marianne, 190–91
Graf, Jay, 44–46, 116, 187–88
Guidant Corporation, 116–18, 120
Gurdjieff, Georgiy Ivanovich, 153

health care industry, 68–69, 197–98,
    200–201

health insurance industry, 79–82,
    181–83
Hemingway, Ernest, 57
Henkel, Herb, 171
Heraclitus (Greek philosopher), 49

Inc. magazine, 90
ineffective change practices, 57–58, 66
Ingersoll Rand, 171
Input / Output Change Model, 53
insurance industry, 34. *See also* health
    insurance
integration
  of culture change, 27–28, 109,
    173–91, 207–9, 213
  of culture, desired, 111
  of Culture Management Tools, 176,
    183–85, 189, 207
Integration Plan, 178, 181–89, 195,
    207–8

Jobs, Steve, 67–68
Journey to the Emerald City, 2–3, 10

Key Performance Indicator meetings,
    169
Kimberly-Clark Health Care (KCHC),
    197–98, 200–201

leaders, 55, 81
  and accountability, 49–50, 83, 126,
    130, 137, 147, 164, 200
  and alignment, 48, 120, 124–32, 162
  and beliefs, 69, 76, 109
  competency of, 48, 116, 172
  and Culture Management Tools,
    147–48
  difficulties / challenges of, 49, 88, 175
  effectiveness of, 42, 87, 113
  and experiences, 89–90, 95, 98
  key role of, 7, 16–18, 172, 205, 210
  mistakes by, 61–64, 67, 69–70, 177,
    208
  and Results Pyramid, 26, 97
  and shifting beliefs, 74–76
  successful strategies of, 194–96
  training of, 1, 27–28, 126, 155–57
  See also leadership skills

Leadership Alignment Process model, 124–32, 156, 195, 210
leadership skills, 18
  to Be Facilitative, 155, 169–72, 195, 210
  and Best Practices, 155–57, 160
  and implementation of culture change, 173, 175–77
  and integration of culture change, 173–91
  to Lead the Change, 154–60, 195
  and Methodology for Changing Beliefs, 161–68
  models for, 153–55, 157
  to Respond to Feedback, 155, 160–68, 195

management teams, 46, 76, 191
  and alignment, 113, 122, 124, 131–32
  and beliefs, 71, 78, 83, 118, 162
  culture of, 107, 109
  and defining results, 32, 34
  and experiences, 106–9
  and Focused Feedback, 187–88
  mistakes of, 61–63
  and Results Pyramid, 27–28
managers, 12–13, 18
  and accountability, 19, 49–50, 64, 106, 130
  and beliefs, 69–71, 75, 86
  and Cultural Beliefs statement, 87–88
  and Focused Feedback, 184–88
  and integration of culture change, 183–84
  mistakes of, 25–26, 67, 69–70
  and results, 7, 30–31, 65
  role of, 16, 56, 204
manufacturing companies, 7–8, 14, 95–97, 106–7, 142–43, 157–60, 189–91
McCoy, Fred, 116–18
McKinsey & Company Global Survey, 194–96
medical industry, 7–15, 44–47, 54, 68–69, 116–20, 142–43, 187–91, 211–13
meetings, 131, 169, 173, 177–80, 182–89, 195, 197, 200, 210–11

methodologies, 10, 15–16, 58, 65, 69, 72, 94, 99, 130, 132. *See also* specific types
Methodology for Changing Beliefs, 161–68
morale, 14, 50–51, 62, 64, 149
motivation, 50, 77, 84, 201

Nickel, Steven, 169–70
nuclear power plant, 74, 187

obstacles, 184
  to achieving results, 16–17, 21–23, 40, 55
  to culture change, 31, 130, 133, 138, 189, 205, 209
online assessment tools, 207–8
optical retail business, 29–30, 51–52, 54, 136–40, 145–51, 183–87
organizational culture, 7–8
  and beliefs, 75–78, 133, 136, 160
  components of, 11–13, 152
  and desired results, 35, 37, 47, 80, 118
  four elements of, 109
  and integration of culture change, 191
  necessary shifts in, 24–25, 27–28, 32, 34–38, 45–48, 68, 78
  optimizing of, 20, 48, 50
  and responding to change, 49, 130
  and three levels of change, 53–54, 62–63
  types of, 17, 20
organizational enrollment, 193–214
organizational systems, 173, 176, 178, 180–82, 187, 195
ownership. *See* accountability
Ownership, Levels of (model), 203–5
Oz Principle, The, 20, 49, 211

Partners In Leadership, Inc., 15, 65, 191
performance
  accountability, 184
  affected by experiences / beliefs, 26
  focus on, 21
  and Focused Recognition, 148
  high levels of, 20–21
  optimizing, 7–8, 50, 214
  organizational, 184

performance improvement, 30
  barriers to, 26, 107, 213
  in companies, 85–87, 97–98, 120
  and Culture Management Tools,
    138, 183
  and "go-to" people, 9–10, 15
  in individuals, 119, 172, 197–98
  need for, 24, 45, 80, 157
PGA Tour, 133–34
pharmaceutical company, 83
Pope, Todd M., 212–13

recruiting strategy, 211–13
restaurant industry, 31–33, 63–66,
    89–91, 133–35
results, current, 24, 29, 35, 37–38,
    43–47, 79, 117
results, desired, 55, 107, 169, 175, 211
  and accountability, 20–23, 43–44
  achievement of, 18, 34–36, 45–46,
    70–71, 109, 111, 113, 137, 181,
    186–87, 191, 207, 214
  and actions, 49–50, 58–61, 63, 65–66
  and alignment, 30–32, 41–42, 48,
    114–15, 132
  and beliefs, 75–79, 81–84, 87
  and Best Practices Map, 3–4
  and the Case for Change, 122–23
  clear defining of, 29–30, 33–34, 39–
    41, 45–48, 119, 123, 125, 135–36,
    183, 195, 197–98
  and Culture Management Tools, 133,
    139–40, 145, 149–52
  and experiences, 89, 100
  and leaders, 129–30, 153, 155, 159, 165
  rating of, 37–38
  and Results Pyramid, 5, 11–13,
    24–28, 39, 46, 66, 72, 193–94
  shifting to, 46–48, 117
results, game changing, 1–3, 5, 14–15,
    28, 32, 47, 76, 111, 118, 128, 133,
    158, 172, 183–84, 189, 196, 213–14
Results Pyramid, 29, 39, 208
  and alignment, 42, 114–15, 117–18,
    120, 133
  application of, 16, 23–28, 46, 48,
    61–62, 109
  and Culture Best Practices, 193–94

and Culture Management Tools,
    143–44
  explanation of, 11–13, 88
  integration of, 113, 175, 184
  used by leaders, 186–87
  using bottom levels of, 56, 69, 72,
    88–89, 97
  using top levels of, 66–67, 70
results, 115, 117–19
retail industry, 19–20, 84–87
risk taking, 18, 23, 78, 119, 158
Rucci, Anthony, 85–87

Schlotterbeck, Dave, 8–15, 18, 28
Schneider, Jeff, 197
Sears, Roebuck and Co., 84–87
Simmons, Amy, 90–91
Smith, Fred, 141
Sony Electronics, 169–70
SSM Health Care, 68–69
steel company, 91–92, 94
Steps to Accountability. See
    accountability: steps to
stock options, 97–98
Stop, Start, Continue analysis, 58–62, 65
success, 1–2, 30, 47, 66, 113, 116,
    118, 169–70, 193–97, 214. See also
    financial success
sustaining
  culture change, 3, 17, 27–28, 173, 191
  culture, desired, 187
  organizational culture, 27–28
  results, desired, 187–88

teams, 20–21, 41, 165, 169–70, 178–79,
    190–91, 196, 205–6. See also
    management teams
tools. See Culture Management Tools
TransEnterix, 211–13

VAIO Service organization, 169–70
Valade, Kelli, 133–34

Wall Street, 9, 47, 66
Whitacre, Ed, 17–18
Wired magazine, 67–68
wireless communications industry,
    67–68

About the Authors

Roger Connors and Tom Smith are co-CEOs and co-presidents of Partners In Leadership, Inc., a leadership training and management consulting company recognized as the premier provider of Accountability Training services around the world. They have coauthored three *New York Times* bestselling leadership books: *The Oz Principle: Getting Results Through Individual and Organizational Accountability*; *How Did That Happen?: Holding People Accountable for Results the Positive, Principled Way;* and *Change the Culture, Change the Game: The Breakthrough Strategy for Energizing Your Organization and Creating Accountability for Results.* They are also authors of the bestselling book *Journey to the Emerald City: Achieve a Competitive Edge by Creating a Culture of Accountability.* Their books have been translated into several languages and have appeared on numerous bestseller lists, including *The Wall Street Journal, USA Today,* AP, *Publishers Weekly,* and Amazon.com lists. They offer the *Three Tracks To Creating Greater Accountability* as a comprehensive training program for helping organizations create greater accountability for individual, team, and organizational results.

Their company has thousands of clients in more than fifty countries and has trained hundreds of thousands of people—from the executive suite to the frontline worker—in understanding how greater accountability can increase efficiency, profits, and innovation at all levels of an organization. Their clients include many of the most admired companies in the world, almost half of the Dow Jones Industrial Average companies, all of the top twelve pharmaceutical companies in the world, and nearly half of the Fortune 50 largest companies in the United States.

Tom and Roger have appeared on numerous radio and television broadcasts, authored articles in major publications, and delivered keynote speeches at numerous major conferences. They have also led consulting engagements and major organizational interventions throughout the world, including most European countries, Japan, North America, South America, and the Middle East. Respected as trusted advisers to senior executives and recognized as the worldwide experts on the topic of workplace accountability, they bring extensive expertise to helping management teams facilitate large-scale cultural transition through their Accountability Training. They both received MBA degrees from the Marriott School of Management at Brigham Young University.

 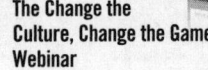 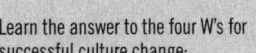 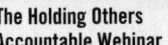